# Historical-Analytical Studies on Nature, Mind and Action

## Volume 1

Historical-Analytical Studies on Nature, Mind and Action provides a forum for integrative, multidisciplinary, analytic studies in the areas of philosophy of nature, philosophical anthropology, and the philosophy of mind and action in their social setting. Tackling these subject areas from both a historical and contemporary systematic perspective, this approach allows for various "paradigm-straddlers" to come together under a common umbrella. Digging down to the conceptual-historical roots of contemporary problems, one will inevitably find common strands which have since branched out into isolated disciplines. This series seeks to fill the void for studies that reach beyond their own strictly defined boundaries not only synchronically (reaching out to contemporary disciplines), but also diachronically, by investigating the unquestioned contemporary presumptions of their own discipline by taking a look at the historical development of those presumptions and the key concepts they involve. This series, providing a common forum for this sort of research in a wide range of disciplines, is designed to work against the well-known phenomenon of disciplinary isolation by seeking answers to our fundamental questions of the human condition: What is there? -- What can we know about it? -- What should we do about it? – indicated by the three key-words in the series title: Nature, Mind and Action. This series will publish monographs, edited volumes, revised doctoral theses and translations.

More information about this series at http://www.springer.com/series/11934

Sarah Borden Sharkey

# An Aristotelian Feminism

 Springer

Sarah Borden Sharkey
Philosophy Department
Wheaton College
Wheaton, IL, USA

ISSN 2509-4793             ISSN 2509-4807    (electronic)

ISBN 978-3-319-29846-7     ISBN 978-3-319-29847-4    (eBook)
DOI 10.1007/978-3-319-29847-4

Library of Congress Control Number: 2016946660

Printed on acid-free paper

This Springer imprint is published by Springer Nature
The registered company is Springer International Publishing AG Switzerland

# Contents

# Introduction

Aristotle often appears in feminist literature, but usually (although not always) as an example of why feminism is needed, and his comments regarding women as "deformed males" is oft-cited. Despite Aristotle's misogyny and mistakes, I think that feminism may be well served by a further investigation of Aristotle and the Aristotelian tradition. Aristotle's hylomorphic model,[1] developed to run between the extremes of Platonic dualism and Democritean atomism, can similarly be used today to articulate a view of gender that takes bodily differences seriously without reducing gender to biological determinations. *Hylomorphism*—in contrast to dualism—thinks that any immaterial features of the person are, first, inseparable from our bodies and, second, only understood and developed through our bodies and material conditions. And hylomorphism—in contrast to atomism, or any simple materialist view—has an account of the structural features that are common to all human beings, features which make possible any scientific study of patterns of human development (at least insofar as that study offers evaluative claims about the fitness of certain patterns in contrast to others). Aristotle's metaphysics of the person can, it seems to me, be used to articulate a particularly subtle and theoretically powerful understanding of gender that may offer an extremely useful tool for making distinctively feminist arguments. The goal of this book is to explore these resources, articulating an understanding of gender that draws from a substantive version of Aristotle's theory of human beings and can be used for truly feminist purposes.

---

[1] The term 'hylomorphism' comes from the Greek words for matter (*hyle*) and form (*morphe*). Aristotle understands human beings to be composed of two distinct but inseparable aspects: matter and form. For more on hylomorphism, see chapter two.

## Summary of Chapters

Aristotle may seem an odd choice for achieving any feminist goal or articulating any adequate account of gender; Aristotle is hardly known to be a champion of women, and surely some of the blame for discrimination against women in the Western traditions needs to be laid at his feet. But I think that Aristotle's thought is better than he himself knew. Oddly, I am not claiming that, if one simply eradicates the misogyny and prejudice in Aristotle's writings, we will end up with a good position. Unfortunately, I do not think that it is merely misogyny infecting Aristotle's claims. Misogyny may be a part of the story, but it is not the whole of it. His criticisms of women are, even worse, at least in part rational ones, the intelligible result of following out his general position. In light of that, his thought does not seem easily reformed or safely used.

Falling prey to the same conclusions Aristotle drew is surely a risk in following his intellectual lead. Nonetheless, it seems to me that Aristotle's general account of the person is extremely helpful for understanding gender. The position I am presenting is *not* Aristotle's, but it will draw heavily from Aristotelian ideas and principles. The first chapter will lay out more fully the case for why we need an Aristotelian feminism. I begin with the most famous current form of Aristotelian-inspired feminism, Martha Nussbaum's 'capabilities approach.' Although the position presented here shares much with Nussbaum's approach, I would like to be more explicitly and thoroughly hylomorphist than Nussbaum, and thus be able to say something more substantive about the role of our differing biologies, and yet without reducing gender to any form of 'biological determinism.' This latter point—that feminism needs to have something substantive to say about our differing biologies—is crucial, and examining both why this is needed and why it is difficult will be the core focus of

Chapter 2 is dedicated to articulating an account of gender drawing on general Aristotelian principles. It will lay out the major tenets of hylomorphism, focusing particularly on how the distinction between a *formal* and *material* principle is useful for addressing questions of sex and gender. It will articulate an account of why gender traits are susceptible to great societal influence and variation and yet also show why gender, on the Aristotelian model, cannot be understood as a mere social construction. It will address a few challenges to understanding both form and matter, and try to articulate an account of each that is true to the 'Aristotelian spirit' but capable of answering more contemporary questions and challenges. Core to the argument of Chap. 2 will be a distinction between *biological matter* and *environmental and cultural matter*. This is not a distinction made explicitly by Aristotle, but is—it seems to me—in the Aristotelian spirit. Matter for Aristotle is not simply physical stuff, but is that in and through which we develop. There are numerous types of conditions for our development, and distinguishing these—and the ways in which they shape our development—is critical for an accurate understanding of gender.

This Aristotelian feminism has a particular and distinct general understanding of the relation of sex and gender, but it can be specified in very different ways. Depending on how one answers certain questions and fills out one's Aristotelian account, one will end up with significantly different understandings of the malleability of gender. Thus there could be quite different claims all of which could count as 'Aristotelian feminism.' Chapter 3 is dedicated to raising those questions and thus pointing to a number of places where the theory needs further development.[2] My aim in this book is not to articulate the theory in detail, but simply to give a broad sketch of the position. I will not take a firm stand on these more detailed questions, but I would like to show why addressing such questions in detail would be significant for presenting a thorough account of gender.

Although I think that a broadly Aristotelian account of gender shows great promise, Aristotle himself was certainly not a feminist. Chapter 4 will be dedicated to examining why Aristotle thought women were naturally inferior, looking both at his texts articulating this claim and his motivations for so understanding women. It will point to various places in Aristotle's thought where contemporary feminists ought to be wary, and lay out three avenues by which Aristotle got to his positions regarding women, including his particular account of human generation, the pressure his understanding of the species-form and its relation to the body places upon his account of what it means to actualize the form, and the role of examples—and thus the lives of the women in his day—in developing his account of the possibilities for women. In Chap. 5, I respond to the evidence and arguments Aristotle puts forward, showing where he went wrong and how one might adopt some version of his hylomorphism without compromising in any way the full equality of women and men.

The bulk of this work is intended to be theoretical. The position has, however, great practical power and can be utilized, I believe, in struggles fighting for women's equality and dignity. Many of these applications may require answering some of the questions raised in Chap. 3—and the way in which someone answers these more specific questions may put one on quite differing sides of certain issues (e.g., pornography, abortion, various religious practices, etc.). But there are certainly more general issues that even a broad version of the position can show are truly *feminist* concerns. Because an Aristotelian feminism focuses on our common human capacities while also taking bodily differences to be significant for gender development, points where our physical differences affect the order and way in which we both develop and use our capacities are of significant concern. One such significant biological difference lies in our patterns of fertility. Males are able to have children

---

[2] Among the questions to be considered are: (i) What is meant by influencing?, (ii) How will the type of hylomorphism one affirms affect one's account of gender?, (iii) How ought we to distinguish the human faculties?, (iv) What kind of impact do our biology and biological conditions have on the development of our faculties—do they affect the order in which the faculties are developed, the patterns of development themselves, the combination of faculties employed in attending to various things, or the objects toward which the faculties are turned?, and (v) Might the influence differ for different faculties? Once again, my goal in the third chapter is not to provide a full answer to these questions but, rather, to show why they are significant issues and to suggest briefly the types of avenues one might pursue in order to answer these questions.

for more years than females, and—related to this—the physical investment of men in the having of children differs from the physical investment of women. Our dominant models of higher education, however, have not yet taken this difference into account, and thus the common patterns by which we develop our higher intellectual and social skills (utilizing a model that is becoming increasingly global) are frequently at odds with women's generative or reproductive capacities. Chapter 6 will give an example of the proposed Aristotelian feminism in use, by looking at the tension between the development of our generative and higher intellectual capacities—and thereby show how the structure of our universities is itself a feminist issue.

## *What Is Meant by* 'Aristotelian Feminism'

As far as I know, the term 'Aristotelian feminist' is not, understandably, in general use.[3] By the description, I mean, first, someone who is committed to the full equality of women and men and understands equality in terms of equal (or common) human capacities; who, second, is committed to working, in whatever ways are fit with her or his broader vocation, to eliminating sources of genuine oppression of women and setting the conditions for the full development of women's human capacities; and, third, who draws in some significant way from Aristotelian ideas. The version of 'Aristotelian feminism' that I would like to present draws from Aristotle's account of the person, and in particular his hylomorphism. It understands gender—using the hylomorphic model—as motivated by both *biological matter* and, what I will call, *environmental and cultural matter*,[4] but not as determined by them. All Aristotelian feminists need to acknowledge that Aristotle himself was not a feminist, and

or compromise the dignity of women but want to preserve that which is worthwhile for understanding ourselves as sexed and gendered human beings.

Although I am calling the position I am articulating an 'Aristotelian feminism,' I am *not* claiming (a) that Aristotle or any particular Aristotelian held this position in the form that I present it, (b) that the reading of Aristotelian principles I present can be fully fit with all of Aristotle's texts, or (c) that this is the only type of feminism which could be developed from Aristotelian principles. There are numerous readings of Aristotle. There are significant and well-justified debates in Aristotle scholarship about what Aristotle really means by primary substance or *ousia*, whether

---

[3] It has, however, been used. See, for example, Avery Kolers's syllabus for PHIL 505/605/SCHG 500, *Special Topics: Global Justice* (http://louisville.edu/~ahkole01/505syll.htm [accessed November 6, 2008]). See also Nussbaum's description in "Aristotle, Feminism, and Needs for Functioning," in *Feminist Interpretations of Aristotle* ed. Cynthia A. Freeland (University Park, PA: The Pennsylvania University Press, 1998), 248–259.

[4] Matter, for Aristotle, is that *through which* one develops—in contrast to form, which is that which develops. I develop the distinction between matter and form more fully in chapter two, as well as distinguishing what I mean by *biological* and *environmental and cultural matter*.

*theoría* or *praxis* is more fundamental, how to reconcile Books I and X of the *Nicomachean Ethics*, whether there is one or many substantial forms, etc. I would like to present a very general account of Aristotelian principles, focusing on a fairly traditional reading of Aristotle's distinction between the formal and material principles. I believe that there is significant basis for this account in Aristotle's texts, but it is not easily reconcilable with all that he has said.

My aim in this text is simply to articulate one theoretical account of gender, drawing from Aristotle and the Aristotelian metaphysical tradition. Although there are feminist theorists who have drawn in very general and 'thin' ways from Aristotle's metaphysics,[5] as well as his ethics[6] and epistemology,[7] such theorists generally attempt to distinguish how their approach can accept aspects of Aristotle's thought without incorporating in any heavy way his metaphysical views.[8] I think, in contrast, that a substantive version of Aristotle's metaphysics can, in fact, be extremely useful for feminists.[9] I will not provide the kind of argument and evidence necessary for a full defense of either this claim or provide a full version of this theory of gender. In this text, I would simply like to articulate, in broad strokes,

[5] A key example would be Martha Nussbaum's 'capabilities approach.' Nussbaum herself denies that her account depends on metaphysical claims. It is not clear to me that this would be true in all senses, although she is certainly only dependent on a very 'thin' version of Aristotelian metaphysics, and insofar as it is one of her 'intuitive starting points,' she is not engaging in metaphysics as Aristotle himself does. See further discussion of Nussbaum's work in chapter one below.

[6] Cynthia Freeland notes, for example: "While his views in metaphysics, epistemology, philosophy of science or logic are often the target of feminist attacks, in the contexts of ethics and metaethics he is often championed by feminist philosophers. There seem to be two key aspects of Aristotle's approach in ethics that feminists wish to appropriate. First, he emphasizes the cognitive value of emotions, that is, their role in aiding people to assess moral situations. He advocates contextual seeing of concrete situations from the standpoint of a particular subject, rather than the impartial, universalizing application of rules; he emphasizes character and virtues rather than rights and duties. In other words, Aristotle's approach in ethics resembles that described as 'feminine' by psychologist Carol Gilligan in her well-known book *In a Different Voice*" ("Nourishing Speculation: A Feminist Reading of Aristotelian Science," in *Engendering Origins: Critical Feminist Readings in Plato and Aristotle*, ed. By Bat-Ami Bar On [Albany, NY: State University of New York Press, 1994], 147). See also further support for these claims in *Feminist Interpretations of Aristotle*, ed. Cynthia A. Freeland (University Park, PA: Pennsylvania State University Press, 1998).

[7] For an example of how Aristotle might so be used, see Lorraine Code "The Impact of Feminism on Epistemology," *APA Newsletter on Feminism and Philosophy* 88, no. 2 (March 1989). (Freeland, however, points out that in other articles in the same volume, the evaluation of Aristotle's epistemology is as less friendly to feminism. See her "Nourishing Speculation: A Feminist Reading of Aristotelian Science," 148.) A broadly Aristotelian cognitional theory has also been put to feminist purposes in, for example, Paulette Kidder's "Woman of Reason: Lonergan and Feminist Epistemology" and Michael Vertin's "Gender, Science, and Cognitional Conversion," both appearing in *Lonergan and Feminism*, ed. Cynthia S.W. Crysdale (Toronto: University of Toronto Press, 1994).

[8] The most significant exception to this is Charlotte Witt's "Form, Normativity, and Gender in Aristotle: A Feminist Perspective" in *Feminist Interpretations of Aristotle*.

[9] Although I will not fully defend the thesis here, I would like to suggest throughout the text that such a substantive use of Aristotle's metaphysics of the person offers resources for responding to some of the dilemmas facing feminist theory today.

*what* such an Aristotelian feminism might look like and why it can truly draw from Aristotle, despite his own claims about women and men. Thus, I would like to present this Aristotelian account of gender as one alternative—a quite promising one, but nonetheless one in great need of further support in order to be fully convincing.

## Acknowledgements

There are many people who have been essential to the writing of this text, including especially Prudence Allen, Mary Lemmons, Deborah Savage, the Siena Circle for Personalist Feminism (an "informal think tank" at the University of St. Thomas, St. Paul), Joseph Koterski, the late Norris Clarke, Chris Manzer, Kevin McDonnell, James Sterba, David Solomon, Alasdair MacIntyre, Kathryn Wales, Elizabeth Kirk, Dan McInerny, Anamaría Scaperlanda Ruiz, Barbara Parsons, Shane Drefcinski, Steven Freddoso, Tom Everett, Greer Hannan, Octavia Ratiu, Dai Li, and, with deep gratitude, the Wheaton College sabbatical program and the Notre Dame Center for Ethics and Culture. The initial work for this book was begun through conversations with the Siena Circle at St. Thomas and through various visits and conversations in St. Paul, MN. The bulk of the work, however, was completed in South Bend; I am exceedingly grateful to Wheaton College, the Myser Family, and the Center for Ethics and Culture for the opportunity to spend a year working through this project. Without that concentrated time and the extensive resources of Notre Dame, this project would likely have lain incomplete in an inchoate form. During the 'Notre Dame year,' Chris Manzer was particularly helpful, reading numerous articles and pointing me toward those most significant for this project and providing editorial comments. In addition, his research on images of women and teachers in the ancient world and early medieval university education profoundly strengthened these sections of the work. Through the following years, I was able to present various chapters to members of my department and the humanities division, as well as Robert Bishop in the natural sciences; this work has been strengthened by their feed-back, objections, and suggestions. Finally, I am profoundly grateful to my husband and co-student in philosophy, Michael Sharkey. He convinced me that this project was important and that I could write it, and he then spent hours reading through drafts of material (even amid his own grading and writing), talking about the possibility of metaphysics, the nature of symbols and their relation to experience, the differing meanings of condition, and how to appropriate the insights and advances of modernity while also retaining the wisdom of the ancients.

# Chapter 1
# Nussbaum, Capabilities, and Biology

The notion of an "Aristotelian feminism," although by no means a dominant approach in feminism, exists in several forms—the most significant of which is Martha Nussbaum's "capabilities approach."[1] Nussbaum presents a compelling and important form of feminism, drawing significant inspiration from aspects of Aristotle's thought. The version I would like to advocate has different foci and goes beyond that of Nussbaum by incorporating more fully Aristotle's metaphysics. But I think that Nussbaum is right that feminism ought to focus on human *capabilities*, or *capacities*,[2] and the various conditions relevant to the development of those capacities. Women historically have had, and continue to have, fewer opportunities to both develop and use the full range of their capacities. And the form of Aristotelian feminism advocated here agrees with Nussbaum that our attention ought to be turned not simply to rights, or equality in terms of job opportunities or distribution of particular resources (as important as these may be), but to *capabilities* and the full set of conditions relevant to the development and full use of these capacities.

I would like to begin by looking briefly at how Nussbaum's 'capabilities approach' is a version of Aristotelian feminism. Nussbaum's focus on capabilities is rooted in an Aristotelian account of human beings as developmental and deeply conditioned by our material circumstances; she defends a version of universal

---

[1] In calling Nussbaum's 'capabilities approach' the most significant form of Aristotelian feminism, I simply mean that it is the best-known and therefore influential version in the English-speaking academic world. There are, however, other positions that could also be described as 'Aristotelian feminism,' including Sybil Schwarzenbach's work in political philosophy, especially *On Civic Friendship* (New York: Columbia University Press, 2009) and Prudence Allen's analysis of the history of women in philosophy, particularly volume III of *The Concept of Woman* (Grand Rapids, MI: Eerdmans, forthcoming).

[2] Nussbaum uses the term 'capability' most frequently; I prefer the term 'capacity.' There are some differences between our uses of these terms (as may become clear in Chap. 2), but for the purposes of this chapter, they can be understood to be interchangeable.

© Springer International Publishing Switzerland 2016
S. Borden Sharkey, *An Aristotelian Feminism*, Historical-Analytical Studies on Nature, Mind and Action 1, DOI 10.1007/978-3-319-29847-4_1

human norms undergirded by an Aristotelian understanding of universal norms; she appeals to an Aristotelian concern for the common good; and even her writing style—a tacking back and forth between particular and universal—reflects a broadly Aristotelian epistemology. Yet unlike Aristotle, Nussbaum is at root a feminist, calling us to look closely at the conditions of all human beings, although especially of women, and to work for greater equality for all, with special attention to the challenges women face. Such an approach strikes me as genuinely both Aristotelian and feminist, and thus I would like to begin by looking at Nussbaum's position, pointing to some of the distinctively Aristotelian elements of Nussbaum's approach and the ways in which she utilizes these in order to defend a substantive feminism.

As substantive as Nussbaum's 'capabilities approach' is, however, and as much as I would like to build upon aspects of her work, she could be both more fully Aristotelian and, as a result, more fully feminist. Nussbaum employs a tremendous number of Aristotelian resources, and she focuses, as is appropriate for an Aristotelian position, on our mortality and bodily life. Nonetheless, she shies away from, and thereby downplays, the significance of our sexually differentiated biologies. She says little about how our bodies as female, male, or intersex are among the significant conditions in which we develop our capabilities. This shying away is understandable. Nonetheless, I do not think that any of us—but women in particular—are well-served by downplaying these biological differences. The task, it seems to me, is rather to incorporate rightly the significance of our different bodies. And, furthermore, I think that Aristotelian metaphysics offers particularly useful resources for doing so.

The following chapter will briefly outline Nussbaum's 'capabilities approach,' showing how it is a truly Aristotelian feminism, and then make a case for greater inclusion of Aristotelian thought in such a feminism. The feature that I think is most in need of greater explication and inclusion is Aristotle's concern for our differing

that so many feminists have been wary of allowing biology to have too great a significance. There are many ways to fail in articulating the import of differing biologies, and our histories are filled with numerous problematic examples (including both 'traditional' positions and certain forms of radical feminism). Nonetheless, I think that it is absolutely critical to do so rightly. Thus, after discussing Nussbaum's general approach, I would like to articulate both why it is difficult to understand well the import of our biological differences as female, male, and intersex and at least some of the reasons why it is critical to do so if we are truly to defend the full humanity and dignity of women.

# Nussbaum's 'Aristotelian Feminism'

## *A Summary of Her 'Capabilities Approach'*

In nearly all of Nussbaum's work, Aristotle is an important source. Although a few people have described Nussbaum's position in feminism as an 'Aristotelian feminism,'[3] she herself uses the title 'capabilities approach,' citing the most important influences for her position as Aristotle, an Aristotelian reading of Marx, and the economic theory pioneered by Amartya Sen. Nussbaum's 'capabilities approach' plays a role in many of her books and is discussed in numerous articles; I would like, however, to focus on her most significant turning of it to feminism in her 2000 *Women and Human Development*.[4]

Nussbaum's most explicit goal in *Women and Human Development* is to articulate criteria for evaluating human development "with a view to shaping public policy."[5] Her project is both theoretical and practical insofar as it is tied to the goal of motivating governments and international agencies to adopt her proposed standards for assessing whether they adequately respect human dignity.[6] Nussbaum thinks that development ought not to be measured in terms of gross national product, expressed satisfaction, or a simple distribution of resources.[7] She thinks, rather, that success ought to be measured in terms of whether each citizen has the material conditions relevant to and necessary for developing her capabilities.[8] That is, what

---

[3] See, for example, Avery Kolers's syllabus for PHIL 505/605/SCHG 500, *Special Topics: Global Justice* (http://louisville.edu/~ahkole01/505syll.htm, accessed November 6, 2008). See also Nussbaum's description in "Aristotle, Feminism, and Needs for Functioning" in *Feminist Interpretations of Aristotle* ed. Cynthia A. Freeland (University Park, PA: The Pennsylvania University Press, 1998): 248–259. Lisa Sowle Cahill refers to Nussbaum's position as a "feminist Aristotelianism" in *Sex, Gender, and Christian Ethics* (New York: Cambridge University Press, 1996), 55.

[4] *Women and Human Development: The Capabilities Approach* (New York: Cambridge University Press, 2000), hereafter WHD. Nussbaum lays out the way in which she roots her position in Aristotle's texts in, particularly, "Nature, Function, and Capability: Aristotle on Political Distribution" in *Oxford Studies in Ancient Philosophy*, Supplementary Volume I (1988): 145–84.

[5] WHD xiii. For a particularly clear cross-disciplinary summary of the 'capabilities approach' and relevant literature, see Ingrid Robeyns, "The Capability Approach: A Theoretical Survey" in *Journal of Human Development*, 6, no. 1 (March 2005): 93–114.

[6] See, for example, WHD 5. She fills out this vision: "My central project is to work out the grouding [sic] for basic political principles to which all nations should be held by their citizens; but an ancillary and related project is to map out the space within which comparisons of quality of life across nations can most revealingly be made" (WHD 116).

[7] It is, after all, always a question how the resources are actually distributed, how much our expressed satisfaction reflects our real conditions, or how the resources actually function to improve people's lives.

[8] She summarizes the key concern: "The central question asked by the capabilities approach is not, 'How satisfied is Vasanti?' or even 'How much in the way of resources is she able to command?' It is, instead, 'What is Vasanti actually able to do and to be?' Taking a stand for political purposes on a working list of functions that would appear to be of central importance in human life, we ask: Is

is most critical for human beings is that they function well, that they are able to flourish in distinctively human ways. Thus, equal distribution of money, professional opportunities, power, or other resources is not sought for its own sake; the goal is not simply one of quantitatively equal allocation. The goal, rather, is equitable distribution, that is, of setting the conditions for each human being to develop and then flourish (if she so chooses) in ways appropriate to human beings. The distribution of money, professional opportunities, power, etc., may be significant insofar as these are critical for setting the conditions for human development, but the fundamental concern is for the development of capabilities; all of the other factors are secondary. This focus—not on resources, distribution of power, etc.—but on functioning well is distinctively Aristotelian, and it provides criteria for evaluating what counts as an appropriate and just distribution of resources, as well as an account of why that distribution is so critical.[9]

The central concept of Nussbaum's approach draws on the Aristotelian account of human beings as developmental and teleological.[10] We have potencies of a particular type oriented toward our own actualization—and this feature of being oriented toward our own development carries, Nussbaum argues, an obligation to provide the conditions so that this development may occur. We do not 'arrive' in the world with a full identity, self-understanding, or fully formed and specified desires. These are developed in and through our quite particular material and social conditions. On the other hand, however, we are not simply molded in limitlessly variable ways by the social, cultural, and material forces of our environments. There is a structure or set of dynamisms—that is, a set of capabilities directed toward their own full development—characteristic of each of us as human beings. All of us long, in some sense, to actualize these distinctively human capabilities and engage in activities that are characteristic of us as human beings, and our various environmental conditions contribute to developing these dynamisms well or ill.[11]

---

the person capable of this, or not? We ask not only about the person's satisfaction with what she does, but about what she does, and what she is in a position to do (what her opportunities and liberties are)" (WHD 71).

[9] In *Sex and Social Justice*, Nussbaum summarizes the import of looking at capabilities: "people have varying needs for resources ....They also have different abilities to convert resources into functioning. ... Unlike the type of liberal approach that focuses only on the distribution of resources, the capability approach maintains that resources have no value in themselves, apart from their role in promoting human functioning" (*Sex and Social Justice* [New York: Oxford University Press, 1999], 34).

[10] See, for example, her discussion on page 43 of *Sex and Social Justice*.

[11] Nussbaum dedicates a tremendous amount of her work to defending the universality of these characteristically human capabilities. In addition to the arguments in WHD, see also "Aristotle on Human Nature and the Foundations of Ethics" in *World, Mind and Ethics: Essays on the Ethical Philosophy of Bernard Williams*, ed. J.E.J. Altham and Ross Harrison (Cambridge: Cambridge University Press, 1995), 86–131; "Human Functioning and Social Justice: In Defense of Aristotelian Essentialism" in *Political Theory* 20, no. 2 (May 1992): 202–246; and "Public Philosophy and International Feminism" in *Ethics* 108 (July 1998): 770–804.

Nussbaum fills out this broad account by listing ten critical capabilities.[12] Her 2000 list includes: (i) life, (ii) bodily health, (iii) bodily integrity, (iv) senses, imagination, and thought, (v) emotions, (vi) practical reason, (vii) affiliation, (viii) relation with other species, (ix) play, and (x) control over one's environment (both political and material).[13] Although she emphasizes the generality of this list, calling it elsewhere a "thick vague conception,"[14] each can be described in a bit more detail. For example, by *life*, she means being able to live a life of a normal length for a human being. Thus, a human being who dies as an infant or even middle-aged has had her capability for life cut short. By *bodily integrity*, Nussbaum means having sufficient sovereignty over one's body that one is not subject to violence, or forced to perform bodily actions or undergo physical changes against one's will. With *senses, imagination, and thought*, she includes a commitment to the ability to use these faculties in "'truly human' ways," that is, in ways "informed and cultivated by an adequate education."[15] Thus, by this capability, she does not mean the simple ability to open one's eyes and see, but a somewhat developed version of sensory, imaginative, and intellectual activity, which would involve some training. And thus, education—although differing in methods and institutional structures—becomes a central condition for the development of this capability. And so forth.

Of these ten capabilities, Nussbaum places special emphasis on two: *practical reason* and *affiliation*. These two are architectonic capabilities, which are particularly central to being human and which inform and organize all of the other capabilities. Practical reason, as she understands it, centers around our ability to "form a conception of the good and to engage in critical reflection about the planning of one's life."[16] It is our ability to evaluate differing goods and choose among them, deciding and committing ourselves to particular kinds of lives. Nussbaum does not understand such choice as unlimited; it is embedded in a life involving all of the various capabilities as well as all of the conditions and circumstances enabling their development. But, nonetheless, choice and freedom play a central role in a flourishing human life. The second of these, affiliation, is not simply the fact that most of us

---

[12] Although I agree with the broad strokes of Nussbaum's capabilities approach, I am not taking a stand on a list of capabilities.

[13] See WHD 78–80. See also the same list presented in *Sex and Social Justice*, 41–42. Nussbaum presents a slightly different list in her 1992 "Human Functioning and Social Justice: In Defense of Aristotelian Essentialism," 216–223 and her 1995 "Human Capabilities, Female Human Beings" in *Women, Culture, and Development* ed. Martha C. Nussbaum & Jonathan Glover (Oxford: Clarendon Press, 1995), 61–104. For discussion of the significance of which capabilities one lists and how one lists these capabilities, see Chap. 3.

[14] E.g., "Human Functioning and Social Justice: In Defense of Aristotelian Essentialism," 216.

[15] WHD 78.

[16] WHD 79. Nussbaum's account of *practical reason* places emphasis on liberal concerns for autonomy in understanding and choosing a life we take to be good. Although certainly focusing on choice, Aristotle places quite a bit of emphasis on the role of practical reason in becoming virtuous, making right judgments, cultivating habits enabling a moral life, etc. It is not clear to me that Nussbaum's and Aristotle's emphases are sharply opposed, but Aristotle's tie between practical reason and a particular set of moral virtues (and a particular kind of good life, understood relatively comprehensively) differs at least from Nussbaum's emphases, if not commitments.

happen to live around other people but involves, rather, an ability to show concern for others, to place ourselves in another's position, to have compassion for another, and to cultivate true friendships and pursue justice. We are social beings, and the various abilities relevant to cultivating our social interactions are central to the development of all of our other capabilities.[17]

In claiming that practical reason and affiliation are architectonic, Nussbaum understands them to infuse all of the other capabilities and to distinguish *human* from less than human versions of those types of functioning. All of the capabilities are interrelated in various ways; one must, for example, have life in order to pursue relations with other species or the natural world, and our bodily integrity is central to having control over one's environment. Nonetheless, practical reason and affiliation are unique in the way in which they "suffuse all the others," offering a particular organization to the capabilities which makes them distinctively human capabilities.[18] For example, there are many lives which could, in fact, be lived for a normal human duration but which would be spent sleeping or in a vegetative state. Such a life, without friendships or substantive relationships and without any free decisions regarding how one wants to live, is not a life we would choose. So also, senses, imagination, and thought can be turned to many things, but most of us, Nussbaum argues, choose to use them in ways that include an orientation toward other human beings and in the pursuit of a particular conception of how a life ought to be lived. Nussbaum takes this concern for versions of the capabilities infused by practical reason and affiliation to be something with which all of us are concerned. We might be able to name someone—perhaps a sociopath—who acts as if these are not her concerns. But most of *us*, when we think of ourselves and what we would pursue (and who *we* would include in the 'we'), would not want such a life.[19] Even those who live lives of solitude often understand their lives of actual isolation to be deeply tied to the good of others. Many of the early Christian Desert Fathers, for example,

as cultivating a certain kind of relation to the divine.[20]

Each of us values our lives, bodily health and integrity, capabilities for imagination, play, etc., and we do so in ways that acknowledge and are tied to our affiliations. So also, our choices regarding the other capabilities are generally made in light of an understanding of what is good and what makes for a good life. Thus, although it is not possible to separate out fully any of the capabilities, the ability to think through and decide regarding what makes a good life (*practical reason*) and

---

[17] Nussbaum expands on this, claiming that this would also involve "[h]aving the social bases of self-respect and non-humiliation; being able to be treated as a dignified being whose worth is equal to that of others" (WHD 79).

[18] WHD 82.

[19] See Nussbaum's arguments in "Aristotle on Human Nature and the Foundations of Ethics."

[20] Many of the Desert Fathers moved outside of the cities, in part, in order to defend those cities against demons and demonic forces, that is, the bringers of disease of various sorts, including physical disease. I am grateful to Sarah Spangler for pointing out this feature of these ascetic motivations.

the ability to do so in a social context (*affiliation*) play a particularly important role in specifically human functioning.[21] Thus, Nussbaum thinks that the conditions for each capability ought to be pursued and in a version that acknowledges and is infused by our practical reason and affiliation.

Although Nussbaum takes practical reason and affiliation to be particularly central, none of the ten capabilities is negotiable. She takes each to be critical for a fully human life, and conditions ought to be set so that each individual may pursue any combination of the ten areas. A government that sets the conditions particularly well, for example, for the development of senses, imagination, and thought (setting up, perhaps, a particularly good educational system) does not thereby get a 'free pass' regarding bodily integrity,[22] or a particular focus on bodily health would not justify ignoring our capabilities for relations with other species or play.[23] Nonetheless, this list is not taken to be comprehensive. There are likely other capabilities that many would consider central,[24] and the list in no way intends to be exhaustive of all that might (or perhaps ought to) be included in an account of a full human life. Rather, Nussbaum takes this list to articulate things most of us, despite our myriad disagreements, could nonetheless agree are important. Thus, it is a list for which there could be great consensus. But it does not comprehensively articulate all of the human capabilities—or even all of the *critical* human capabilities.[25]

Further, Nussbaum does not think that all of us as individuals need to actualize all of our capabilities equally. Although governments and governing groups should set the conditions for the use of all ten capabilities, each of us may self-limit, deciding—for various reasons—which among our human capacities we will actualize and use more fully and regularly. In some cases, individuals may significantly downplay, or simply not develop, certain of the capacities. For example, someone might prioritize relations with other species over certain forms of intellectual development, or—for various reasons—refuse to cultivate certain types of emotional

---

[21] See Nussbaum's "Aristotle on Human Nature and the Foundations of Ethics" for an interpretation of Aristotle that places these two at the crux of Aristotle's account of human nature.

[22] We might think here of a state with excellent educational resources, which nonetheless allows female genital mutilation.

[23] We might think here of a Western nation with a great health care system but an excessive emphasis on work or a problematic relation to the environment.

[24] For example, Lisa Cahill suggests adding, as distinct capabilities, both kinship and religion. See *Sex, Gender, and Christian Ethics*, 59–61.

[25] Nussbaum further states that the list is open to revision. See WHD 76–77. These features of Nussbaum's list, although important for her political goals, may indicate corresponding weaknesses. She does not tell us which of these ten capabilities, beyond practical reason and affiliation, are most central, which ought to be prioritized, which to pursue when all are beyond some basic threshold, etc. In cases of limited resources, which should be de-emphasized in favor of more central capabilities? Or should something else, not on the list, be prioritized? Insofar as practical reason and affiliation 'organize and suffuse' the others, they appear to take pride of place; Nussbaum does not, however, state the implications of this explicitly, nor is it clear that she could (or should), given her emphasis on political consensus rather than a more metaphysical account of human nature.

development. Such self-limitation is occasionally both necessary and appropriate.[26] Self-limitation is also, however, tied to our conceptions of the good life. If one understands certain religious texts as central, she might engage in ascetic practices that compromise bodily health. Or she may be committed to certain affiliations and may quite willingly sacrifice her political control, or even her life, for the sake of these. Such decisions are fundamentally tied to our practical reason and our judgments regarding what makes for a good life. Nussbaum takes these decisions regarding self-limitation to be left appropriately to individuals; they ought not to be part of the ideal aimed at by governments or international agencies. Such larger organizations ought to set the conditions sufficient for each individual to use all of the capabilities, even if those individuals may choose not to do so.

Nussbaum emphasizes this distinction between *capability* and *functioning* quite strongly. The capability is simply the ability to use or function in a certain way. She sees functioning as a matter of choice. Once a capability is developed and we have the conditions necessary to use it, each of us can, however, choose not to do so. To use one of her examples, an individual may choose not to be healthy—she might prioritize caring for another over her own physical health, or she might choose a life of extreme asceticism. But someone who is starving because of a lack of food does not have that choice; she is simply starving and has not chosen *not* to function well. Or, to cite another of Nussbaum's examples: we can choose to remain celibate or enter into pleasurable sexual relations, but having basic bodily integrity—i.e., not having been subjected to genital mutilation—would seem to be fundamental to making this a true choice. The role of the state is not to make the choice between these two for an individual, but to provide the conditions so that each individual has the capabilities and these thus are genuine choices.[27]

Like Aristotle, Nussbaum understands the development and use of our full range of human capabilities to be the ideal for each individual; the good life is one in

ing well ought to be the ideal of governing organizations.[28] Whether an individual *uses* a capability ought to be left to the individual. Thus, governments ought to set

---

[26] Self-limiting at too low of a level will significantly hinder the development of the other capabilities. But none of us can develop equally all of our capabilities to their fullest possible extent; time and energy are limited. Thus, self-limitation in some form is necessary, even if holistic development of some kind and to some degree is also necessary in order to use any of the capabilities well.

[27] See, for example, *Sex and Social Justice*, 44. This distinction between *capability* and *functioning* is useful and important, and it can be made, to some degree, as Nussbaum's examples show. It is not clear, however, that it can be very finely made. Insofar as capabilities are developed by *using* them, one cannot have capabilities ready for use without functioning. Nussbaum acknowledges this in a number of places. But given the significance of *functioning* for the having of a capability at least ready for use, and given the role of our social relations for the development of all of our capabilities, I am not sure that these distinctions do not become so problematic that something closer to a full metaphysic of the person is necessary in order to maintain these distinctions. For a different version of this critique, see Phillip McReynolds, "Nussbaum's Capabilities Approach: A Pragmatist Critique" in *The Journal of Speculative Philosophy* 16, no. 2 (2002): 142–150.

[28] This raises the question of whether it ought to be part of the ideal of non-governing groups. Perhaps governments ought not to have functioning (rather than capabilities) as part of the ideal.

the conditions so that the use of our capabilities is a genuine option, but without requiring that we do so. When the conditions are set, then individuals are truly free to decide whether and how to use their capabilities. Thus, she claims that her position aims at *capabilities* and not *functioning*—not because functioning is not part of the ideal (it is) but because *freely choosing* to so function is even more central.[29]

This point should, however, be qualified. The distinction between functioning and capabilities can only be loosely made. We must after all *function* to some degree in certain basic versions of our capabilities in order to then develop further, advanced versions of those (and other) capabilities. For example, one's ability to imagine to some degree what her mother or neighbor is experiencing is essential for more complex imaginative tasks such as creating a full world of a novel or work of art. So also, our intellectual capabilities must be developed to a certain degree in order to have the opportunity to develop further skills relevant to obtaining paid employment (and thus having certain forms of material and political control over one's environment). Nussbaum is not requiring that every adult choose to write novels or pursue employment, but in order for either of these ever to be options, certain basic early training in imaginative and intellectual functioning is necessary. Thus, required basic education might be a pre-requisite necessary in order for each of us to have a true choice regarding advanced imaginative work or any paid employment. Given this, although the general goal is capabilities and not functioning, Nussbaum will make functioning a requirement where basic functioning is a pre-requisite for having the opportunity to develop any meaningful version of the capability. She says:

> In general, the more crucial a function is to attaining and maintaining other capabilities, the more entitled we may be to promote actual functioning in some cases, within limits set by an appropriate respect for citizen's choices.[30]

Thus, *functioning* might be required for basic capabilities—or basic versions of the capabilities—even if it is not for more advanced ones.[31] The goal of governing groups ought, however, to be to provide the material conditions (which might include requiring functioning in certain ways) necessary for every individual—both women and men—to meet at least some basic threshold for the use (if she or he so chooses) of a truly human version of each and every fundamental human capability.

Thus, like Aristotle, Nussbaum places the focus on capabilities and, like Aristotle, she understands the *polis* as a central place where the conditions are set for the development of human capabilities. Unlike Aristotle, however, and more in keeping

---

Should, however, a private school, the YMCA, an activist group, relief agency, or non-governing political party have such an aim?

[29] See "Aristotle, Politics, and Human Capabilities: A Response to Antony, Arneson, Charlesworth, and Mulgan" in *Ethics* 111 (October 2000): 124. See the same article, pages 108–109 for a summary of some of her points of departure from Aristotle.

[30] WHD 92.

[31] Nussbaum distinguishes among, what she calls, *basic capabilities, internal capabilities,* and *combined capabilities.* See WHD 83–85 and *Sex and Social Justice,* 44. She claims that "[t]he aim of public policy is the production of *combined capabilities*" (*Sex and Social Justice,* 44).

with modern liberal concerns, Nussbaum distinguishes between *capabilities* and *functioning*, or *use*, of those capabilities. Nussbaum understands the state and various international organizations to focus, ideally and for adults, on capabilities rather than full use of those capabilities, with the recognition that certain basic functioning might, however, be a condition for other fundamental capabilities. In such instances, functioning can be prescribed. But, in general, out of respect for individuals and the centrality of human freedom, broader groups ought to focus on capabilities rather than full human functioning and flourishing.[32]

## The Capabilities Approach *as Aristotelian*

An Aristotelian account of the person—in contrast to, for example, a Platonic, Hobbesian, Lockean, or Foucaultian—informs Nussbaum's approach. She takes the position she articulates to be compatible with a number of metaphysical views, and she advocates acceptance of the position on political and not necessarily metaphysical grounds. Nonetheless, there is deep Aristotelianism undergirding the theoretical approach. There is implicit in the notion of capabilities an understanding of potencies moving to act, and she is clearly committed to the critical role of our particular material and social conditions for this process of actualization. So also, the way in which Nussbaum articulates and defends the universal character of these capabilities is distinctively Aristotelian. One of the great strengths of Nussbaum's work is her global focus.[33] Nussbaum understands the list of capabilities to be relevant to each and every human being, regardless of historical or social context.[34] She says of her universalism (something fit for an Aristotelian):

losophy that is strongly universalist, committed to cross-cultural norms of justice, equality, and rights, and at the same time sensitive to local particularity, and to the many ways in which circumstances shape not only options but also beliefs and preferences.[35]

---

[32] And, unlike Aristotle, Nussbaum emphasizes that the focus ought to be on *everyone's* capabilities and not those of a few. For further discussion of this point, see the concluding section of Chaps. 4 and 5 below.

[33] This feature has been criticized as well. See, for example, L.H.M. Ling, "Hegemonic Liberalism: Martha Nussbaum, Jörg Haider, and the Struggle for Late Modernity," conference proceedings, International Studies Association, 41st Annual Convention (March 14–18, 2000), available at http://www.ciaonet.org.isa/li101/, accessed April 1, 2009, and Karin Van Marle, "'The Capabilities Approach', 'The Imaginary Domain', and 'Asymmetrical Reciprocity': Feminist Perspectives on Equality and Justice" in *Feminist Legal Studies*, 11 (2003): 255–278.

[34] She says, for example, "I believe, however, that the human personality has a structure that is at least to some extent independent of culture, powerfully though culture shapes it at every stage" and that personality is "not thoroughly the creation of power" (WHD 155). See also WHD 6. Nussbaum makes a detailed defense of universalism in general. See especially WHD 31ff.

[35] WHD 7.

She is truly interested in cross-cultural and transhistorical norms relevant to all human beings. This universalism is not, however, Platonism. The Socrates of the *Republic* takes variation to be an imperfection, that is, a failure to express adequately that which is perfect in only one proper expression. Universal, for Plato, means repeatable or present in more than one case; universality does not, however, indicate multiple, appropriately varied expressions. On Plato's account, there is one — and only one — truly appropriate expression of the universal (i.e., the Form in its immaterial state). Aristotle, in contrast, understands universality to include variation; such differences in particular expression are essential to the universal structures themselves. There is no single expression of a structure that is the ideal. There is, according to Aristotle, a structure, and we can judge certain expressions to be more and less appropriate developments of that structure, but no single existing version would count as the permanent ideal. Sylvia Plath, Gabriel García Márquez, Herman Hesse, and Czeslow Milosz are all great writers, and they can be rightly judged to be so in comparison to, for example, most Composition 101 students and the majority of novels in the average airport bookstore. But this does not mean that there is a single example of ideal writing against which these four are measured. Rather, the four differently but excellently express the common human capacity to communicate ideas, images, stories, and thoughts through written language. Such variation in expression is essential to the Aristotelian understanding of what is universal.

Nussbaum, like Aristotle, finds the universal structures in the particulars, and she takes the universal capabilities to express themselves in quite differing ways in different contexts.[36] A well-developed sense of play might, for example, be expressed through boisterous laughter and energetic, highly organized games, or it may be expressed in more muted smiles and subtle teasings. So also, what is involved in the development of our capabilities may differ quite significantly. Someone living in a small tight-knit farming community in a culturally static region of an industrialized nation develops her practical reason in a very different context than someone living in a large, cosmopolitan city in a region undergoing tremendous social and cultural change. The development of her capabilities may be importantly tied to access to official cultural centers in one context, but not necessarily in the other. Although the general capabilities are common, the expression of these capabilities and the resources necessary to develop them differ significantly.

On one hand, to give up on the project of articulating universal norms would, Nussbaum argues, seriously risk our becoming pawns of powerful and often partisan non-moral concerns.[37] The articulation of universal ideals, structures, and

---

[36] In an earlier article, she describes her account of capabilities as a "thick vague theory of the good"; it is vague because "it admits of much multiple specification in accordance with varied local and personal conceptions" ("Human Functioning and Social Justice: In Defense of Aristotelian Essentialism," 214 and 215).

[37] She says, for example: "I am convinced that this wholesale assault on theory is deeply mistaken, and that the systematic arguments of theory have an important practical function to play in sorting out our confused thoughts, criticizing unjust social realities, and preventing the sort of self-deceptive rationalizing that frequently makes us collaborators with injustice" (WHD 36).

capabilities common to all of us provides theoretical ballast against such threats and a non-arbitrary position from which to critique such forces. On the other, however, to attempt to understand those norms as expressed in an identical manner in each situation is to overlook important cultural and material differences. It is to forget that we become ourselves through our particular circumstances. There will thus be—and ought to be—variation in how life, bodily integrity, affiliation, play, control of environment, etc., are realized in our very different social, economic, religious, and physical environments. Thus, Nussbaum is committed to a genuine universalism, but an Aristotelian rather than a Platonic universalism.

Nussbaum's focus on capabilities is itself Aristotelian, even if she differs in some details from Aristotle's account of their relation to the polis (and rootedness, or not, in a metaphysical theory). Her emphasis on the centrality of practical reason and affiliation draws from her reading of Aristotle's account of human functioning. Her vision of the universal as expressible only in quite differing particular circumstances expresses well Aristotle's understanding of universality, in contrast to Plato's. So also the very style in which she presents her position exemplifies an Aristotelian account of how we come to understand.[38] Nussbaum does not simply write a treatise, laying out her basic claims. Instead, she begins with particular case studies, telling us the stories of two quite different women in India. She regularly returns to these examples and exemplifies each point with particular cases—and yet she does not avoid making general claims, claims that are cross-cultural and transhistorical. She brings us to the general claims through an appreciation of particular instances, and our understanding unfolds through investigation into particular instances. But the universal is not reduced to a set of particulars. Nussbaum thus proceeds in a broadly Aristotelian manner, with a continual tacking back and forth between the universal claims and particular examples.[39]

Finally, Nussbaum maintains an Aristotelian concern for the common good. This

liberal commitments. In *Sex and Social Justice*, for example, she reaffirms these, emphasizing her liberal commitment to "the equal importance of each life, seen on its own terms rather than as part of a larger organic or corporate whole."[40] Later in the same text, she elaborates on the point:

In normative terms, this commitment to the recognition of the individual separateness means, for the liberal, that the demands of a collectivity or a relation should not as such be made the basic goal of politics: collectivities, such as the state and even the family, are composed of individuals, who never do fuse, who always continue to have their separate brains and voices and stomachs, however much they love one another. Each of these is separate, and each of these is an end. Liberalism holds that the flourishing of human beings taken one by one is both analytically and normatively prior to the flourishing of the state or the nation or the religious group: analytically, because such unities do not really efface the

---

[38] Exemplifying it better, in many ways, than Aristotle's own style of writing—at least in the texts we now have.

[39] Nussbaum's style reflects a general Aristotelian epistemology. I will leave aside whether it would do so given a more detailed analysis of Aristotle's theory of knowledge.

[40] *Sex and Social Justice*, 10.

> separate reality of individual lives; normatively because the recognition of that separateness is held to be a fundamental fact for ethics, which should recognize each separate entity as an end not as a means to the ends of others. The central question of politics should not be, How is the organic whole doing?, but rather, How are X and Y and Z and Q doing?[41]

It is clear in this passage—and Nussbaum means to make it clear—that she is not committed to an account of the common good as understood by many Aristotelians. Aristotle himself, in contrast to Nussbaum, was willing to organize the polis with an eye to the flourishing of certain members (but not all) of that society; he certainly appeared willing to subordinate some members—for example, women and 'natural slaves'—for the sake of the whole.[42]

A focus on the organic whole *at the expense of individuals* is not, however, central to Aristotelian claims regarding the common good.[43] What characterizes an Aristotelian focus on the common good—in contrast, to a more Hobbesian position, for example—is that living in political societies is seen as appropriate, fit, and even natural for human beings. Hobbes thinks that our political arrangements are a way to manage our fears; they are seen as a necessity for avoiding the absolute worst, that is, the battle of "every man against every man." In contrast, Aristotle understands living in such political societies as something fit to us as social beings and essential to our full flourishing as human beings.[44] Nussbaum shares this Aristotelian emphasis, and she not only places *affiliation* among the list of ten capabilities, she makes it one of the linchpin capabilities organizing and "suffusing" the whole.

So also, the Aristotelian common good tradition emphasizes goods held in common, that is, goods which are *ours* collectively, but not properly belonging to any one individual (for example, sanitary water, clean air, our governing institutions, etc.). There is thus a need to cultivate an understanding of ourselves as part of a community, sharing experiences, resources, and goods within that community. Generally tied to this is a concern for a common heritage, common social practices,

---

[41] *Sex and Social Justice*, 62.

[42] What Aristotle does not argue, however, is that women and 'natural slaves' are equally able as free males to flourish as human beings but, nonetheless, still ought to be subordinated. It seems to me plausible to read Aristotle as being willing to organize the state for the good of free males because, he thinks, only free males are truly able to enjoy such goods. Women and 'natural slaves' can enjoy lesser goods corresponding to their lesser abilities, and thus they are rightly, on Aristotle's view, accorded a lesser place, but a place where they can nevertheless flourish as the types of beings that they are. It is not clear to me, however, that, if Aristotle had changed his mind regarding the inferiority of women and 'natural slaves,' he would have continued to maintain his account of the overall organization of society. See also Nussbaum's "Nature, Function, and Capability: Aristotle on Political Distribution" in *Oxford Studies in Ancient Philosophy*, Supplementary Volume I (1988), especially 171–172.

[43] And it may not be a part of Aristotle's understanding of the common good at all, as suggested in the previous footnote.

[44] In *History of Animals*, Aristotle writes: "Social creatures are such as have some one common object in view .... Such social creatures are man, the bee, the wasp, the ant, and the crane" (1.1.488b8-9). See also *Politics* 1.1 and the discussion of 'civic friendship' in *Eudemian Ethics*. Nussbaum has a beautiful discussion of this dimension of Aristotle's thought in "Aristotle on Human Nature and the Foundations of Ethics," especially sections II and III.

and the social dimensions of our formation and development. Such elements may be seen as constraining our choices and hindering our understanding of the self as an 'autonomous individual,' but they can also be seen—and, Aristotle would argue, are more properly seen—as opening up possibilities, making us *free for* certain kinds of life that are not possible outside of the community (e.g., certain forms of education), and creating the conditions necessary for any of us to develop any degree of independence or autonomy.[45]

There are significant differences and disputes between more liberal and communitarian thinkers, and Nussbaum's identification of herself as standing within the liberal tradition is worth noting. Her particular form of liberalism has not forgotten, however, the Aristotelian insight into the common good. She focuses on the conditions—many of which are social—for the development of our capacities[46]; her work addresses the ideals that ought to be held by governmental and international agencies, i.e., those agencies called to promote the common good; and she regularly emphasizes, through both her examples and claims, the import of more localized communities and relations. Among the goods that she calls communities to hold as common goods are the conditions essential for the use of our capabilities. These will differ in varying contexts, but they involve, in each case, certain truly common goods. Although many of the values Nussbaum continually emphasizes are more traditionally liberal (e.g., autonomy and choice, dignity and rights), she does not focus on these to the exclusion of communal concerns. Hers is not a liberalism that focuses exclusively on autonomy and rationality, or even versions of autonomy that prioritize negative freedom or a largely acontextual rationality.[47]

Although there are certainly features of Nussbaum's account that differ from Aristotle's (e.g., her focus on *capabilities* rather than *functioning*, her claim that these are not comprehensive, her focus on more physical capabilities and less on virtues), and her interest in gaining political consensus differs significantly from

Aristotelian, and her arguments (including both content and style) are more fully illuminated when seen within their Aristotelian context.

---

[45]This is not meant to deny the reality that many (and perhaps even all) traditions, communities, and social relations have been hindering, deeply damaging, and severely limiting of autonomy and independence in various ways. The claim is not that communities are always good but, rather, that—because we are fundamentally social beings—we cannot develop our capabilities, become independent, or cultivate autonomy outside of all social relations. The constraints and hindrances need to be seen on the backdrop of our social nature. See Nussbaum's discussion in "Human Functioning and Social Justice: In Defense of Aristotelian Essentialism," esp. 225–226.

[46]She writes: "We see the person as having activity, goals, and projects—as somehow awe-inspiringly above the mechanical workings of nature, and yet in need of support for the fulfillment of many central projects" (WHD 73). Her comments about the family (at, for example, WHD 251ff) may, however, be in some tension with these commitments.

[47]It is certainly true that Nussbaum prioritizes these more highly than other, non-liberal Aristotelians (e.g., Alasdair MacIntyre). See also footnote 16 above. The point here is not to deny the significance of liberalism for Nussbaum's position, but to note the ways in which it differs from classic liberalism in its adoption of some, fairly substantive version of the common good.

## The Capabilities Approach *as Feminist*

What makes Nussbaum's approach *feminist* is that she thinks we ought to look with special attention at failures in reaching these goals for women. She opens her book by saying:

> Women in much of the world lack support for fundamental functions of a human life. They are less well nourished than men, less healthy, more vulnerable to physical violence and sexual abuse. They are much less likely than men to be literate, and still less likely to have preprofessional or technical education. ... women have fewer opportunities than men to live free from fear and to enjoy rewarding types of love.... In all these ways, unequal social and political circumstances give women unequal human capacities. ... These are not rare cases of unusual crime, but common realities. According to the *Human Development Report 1997* of the United Nations Development Programme, there is no country that treats its women as well as its men, according to a complex measure that includes life expectancy, wealth, and education.[48]

She thinks that, given the greater suffering of women across the globe, "international political and economic thought should be feminist, attentive (among other things) to the special problems women face because of sex in more or less every nation in the world."[49]

This focus on global questions—on the problems faced by women in the poorest countries and in the poorest regions of wealthy countries—is, I think, one of the greatest strengths of Nussbaum's approach. Suffering anywhere is an evil, and thus even the milder forms of oppression of middle-class, Western, or more privileged women ought to be addressed. Betty Friedan's *The Feminine Mystique*, for example, is not simply middle-class complaining; people write what they know of, and sometimes it is necessary to develop a sufficient sense of oneself before one can advocate effectively for another.[50] On the other hand, however, it is also time for Western feminism in particular to become more explicitly global, attentive to the most acute forms of suffering throughout the world and welcoming of global perspectives. This has been a trend in feminism more recently,[51] and Nussbaum's work importantly contributes to this shift.

Although embracing a more global concern, Nussbaum's focus is, nonetheless, not simply on the greatest sufferings but on the challenges for women in particular. That is, she thinks that we ought to look at women as a group. When addressing questions of justice or considering whether the conditions are set for the development and use of capabilities, we ought to ask how the various programs, resources, structures, etc., affect women and about whether women's capabilities in particular

---

[48] WHD 1–2. The *Human Development Reports*—in contrast to other forms of measure—were developed with an eye, at least in part, to capabilities.

[49] WHD 4.

[50] Although positioned as originating in suburban housewife experience, Friedan's great work may not be best understood as arising from middle-class concerns. See Daniel Horowitz, *Betty Friedan and the Making of the Feminine Mystique: The American Left, The Cold War, and Modern Feminism* (Amherst, MA: University of Massachusetts Press, 1998).

[51] This has been developed both through global feminism and various forms of third-wave feminism, focusing on the intersection of particular cultural, racial, and class features with sex.

are enabled. This focus is motivated, as she notes in the opening passages, by the conviction that women as a group are less well off than men and that women have suffered more in terms of capability-deprivation than men. Thus, one might argue that her concern is for suffering per se, rather than women as a group, and the focus on women is, for Nussbaum, simply a way of focusing on those more likely to suffer. Regardless of the reason, however, the approach can be counted as a legitimately feminist one. Nussbaum's focus is quite attentive to the situation of women, and her capabilities approach offers resources for both understanding the nature of women's inequality and offering reasons for working to overcome it.

It seems right to give Nussbaum's work the title of 'Aristotelian feminism'; our capabilities are, in Nussbaum's hands, as in Aristotle's, potencies distinctive to being human, which must be developed (insofar as they are) in and through our material conditions, and they can be developed well or ill. Like Aristotle, she understands these capabilities to be universal, applicable to all human beings, even though expressing themselves in distinctive ways in differing material and cultural conditions. Although perhaps less obvious because of her explicit liberalism, Nussbaum is also committed to a substantive version of the common good. Her focus is not simply on what individuals ought to do but, more fundamentally, on how governments, international agencies, and other communities of people ought to organize themselves, what they as groups ought to value, and thus what broad values *we* as human beings ought to hold in common. Many aspects of the content, although not all the details, are distinctively Aristotelian, while her emphasis on women and women's development is clearly feminist. Nussbaum thus provides a model for using Aristotle in a positive way for feminist purposes.

Nussbaum provides a critical model of Aristotelian feminism; nonetheless, I would like to advocate for an even more fully Aristotelian form of feminism. An Aristotelian account of the person is implicit, for example, in Nussbaum's focus on capabilities. An even more explicit version could, however, help address at least one point Nussbaum avoids and thereby enable us to be more fully feminist. One of the challenges Nussbaum faces is articulating an adequate account of how to run between the two extremes of *biological determinism* (that is, seeing our differing bodies as simply creating our gender) and full-blown *social constructivism* (that is, seeing gender differences as simply a result of social forces and not tied in any significant way to biological differences). Near the end of *Women and Human Development*, Nussbaum says:

> Particularly in the area of sex difference we have a great deal of evidence of cultural shaping at an early age. We cannot use such evidence to rule out a biological component in sex difference with regard to love and care; but we can point out that we are still where Mill

thought we were—in absolutely no position to know what that component may be, so early and pervasive are the environmental differences.[52]

This is an interesting claim. There might be a biological component to gender, she says, but because of the role of environment—that is, various social conditioning—we are "in absolutely no position" to know what kind of role biology may play. Similarly, just a few pages earlier, she argues:

> The tendency for women to focus their energies on care for children and family may well have biological roots; at one time in human prehistory such a division of roles may have had adaptive significance. Evidence concerning the human species is still too thin and indeterminate to say much with confidence, but there is at least some reason to think this may be so. But we should remind ourselves from the start that, insofar as such biological differences obtain, they are differences in tendency only, and they give us no reason to promote traditional roles for women or to fail to promote them for men—any more than the putative linkage of aggressive behavior with maleness (far more convincingly demonstrated—for example, by violent crime statistics everywhere in the world), gives us reason to relax the restraints of the criminal law or to view male aggression with special indulgence.[53]

Although the traditional division of labor may have some biological basis, the evidence for this is, first, "thin and indeterminate" and, second, it would—even if sufficient—only indicate tendencies which would not justify promoting traditional sex-differentiated roles. Her final analogy with aggressive behavior and males is, I take it, intended to make the point that, even if there were biologically-based differences, we must still ask the moral question of whether differing behavior arising from those tendencies ought to be encouraged.

In neither of these passages does Nussbaum deny that there are biological differences nor that such biological differences might have some significance for the development of our capabilities. But her emphasis, first, on our lack of ability to know whether there are truly biologically-based gender differences and, second, on our lack of clarity regarding our moral obligations, even if there are such differences, is used to justify a downplaying of biological difference. Because we are not yet in a position to deal with these questions, Nussbaum leaves them to the sidelines.[54]

Nussbaum makes a similar move in her 1999 *Sex and Social Justice*. She writes:

> Experiments that allegedly show strong gender divisions in basic (untrained) abilities have been shown to contain major scientific flaws; these flaws removed, the case for such

---

[52] WHD 267.

[53] WHD 264. For another discussion of these concerns, see "Human Capabilities, Female Human Beings," section 8.

[54] Nussbaum likely has other reasons for leaving aside these questions. She writes in "Human Functioning and Social Justice: In Defense of Aristotelian Essentialism": "There is much disagreement, of course, about *how much* of human experience is rooted in the body. Here, religion and metaphysics enter the picture in a nontrivial way" (217). Nussbaum repeatedly makes clear in WHD that her project is not metaphysical and that she is working for a political goal and thus aiming for the greatest consensus. I assume that at least part of why she hesitates to answer these questions is that doing so would engage her in more explicitly metaphysical projects and thereby compromise the more political goals.

differences is altogether inconclusive. Experiments that cross-label babies as to sex have established that children are differentially handled, played with, and talked to straight from birth, in accordance with the handler's belief about the child's biological sex. It is therefore impossible at present to separate 'nature' from 'culture.' There may be innate differences between the sexes, but so far we are not in a position to know them—any more than we were when Mill first made that argument in 1869.[55]

Nussbaum acknowledges that there may be a biological basis for certain aspects of gender; she acknowledges that our bodily differences as female and male might matter, but—she quickly says—because it is too difficult to distinguish the biological from cultural, we cannot pursue the question of how our differing bodies might matter.

Nussbaum is surely right that this is a difficult question to answer and that tremendous data (as well as better theoretical models) are still necessary in order to answer the questions well. Her general tack, however, is to downplay the significance of biological difference and emphasize rather the points of commonality among all human beings, while also looking at the places where women in particular have had fewer opportunities to develop those common capacities than men.[56]

Nussbaum's downplaying of questions of biological difference and their possible significance is understandable. When we claim that women and men are equal, there is a corresponding tendency to emphasize the relevant similarities, the ways in which we are the same and thus equal. When we emphasize differences, however, and particularly differences that have any kind of 'innate' or biological basis, there is then a temptation to see one version as superior to another—as Aristotle himself did. But in failing to take up this question of the significance of biological differences, or at least acknowledge more fully its import, Nussbaum neglects factors that open women up to certain kinds of abuse. If our biological differences *do* make any significant difference, then failing to take them into account will be damaging to

unjust situations. But it is not clear that in avoiding that one form of injustice, we

---

[55] *Sex and Social Justice*, 52. The position she is criticizing at this point in the text is a significantly stronger one than I will defend at any point—i.e., one claiming that there are innate differences of *capacities*.

[56] This hesitation to embrace any strong notion of the significance of biological difference is a relatively common and understandable one in contemporary feminist discussions. For example, in her highly influential and widely read *Justice, Gender, and the Family*, Susan Moller Okin similarly downplays the significance of biological differences, claiming that "the rejection of biological determinism and the corresponding emphasis on gender as a social construction characterize most current feminist scholarship" and "the new meaning of the word [gender] reflects the fact that so much of what has traditionally been thought of as sexual difference is now considered by many to be largely socially produced" (*Justice, Gender, and the Family*, 6). Nussbaum and Okin both downplay the significance of biology for gender. It would be a mistake to claim that they simply deny any significance to our differing biologies, but such differences are made inessential to the account. (This tendency to emphasize the social dimensions relevant to gender over any biological features continues to be a dominant one, as can be seen by looking at the Spring 2009 websites of women's studies programs at, for example, Smith College, Dartmouth College, University of California-Irvine, University of Notre Dame, Emory University, DePaul University, Fordham University, and Duke University.)

avoid the opposite error. Aristotle, after all, regularly warns us to beware of two errors, and not simply one.

Wendy Williams in her oft-anthologized 1982 article brings the question out clearly. Williams argues that if women, as many liberal feminists have been arguing, are truly no different from men—if in all significant ways women are equal to, because they are the same as, men—then it is time for women step up and shoulder the responsibilities, as well as the privileges, of an equal society. If women are truly fundamentally like men, they should be treated like men. There should thus be no exemption of women from combat or, if reinstated, the draft. Rape law should work in an identical way whether one is dealing with a raped female or male, and there should be no special treatment of pregnancy. Whatever benefits are offered to one sex ought to be offered, in an equal and perhaps identical way, to the other.[57] And it strikes me that Williams is right—unless we can give an account of how women and men are both truly and fundamentally equal and yet also different.

There may, however, be places where biological differences matter for the ways in which our capacities are developed. I do not know where or exactly how these differences will influence development in each case.[58] This book is not making a claim about *what* biological differences exists between (or among) the sexes, nor *how significant* those differences are for our development. My project is to lay out a theoretical model for incorporating biological differences into a more adequate understanding of gender development. This text is, thus, philosophical, offering a theoretical model, rather than scientific or psychological.

Although much more would be needed—including scientific data—in order to make very many specific claims about how capability-development would be affected, a more adequate theoretical model is, nonetheless, essential.[59] I worry that current models—for example, models such as Nussbaum's, which downplay biological differences, focusing nearly exclusively on the social construction of gender—discourage us from attending to biological differences. It is surely true that many traditional understandings of gender have missed the great significance of the social dimension of gender development. (This is, as I will argue in Chap. 5, one of Aristotle's significant failings.) And this failure has had devastating effects on many women's lives. But the contemporary feminist tendency has been to swing toward a social constructivism regarding gender—or at the very least, toward positions that inadequately articulate how they differ from such full-blown social constructivism. This swing leaves women vulnerable in a number of critical ways and compromises Nussbaum's project of pursing full capabilities development for all human beings. Before turning to a fuller discussion of why we need models that incorporate a more nuanced understanding of the significance of biological differences, I would like to

---

[57] Wendy W. Williams, "The Equality Crisis: Some Reflections on Culture, Courts, and Feminism," *Women's Rights Law Reporter*, 7, no. 3 (Spring 1982): 175–200.

[58] And thus, even if I am correct about differences, we might want to accept William's suggestions for the particular examples she discusses.

[59] I will, however, give one example of where this model could be used to understand educational institutions in Chap. 6.

look briefly at why many feminists—Nussbaum included—have tended to downplay biological differences.

## Reasons for Downplaying Biological Differences

It is understandable that Nussbaum and so many other feminists have downplayed
biological differences. There is no doubt that abilities previously thought to be tied
directly to biology are not so connected. It has been a hard-fought battle to show that
women's biology does not hinder their ability to succeed in, for example, professional realms. Nussbaum cites an 1873 U.S. Supreme Court case (*Bradwell v
Illinois*), decided in support of an Illinois law prohibiting female lawyers. Justice
Bradley wrote the decision, saying:

> The harmony, not to say identity, of interests and views which belong or should belong to
> the family institution, is repugnant to the idea of a women adopting a distinct and indepen-
> dent career from that of her husband…The paramount destiny and mission of woman are to
> fulfill the noble and benign offices of wife and mother.[60]

This is a strong claim—it is "repugnant," he says, for women to work in, in this case,
the legal field.[61] Biological difference (e.g., the fact that women can be mothers) has
been both an implicit and explicit justification for limiting women's access to property ownership, any significant role in the state, certain forms of formal education,
etc.

There is no doubt that an overemphasis on biological difference has been used as
a justification of much that has significantly hindered women's development. The
focus on biological differences has been precisely the concern of so many feminists.
differences, if we allow differing biology, for example, to be taken too strongly into
account, we will end up undermining equality, as much of our history has shown.[62]
It will be a way of eliminating professional opportunities for women and encouraging a lesser development of women's full range of abilities.

In 2006, Lawrence Summers resigned from his position as President of Harvard
University. Among the things prompting this resignation was outcry over comments
Summers made at a private conference in 2005 on the status of women and minori-
ties in the science and engineering fields.[63] In his lunchtime remarks, Summers

---

[60] See WHD 253.

[61] For more on the history of women lawyers in Illinois, see Meg Gorecki's "Legal Pioneers: Four
of Illinois' First Women Lawyers" in *Illinois Bar Journal* (October 1990): 510–515, found at
http://womenslegalhistory.stanford.edu/articles/legalpioneers.pdf (accessed May 2, 2009).

[62] Aristotle can certainly be cited as a case in point. For Nussbaum's articulation of this fear, see *Sex
and Social Justice*, 51–52.

[63] See, for example, Marcella Bombardieri's "Summers' Remarks on Women draw Fire" in *The
Boston Globe*, January 17, 2005, at http://www.boston.com/news/local/articles/2005/01/17/sum-
mers_remarks_on_women_draw_fire/, accessed May 12, 2009.

discussed a number of theses about why there are fewer women in these fields, including the idea that there are innate differences in relevant abilities between women and men. Although discussing various hypotheses and simply synthesizing the available data, as he described his approach later, he provoked a great deal of controversy with these remarks. Part of what made it so controversial is that Summers was, as president, the most visible person at one of the world's most prestigious universities. His raising of questions regarding possibly inferior innate abilities in women could not help but put doubts into the minds of girls world-wide about their potential to succeed in certain fields. And there are rightly fears that if such differences are chalked up to biology, there will be less motivation and commitment to discerning (and changing) the social factors that have contributed to the differences. Much work in the last few decades has uncovered differing social conditions and socialization, and changes in these conditions have enabled women to succeed in ways and in places where they were long thought 'not to belong.' Summers' call to look again at 'innate' differences threatens to undermine these successes. (And it is surely not insignificant for this controversy that, during his time as president, there had been a decline in tenure-track positions offered to women, dropping to only 4 out of 32 offers in the division of Arts and Sciences in the year prior to the famous speech. Summers was himself disturbed by this trend, calling it "unacceptable," and yet a decline in offers continued during each year of his presidency.)

Thus, on one hand, we have histories which have used biological differences between women and men (particularly, differences regarding reproduction, although certainly not exclusively) in order to justify a lesser concern for women's capabilities development. These claims to biological difference have been used to justify not encouraging (or actively discouraging) women to pursue certain fields—and often those fields which are the most economically, politically, and socially advantageous. On the other, there is credible scientific data that indicates that certain points of presumed biological difference may, in fact, be the result of socialization rather than biology.[64] A number of authors rightly caution us about overemphasizing sex-based biological differences. Anne Fausto-Sterling, for example, (in a text cited by Nussbaum) looks at research into the supposed differences between girls' and boys' abilities in mathematics, emotional variability, and aggressiveness. She concludes, in each case, that the data is simply not sufficient to justify any claims to a marked difference. In studies of girls' and boys' success in mathematics, for example, it was found that many studies failed to take into account the fact that the boys tested had often taken more math classes than the girls tested. Such differences in training undermine any attempt to use such studies for claims regarding innate ability.[65]

---

[64] Two nearly classic texts from the 1980s arguing this point are Anne Fausto-Sterling, *Myths of Gender: Biological Theories about Women and Men* (New York: Basic Books, 1985) and Ruth Bleier, *Science and Gender: A Critique of Biology and its Theories on Women* (New York: Pergamon Press, 1984).

[65] See Fausto-Sterling, *Myths of Gender*. In her more recent *Sexing the Body: Gender Politics and the Construction of Sexuality*, Fausto-Sterling returns to some of the same concerns. The themes of

Even in some of the seemingly obvious things—e.g., differences in athletic ability—the differences may not be as obviously biological as it, at least traditionally, has been thought. It has been agreed, for example, that, while women may be more skilled at precision archery (but not distance archery), gymnastics, and long-distance swimming, men are naturally faster at running and are overall stronger.[66] Men surely have greater upper body strength, and their legs are better fitted for running. Fausto-Sterling argues, however, that even these differences in athletic ability may not be quite as simple as they first appear.

First, the critical role of early childhood training through play provides a critical basis for the development of all of our athletic skills. Athletic ability requires training, and training women to any high level of athletic skill has not been a priority for much of our history. Women neither participated nor watched the ancient Greek Olympic games, and women did not officially run in the modern Olympic marathon until 1984.[67] It has long been assumed that women would be slower runners than men, were they to compete under any kind of equitable conditions. It is rather striking, however, that in the 20 years between 1964 and 1984, "women marathon runners have knocked more than an hour-and-a-half off their running times, while men's times during that same period have decreased by only a few minutes."[68] Fausto-Sterling cites the 1983 times, for a woman (Joan Benoit), as 2 h, 22 min, and 43 s and, for a man (Alberto Salazar), as 2 h, 8 min, and 13 s. The 2008 records stand at 2 h, 15 min, 25 s for a woman (Paula Radcliffe) and 2 h, 3 min, 59 s for a man (Haile Gebrselassie). The gap between the men's and women's records has been getting increasingly smaller: Between 1964 and 1984, it fell from just over an hour and 15 min difference between the record times to a mere fourteen and a half minutes, and between 1984 and 2008, the gap fell again to just under eleven and a half minutes. The fact of this decreasing gap and the persistence of the decrease (impressive in the first 20 years, but continuing through a second 20-year span)

formance is due to social and environmental factors rather than biological ones.

Fausto-Sterling calls our attention to our physical composition, noting that, although the percentage of body fat in nonathletic women is generally greater than that in untrained men (25% in women to 15% in men), this difference nearly disappears with athletic training.[69] Fausto-Sterling says, regarding differences in strength:

---

*Sexing the Body* are a bit broader than her earlier book, but she includes discussion of the development of gender and supposed differences between girls' and boys' brains, as well as extensive discussion of intersexuality.

[66] These are among the differences Edward O. Wilson points to in his *On Human Nature* (Cambridge, MA: Harvard University Press, 1978), 127.

[67] See Fausto-Sterling, *Myths of Gender*, 214.

[68] Fausto-Sterling, 218–219.

[69] See Fausto-Sterling, 216, citing a 1974 article in the journal *Women Sports*. We might also ask how much cultural factors play into our assumptions about what it means to be un-athletic for women and for men.

> The average strength differences between men and women result at least in part from men's larger size. The upper body strength of the average female (that is, strength derived from arms and shoulders) is about half that of the average male although, when matched for size, a woman has 80 percent of a man's upper body strength. The lower body strength of the average woman reaches 70 percent of the average man's, and when the comparison is made between individuals of the same weight a woman's lower body strength approaches 93 percent of a man's. Leg strength measured relative to lean body weight (leaving out the fat differences) actually shows women's legs to be 5.8 percent stronger than men's.[70]

Fausto-Sterling acknowledges differences in strength between women and men, but she notes that these differences are much smaller than might be commonly assumed and that the differences between human females and males are smaller than those between females and males of certain other species (e.g., gorillas).[71]

Although there are likely some permanent differences, the exact differences in height, weight, strength, and body fat ratios between women and men cannot be easily separated out from environmental factors such as early training and exercise, nutrition, and the role of both of these for the onset (and nature) of critical hormone changes. There may always be some differences between the average height and strength of women and men; it is, however, difficult to say exactly how much these will 'naturally' differ because of the critical role of more environmental factors.

Furthermore, the things that we think are different between women and men affect how we train girls and boys, in both overt and subtle ways. If it is believed that boys are faster runners or better in mathematics than girls, for example, care-takers (e.g., parents, teachers, the media and other sources of role models) are likely to encourage those boys to continue making efforts where they might not for the girls. The care-takers may maintain lower expectations for the less-'endowed' group and may divert resources to those thought more capable of using them, etc. These encouragements and various social resources are not unimportant for which skills are, in fact, developed, and these skill differences can—as Fausto-Sterling shows—come to exhibit themselves as *physical* differences, affecting our body composition, hormone levels, brain structure, etc.[72] The subsequent development of skill can then be used to justify the original judgment of which sex is more naturally suited to some activity.

This interaction between nurture and nature—between how we treat children and how they develop physically—raises important and difficult questions about how we can recognize genuine biological differences.[73] Nussbaum is right that it is not

---

[70] Ibid., 217.

[71] Ibid., 215.

[72] Fausto-Sterling notes: "*The physical structure of the adult brain—its size, number of cells, and most importantly its neuronal pathways—establishes itself in intimate interaction with the environment of the developing individual.* Nutrition, exercise, physical contact with other humans, exposure to varying sorts of visual and cognitive stimuli, all these and more influence brain structure" (*Myths of Gender*, 74).

[73] Ruth Bleier makes the point quite strongly: "But, most importantly, it is *not* possible to tease apart genetic and other biological factors from environmental and learning factors in human development. That is, in fact, a meaningless way to view the problem, since, from conception the rela-

easy to pick out and rightly evaluate the significance of these differences. Because we are social beings, we never encounter versions of biological difference uninfluenced by environmental and social conditions. There are no uninterpreted biological givens.

These cautions need to be taken seriously. The tendency in Nussbaum to downplay the role and significance of biological differences is not an accident, and Nussbaum and Fausto-Sterling are surely right that much that was once considered innate or biologically-based—e.g., women's unfitness for competitive team sports—has been clearly shown to be false. Such progress could not have been made without significant questioning of the biological bases of the assumptions regarding difference.

So too, advances in technology—including machines that make differences in strength, for example, less significant and technologies that have changed our relation to child-bearing and early childcare (e.g., breast pumps and infant formula)—have changed even our relation to what biological differences might be thought more permanent. Although it is still the case that, thus far, only individuals with female reproductive systems can carry and give birth to children and lactate, various technologies allowing control over the timing of reproduction and certainly technology separating the feeding of young children and women's bodies have substantially changed the way in which biological differences affect our lives. Thus, even where there are remaining biological differences, there are still questions regarding the *significance* of these differences. We can, as societies, make changes so that biological differences become less significant for how work and time are allocated to differing projects.

---

tionships between the actions of genes and the environment of fetus are inextricable. The very structure and functioning of the brain, the organ of mind and mediator of behavior, are influenced by environmental input both before and after birth. Thus, whatever the genetic and hormonal influences are on the development of our fetal and newborn brains, they are inextricable from the influences of the environmental milieu, from sensory input and learning. In addition, in its structure and function, the human brain is qualitatively and quantitatively different from the brain of other animals. Its capacity for learning, consciousness, memory and intent, motivation, intelligence, innovativeness, and flexibility frees us from predetermined and stereotypic behavior patterns, and it also has created cultures of staggering complexity and sophistication that affect our behaviors from the time of birth. No science or discipline can peel off layers of culture and learning and find an untouched core of biological *nature*. Rather than biology acting to constrain and limit our potentialities, it is, in fact, the supreme irony that our magnificent brains, with their nearly limitless structural and functional potentiality for learning, flexibility, and choice-making, have produced *cultures* that constrain and limit those potentialities" (*Science and Gender*, 6–7).

## *Reasons Not to Downplay Biological Differences or Uncritically Embrace Constructivism*

It is surely right both that social conditions shape, in deep ways, the ways in which our biology develops and that technologies and social conditions shape the significance of biological differences. But neither of these points, as critical as they are, yet justifies concluding that we cannot or ought not to distinguish, on one hand, biological differences which cannot easily be changed from, on the other, those amenable to significant change, given certain sociological factors. It is surely true that our biology always develops under distinct social conditions; this does not, in itself, show that we cannot or ought not to point to that which is amenable to greater or less social conditioning. It would be a mistake to think of any biological differences as expressing themselves outside of social contexts or developing in a way uninfluenced by social context. I fully agree that there are no simple biological givens. But granting these points does not mean that there are no recognizable biological differences among human beings, including sex-based ones, nor that we cannot say something about the degree to which those differences are amenable to various kinds of conditioning. One can make a *distinction* between things that are nonetheless inseparable.

Aristotle is fully committed to the thesis that distinction is possible even when separation is not—and it strikes me that he is right in this mereological point. We regularly distinguish, for a mundane example, between the color of a thing and its shape, even though no physical, colored item can exist without *some* shape (and vice versa). The shape can be varied, and the color can be varied. But shape cannot exist without color also existing, that is, the inseparability of shape and color in no way indicates that shape is indistinguishable from color. Furthermore, there can be 'lawfulnesses' relevant to shape which differ from those relevant to color. Colors, for example, move in a graded spectrum and certain colors look good with some colors, but not others. The 'rules' of fitness regarding shapes differ from those regarding color (shapes do not, for example, have the same kind of graded spectrum)—and we can distinguish these differences, recognizing the range of possibilities appropriate to each. Thus, in itself, inseparability does not indicate indistinguishability.

The inseparability of our biological development from our social conditions is a key point that needs to be made and has been well argued by Fausto-Sterling, among others. Fausto-Sterling points out well that we need to be cautious in making distinctions between our biological features that are more and less amenable to social factors, such as early training and investment of appropriate attention and resources. The point about the inseparability of sexual-differentiated features and social environment is one often overlooked in our histories and in need of making. But that point is not the same as, nor does it entail that, they are, in principle, indistinguishable.

Nonetheless, the particular types of interaction between our biological and social conditions may present particular challenges, at least in certain cases, to making proper judgments about whether some difference is more biological or environmental. These difficulties require us to use great care and to cultivate a rich self-awareness as we proceed, but the fact that we regularly make distinctions in other cases where there is a strong and intimate interaction between the biological and the environmental show that it is, at least in principle, possible to make these distinctions.

It has recently become popular to label food in the United States as 'organic' or 'natural.' Such labels are intended to point to foods which have been, in some sense, less changed by human interference than other foods (i.e., not using chemical pesticides or fertilizers on vegetables, and avoiding antibiotics and growth hormones in animals). None of the food in the grocery stores can claim to be free of social influences. The fact that the food is present there at all, that these foods rather than others have been chosen as healthy or fit for human consumption are socially-conditioned decisions. There are similarly numerous social choices and processes by which the seed for the plants is obtained, the plants are protected from insects, disease, etc.; the food is further labeled and priced so that it may be purchased at all—and all of these involve highly socially-conditioned processes. Further, there are numerous controversies about what counts as 'natural,' about what criteria a food would need to meet in order to be described as 'all natural,' and whether the government-sponsored criteria for labeling something as 'organic' are sufficient or even appropriate. These debates reveal the difficulties of distinguishing what counts as 'natural.' None of the parties are, however, attempting to separate out fully the biological, or natural, from the social but, rather, to articulate which practices are socially conditioned in problematic ways (at least for describing something as 'natural' or 'organic') and which are appropriate and in keeping with what is 'natural' or 'organic.' The debates within the food industry reveal how difficult such judgment calls can be, but they also show that making such distinctions is possible. Full sepa-

biological creates challenges—but these are also challenges that we regularly meet, more and less well.

If separability is not a requirement of distinctness, then the question for an Aristotelian feminist becomes: *How* do we recognize the properly biological in contrast to the properly environmental or cultural? What are the marks by which we recognize each, and under what conditions can we responsibly make these judgments? These are the questions each discipline addresses insofar as it does its work well, and they are part of everyday theoretical work. Making these distinctions in any particular case requires employing the methods fit to the relevant disciplines (e.g., biology, sociology, psychology). The methods of the natural sciences, the human sciences, the arts, and the humanities each differ in ways that are, under ideal conditions, fit to and appropriate for the particular subject to which they are dedicated. Insofar as the methods are good ones, they will be attentive to the marks of distinctness in and amid the interconnected features and thus able to isolate—more and less well—what is significant for answering the particular question pursued.

It is certainly true that the methods developed in each discipline have not always been ideal, nor have practitioners always well employed even good methods.

Feminist theory has been particularly important for calling attention to the places where the disciplines have not been sufficiently rigorous or true to their own ideals insofar as they have overlooked, for example, women's experiences and where the particular questions asked have obscured critical data related to women. There is yet much work to be done within the differing disciplines to ensure that they can well pursue questions as they relate to sex and gender. But the success of feminist theorists in pointing to these lacuna and the subsequent changes in many of the disciplines gives hope that critical methodological improvements can be made.[74]

It strikes me, first, that work distinguishing (but certainly not separating) 'nature' and 'nurture' can be done, and, second, that it ought to be done. If there are such biological differences, recognizing them is critical for understanding the conditions under which women, in contrast to men, develop their capacities. Even more significantly, if there are significant biological differences but we fail to notice this, then we are extremely likely to end up presuming a male biological model rather than a female one. Many of our structures, institutions, traditions, and practices—much of which has been set up in order to enable capability-development—have been inherited from societal patterns that prioritized the development of (certain) males. By and large (although certainly not universally or exclusively), more of our social resources have been dedicated to developing the physical, intellectual, social, and artistic capacities of males rather than females. For example, most of our universities worldwide have only been opened up to women in the last century or so.[75] And practices enabling greater political involvement (e.g., the opportunity to own property, vote, hold political office, etc.) have been evolving at a very rapid rate during the last several centuries. These changes have enabled women to cultivate and use their human capacities in different ways than in earlier eras. Such changes in the structures relevant to capability development and use are laudable and absolutely critical. But we still need to ask whether the changes have been pursued in ways that acknowledge equally women's development and men's development, conditioned by somewhat different biological features. Failing to do so may lead us to accept too easily institutions and expected patterns of development that favor a male biologically-conditioned development over a female (or intersex) one.

Once again, it is understandable that so many contemporary theorists have downplayed biological differences. But even if understandable and praise-worthy in certain respects, it is also dangerous. Further, it seems to me that an Aristotelian account of bodies—in contrast to either a dualist or materialist account—can provide us a nuanced account of the significance of biological differences for gender and gendered capabilities development. Thus, it seems to me both problematic and

---

[74] Methodological questions are, thus, I think best addressed from within and by the disciplines most relevant to particular questions posed. This is not to deny that more interdisciplinary work is necessary, nor that certain traditional divisions may need to be re-thought. But the particular method appropriate to answering any specific question regarding the influence of biological matter on gender formation depends upon the specific question asked, the particular capacity considered, etc.

[75] See the discussion of university education in the sixth chapter.

unnecessary to downplay in quite the way Nussbaum does our biological life and the significance of biological differences.

## Qualifying Note

In the concluding section of a 1995 article, Nussbaum asks whether there is a single human norm or two (a female and male norm). In that piece, she discusses claims that there are feminine and masculine roles (e.g., caretaker and breadwinner) and claims that there are feminine and masculine capabilities (e.g., more connected, relational ones and more detached, abstract ones). The claim that biology and biological differences matter is *not* a claim that such differences would lead women and men to differing roles in society.[76] And I absolutely reject claims that there are gender-exclusive traits. Nussbaum is right to claim that the capabilities are fundamentally human ones and not female or male. Anything that genuinely counts as a capability can be developed by both women and men. But one can accept that biological differences matter without positing female and male norms in either of the senses Nussbaum discusses.

Thus, in focusing on women's capabilities and the biological conditions for women's development, I am in no way suggesting that women possess distinctive capabilities which differ from those of men. But I would like to suggest that the *conditions under which* we develop our capabilities include our own biology and not simply other material and social conditions. It is absolutely true that biological differences have often been used to justify too much. There is a real danger to reading gender differences in any simple way off of biological ones. There is also, however, a danger in failing to acknowledge any genuine biological differences and any

attend to all of the conditions relevant to women's capabilities development if we do not attend to differing biological conditions (even while acknowledging the role of social conditions in our interpretation of the significance of those biological conditions).

---

[76] I can imagine some very, very limited situations where such roles might allow the fullest possible (given the overall circumstances) opportunity for capabilities development for both women and men. Such cases would, however, be exceedingly rare. Thus, I agree with Nussbaum that positions advocating such different and exclusive roles should be treated with extreme caution, if not outright rejected. See section VIII ("Women and Men: Two Norms or One?") in "Human Capabilities, Female Human Beings" in *Women, Culture, and Development* ed. Martha C. Nussbaum & Jonathan Glover (Oxford: Clarendon Press, 1995).

## Firestone's Radical Feminism

Nussbaum's tendency, and that shared by many feminists, is to downplay the significance of biological differences. There has, however, been an opposite move among certain feminists. Shulamith Firestone, in her classic *The Dialectic of Sex*, for example, argues that our biological differences are real and absolutely central for genuine feminism. Because we have different bodies, because women carry each child born in their bodies for, on average, nine months, because women have traditionally provided children's first food from their own bodies, and have thus been the primary ones responsible for the survival of human infants in what is a very long period of great vulnerability, there has been an inequitable division of labor written into nature itself. She states outright that these differences—and not simply the societal meanings attached to them (although also these)—are the reason for our history of inequality.[77] The solution, she claims, is quite simple: overcome our biology. If our inequalities originate in nature, then change nature. We have already done so partially, making differences in strength, for example, unimportant for much of the work we do. The development of machines and technology that overcome size differences is a great step forward. So also, we have developed technologies relevant to our reproduction. Women have more numerous options for control over when they get pregnant and with whom, and breast-feeding has become unnecessary, at least for those with certain financial resources. The ultimate goal is to make reproduction and child-rearing unconnected to sex, so that men as well as women can carry babies, or babies can simply be formed in an artificial womb independent of either women or men.[78]

Firestone's strong claims about the significance of biology, and the related need to overcome it in order to achieve equality, stand in contrast to Nussbaum's downplaying of such differences. In claiming that biology matters, I am not arguing for as tight a tie between biology and gender as Firestone advocates. One can claim that biology matters without claiming, like both the more traditional and the radical feminist positions, that it matters quite this much.

---

[77] Firestone attributes significant economic, social, and cultural (including the very notion of culture) differences to our biological differences. Thus, biology on her account has played a profound role in the whole history of inequality. For a brief summary of the critical biological differences, see Firestone, *The Dialectic of Sex: The Case for Feminist Revolution* (New York: Farrar, Straus and Giroux, 1970), 9.

[78] She says, for example: "The reproduction of the species by one sex for the benefit of both would be replaced by (at least the option of) artificial reproduction: children would be born to both sexes equally, or independently of either, however one chooses to look at it; the dependence of the child on the mother (and vice versa) would give way to a greatly shortened dependence on a small group of others in general, and any remaining inferiority to adults in physical strength would be compensated for culturally. The division of labour would be ended by the elimination of labour altogether (through cybernetics). The tyranny of the biological family would be broken" (*The Dialectic of Sex*, 11). See also Chap. 10 of *The Dialectic of Sex* for Firestone's development of these alternatives.

Firestone's solution—overcoming, by changing, our biology—is not an obviously Aristotelian response. For an Aristotelian, there is a dignity to matter.[79] Aristotle is not a dualist. We are not souls or minds who happen to be chained to matter. Matter and our material life is not incidental, unimportant, or undesirable. On the contrary, our biology is part of who we are and has its own dignity. One of the key themes of hylomorphism is precisely its emphasis on the dignity of matter and the material world. Hylomorphism understands us not simply as souls stuck in bodies but, rather, as bodily, material, cultural beings. Hylomorphism does not reduce us in any simple way to our bodies, but it does claim that bodily, material life is an element to be celebrated. Thus, the radical impulse expressed by Firestone to overcome our bodies is not the hylomorphic, Aristotelian sensibility. Although both Firestone and an Aristotelian feminism of the sort I am advocating agree that our biology matters more than Nussbaum, for example, acknowledges, I will not argue that our primary goal ought to be eliminating biological differences. Rather, our focus ought to be on changing the various cultural conditions and institutional structures that fail to encourage full capability development for individuals developing under varied biological conditions—including female and male biology.[80]

This focus on the positive significance of the material world does not mean that all biological or material changes should be rejected. Aristotelians certainly support, for example, artificial hearts, limbs, etc., that is, changes to the biological conditions encouraging the full flourishing of the human being.[81] Claiming that there is a dignity to matter (including female biology) does not mean that all changes to our bodies are unnecessary or inappropriate. What is critical is the development of our *human* capabilities. If the biological changes enable that, then they are appropriate.

---

[79] Aristotle himself saw the form as being superior to matter. See, for example, *The Generation of Animals* 732a5-10. And when this is coupled with his association of the female with matter and the matter, matter clearly has some kind of significant dignity in the Aristotelian account, and Aristotle's explicit comments critical of matter does not lead him into the kind of denigration of matter present in most dualist accounts (and certainly important to Plato's dualism, especially as articulated in the *Phaedo*). Furthermore, we can dispute Aristotle's problematic association of women with matter (see Chap. 5) without thereby rejecting the general Aristotelian hylomorphism.

[80] Firestone's radical solution, though provocative in many important and good ways, raises a number of further questions. First, it is not obvious that all differences need be oppressive. Certainly, most human cultures have treated some differences, at certain points, in ways that are problematic; but all cultures have also celebrated certain differences. Differences can, but need not, be treated in ways that are oppressive. Thus, differences per se are not obviously problematic. Second, it is not clear that we ought to devote so many resources to such radical changes in our biological structures rather than dedicating those resources to something else (e.g., eliminating hunger, funding AIDS research, better care for elderly, fighting sex slave trade, etc.). I am not convinced that our resources are best used for the projects Firestone recommends. And, finally, Firestone's solution suggests that she takes the root problem to be something best addressed by a technical solution, rather than a problem that is fundamentally relational or moral. Although there will surely be technical dimensions to both the problem and best solutions, I am not convinced that a technicist rather than a moral (and social) solution will ultimately be most successful.

[81] See Chap. 2 for further discussion of the relation of form and matter.

But any such change would not aim at overcoming our matter and materiality per se, but at creating material conditions which better serve the development of our human form and all our human capacities.[82]

# Conclusion

I am convinced that a concern for biological difference can be rightly incorporated into a nuanced account of gender. The account I would like to defend understands human beings as developmental, emphasizing—like Nussbaum—that we do not enter the world with as a full-blown self but must instead *become* ourselves. This view agrees with Nussbaum's approach in claiming that there is a basic set of human capabilities or capacities whose development is essential to our full human flourishing (although, unlike Nussbaum, I do not take a stand on *what* these are). Further, it agrees that our conditions are critical for how our capabilities are developed—and thus our early childhood experiences, our relations with our primary caregivers, examples and role models around us, societal expectations, as well as various physical resources such as food and shelter, etc., are all critical components of our development, including gender development. But in addition to these features, our biology itself (that is, our genes, hormones, reproductive systems, etc.) plays a role and is among the conditions in which we develop. Because of the role of biology—including sexual biology—our gender development is not solely the result of social forces, nor is it limitlessly malleable.

In making this final claim, it is worth noting that there are a number of senses of non-malleability or limited alterability. We might make the claim of *individuals* (claiming, for example, that there are limitations to how much social forces can mold a particular individual's gender), or of *groups* of individuals over a longer period of time (claiming, for example, that, although certain isolated individuals may be molded in nearly limitless ways, such limitless shaping power cannot be sustained over the long run).[83] Surely social and cultural forces can have a tremendous influence over both individual gender development and group understandings of gender, and it is a mistake of more traditional positions to underestimate the shaping power of social and cultural forces. But I am not convinced that these forces can tell the whole story. (I am not, however, committed to any particular account of limited malleability.) I think that we need to take biological differences into account in understanding gender differences, even while acknowledging that biology is affected and shaped by culture and that biology can be changed. It is not clear to me, however, that biology ought, in all cases, be changed, nor that biologically-motivated gender differences may not be themselves valuable. The goal is not, I think, to

---

[82] It is in this sense that matter serves form.

[83] Or one might make a different claim, arguing that individuals may only be molded in incremental ways, but—over the long run—some group (e.g., women) can be molded in nearly limitless ways. Each of these claims is slightly different.

overcome gender or even gender differences but, rather, to overcome inequality—and particularly inequalities in opportunity for capability development. Overcoming these inequalities in certain cases will require looking at points of biological difference and re-thinking and re-structuring, for example, some of our models of development, patterns of education, and institutions. Thus, I am interested in maintaining some notion of femininity and masculinity—some version that is not exhaustively understood as a social construct, although certainly developed in social contexts as well as biological ones.

Finally, although emphasizing throughout this book the import of biology, I will not be taking a stand on the question of *what* biological differences are relevant nor what descriptions of development should be considered more 'feminine' or 'masculine.' It strikes me as possible that we could articulate certain broad tendencies as 'feminine' and others as 'masculine,' but I will take no position here on which traits or tendencies ought to be so designated. This makes this book both less controversial and less interesting than it could be. But, unfortunately, I think that there are a number of issues (both philosophical and scientific) that must to be addressed before we can give more content to our notions of 'femininity' and 'masculinity,' and, since these go beyond the limits of this text, I want to save those questions for a time when they can be addressed more fairly.

In order to achieve these things, I would like to turn to Aristotle. Aristotle—and in particular Aristotelian metaphysics with its hylomorphic understanding of the person—offers us tremendous resources for running between the dual errors of biological determinism, which overemphasizes differences, and full social constructivism, which denies substantive differences, while still affirming full and complete equality between women and men. Despite his own avowed positions regarding women, Aristotle offers us something useful for understanding both why matter matters, that is, why our differing biology (among other things) is significant, with-

My claim is absolutely *not* that, because women can bear children and men cannot, women ought not to develop their other human capacities, that there should be limits in principle on the involvement of women in the professional world, etc. But I am claiming that, if there are differences of any significance between women and men, it is neither just nor feminist to fail to take those into account. We must, of course, be exceedingly careful about how we articulate those differences. But it is not progress for women—particularly for women who must struggle on so many other fronts—to pretend that there are no differences. And it weakens all of us not to acknowledge genuine strengths and distinctivenesses where each of us has them. One thing that we have surely learned from the history of medicine and psychology (among other fields)—something brought out so clearly by Carol Gilligan—is that: if there are points of difference between women and men and these are not noticed and made explicit, then the models that dominate will be male or masculine ones. If there are significant, non-malleable differences between women and men, it is rarely good for any of us, but *women in particular*, to ignore them.

It seems to me that one of the challenges facing feminists in general—Nussbaum included—is maintaining a full and true commitment to women's genuine human equality and dignity, fighting for the conditions essential for the development of the full range of human achievements for women in all areas of life, while also having something substantive and helpful to say about the ways in which women's differences from men become significant. The two dominate feminists temptations have been either to downplay such differences—as Nussbaum and most more liberal feminists have done[84]—or to overemphasize those differences. This overemphasis on difference has been the same temptation for both more 'traditional' positions—such as Judge Bradley's—and radical feminists, who think that the solution is to use technology to overcome biology. None of these, however, strikes me as a satisfying answer. Each runs the risk of overemphasizing that which is only an aspect of our development. It is time, however, for a more nuanced and full account. And thus it is time to return to Aristotle and find in his broad metaphysical principles, an understanding of us that can be more fully feminist.

---

[84] This is not only, however, the tendency of broadly liberal feminists. Insofar as Nancy Chodorow, for example, focuses on our *parenting practices* and not more biologically based features as accounting for the psychological sources of gender, she too downplays the role of the biological.

# Chapter 2
# An Aristotelian Account of Sex and Gender

We all grow and develop and must do so 'where we are planted,' in the time and era in which we live, among and with our contemporaries. Aristotelian hylomorphism, although perhaps a bit simple in its original form in light of contemporary biology,[1] nonetheless provides a set of useful concepts and distinctions, ones that can acknowledge our deeply situated character without giving up a commitment to fundamental structures common to all human beings. Key to Aristotle's account is the distinction between form and matter, or the formal and material principles. The first refers to the general pattern of development—e.g., the general developmental pattern characteristic of human beings in contrast to baboons or Arabian horses—while the latter refers to the conditions under which the development occurs. This distinction allows Aristotle to affirm that all members of one species can genuinely be said to share something significant and yet also so obviously and truly differ. All of us, according to Aristotle, share the same type of form—or principle of growth and development—and yet also differ in ways that are not insignificant. These differences are due to our differing material conditions, including not simply our differing physical matter but also our different cultural, social, historical, and linguistic influences as well as our choices and previously habituated patterns.

Aristotle's general account strikes me as possessing great explanatory power. It can provide a substantive account of commonalities among human beings and our human development—commonalities that make disciplines such as psychology and

---

[1] In claiming that Aristotelian biology—and thus Aristotelian hylomorphism insofar as it relies on that biology—needs to be updated, I am not making a claim about Aristotle's scientific method or his more general biological claims. I am not taking a strong stand on precisely how much would need to be preserved. For a defense of aspects of Aristotle's scientific method and general scientific claims regarding substances and essences, see Baruch A. Brody's "Towards an Aristotelian Theory of Scientific Explanation," *Philosophy of Science* 39, no. 1 (March 1972): 20–31 and "Why Settle for Anything Less than Good Old-Fashioned Aristotelian Essentialism," *Noûs* 7, no. 4 (November 1973): 351–365, as well as Richard J. Connell's *Substance and Modern Science* (Houston: Center for Thomistic Studies, 1988).

© Springer International Publishing Switzerland 2016
S. Borden Sharkey, *An Aristotelian Feminism*, Historical-Analytical Studies on Nature, Mind and Action 1, DOI 10.1007/978-3-319-29847-4_2

biology possible—and yet do so in a way that does not undermine or make insignificant our true individual differences.[2]

Certain specific aspects of the Aristotelian account of human beings are certainly in need of re-articulation and development in light of more recent philosophical and scientific developments,[3] but I think that core Aristotelian insights should be preserved. The following will not attempt to do that work of "creative retrieval" in any area but that of gender. As such, it is woefully inadequate to the larger task of updating or defending hylomorphism. I hope, however, that it will offer a plausible account of the striking commonalities among all human beings and among all women in contrast to men, and vice versa, while also acknowledging and accounting for the deep and significant differences among all of us as individuals. The general account I want to articulate will draw heavily from Aristotle, but it is not, and does not intend to be, a faithful commentary on or exposition of his positions. Rather, it is inspired by and draws from his writings, but departs—both in emphases and on a number of critical points—from his claims. The following chapter begins by presenting a general account of hylomorphism and the particular account of matter I would like to follow. I then lay out how this hylomorphism would be relevant to an account of sex and gender.

## General Aristotelian Picture of Human Beings

The Aristotelian hylomorphic vision of the human being understands each of us as a unity of *form* and *matter*, or the formal and material principles. Form is that which is responsible for our commonality; each human being has the same basic human structure or pattern of development. Matter is that which is responsible for differ-

human[4]) in a living human being. Thus, hylomorphism runs between the extremes

---

[2] Some, such as John Duns Scotus and Edith Stein, would strongly disagree with this claim that Aristotle preserves the significance of our individuality, and thus Scotus and Stein—albeit in quite different ways—posit formal principles of individuality. I do not yet see, however, that it is necessary to follow the Scotist and Steinian lines, so long as one has a sufficiently charitable read of how our material conditions and freedom are involved in our individuality. For more on this, see my *Thine Own Self: Individuality in Edith Stein's Later Writings* (Washington, DC: Catholic University of America Press, 2009).

[3] I think that both philosophical developments, especially Kantian and phenomenological developments, and scientific developments, especially in evolutionary theory and genetics, need to be addressed and incorporated. Work has been done in both of these areas, including, to name two among many, Edith Stein's writings, especially *Finite and Eternal Being*, and Bernard Lonergan's, especially *Insight*.

[4] Some qualified hylomorphists—for example, Thomas Aquinas—claim that, insofar as we are fully human, form and matter are inseparable. But temporary separation is possible. Thomas understands our form as responsible for more than formation of the body. It has, in addition, higher, non-bodily powers (e.g., mathematical and abstract reasoning) in virtue of which the soul

of *dualism*, which understands us as composed of two distinct and separable parts (usually a body and a soul, or mind), and *monism*, which in contemporary times is usually some form of materialism and understands us to be composed of a single type of thing. *Hylomorphism*, in contrast to both, understands us as composed of two types of principles, which are truly distinct and following distinct lawfulnesses, but nonetheless inseparable. Thus, we are, according to Aristotle, not a body and a soul but, rather, a body-soul, or matter-form, composite.

Aristotle describes the unity of form and matter as a substance. It is quite common since Locke to understand substance as a static 'thing'—and even more common to critique such 'substance ontologies.' This Lockean parody of substance is not, however, Aristotle's. Aristotle's substantial form in living things is primarily the center of unity providing a temporal pattern of growth and development.[5] Each form, as a pattern of growth and development, is growing and developing toward some goal or telos. The form is thus, for example, the baby squirrel's way of aiming at being an adult squirrel, with, presumably, four legs, a bushy tail, measuring within such-and-such a range of size, living on such-and-such foods, etc. Each type of form has a distinct set of directednesses and a telos making it to be *what* it is, and each form aims at full development. According to the Aristotelian tradition, form does not 'arrive' in the world fully developed. Form is rather a set of capacities or potentialities that must develop—gradually and over time—through our matter and in particular, historical conditions. Thus, for example, we develop our capacities for physical growth by eating sandwiches, apples, and pizza; our capacities for reasoning by playing with childhood toys or trying to figure out how best to comfort someone who has been hurt; etc. Matter, in contrast to form, has no directedness or distinct telos. *Qua* matter, it is simply plasticity for formation. Thus, matter's primary 'determination' is to be undetermined and capable of taking on the determination of the form. What it is to be matter is to be informed by the form, and what it is to be form[6] is to inform matter.

Core to the Aristotelian position is the claim that the elements in question are *principles* and not *pieces*. That is, the two elements are truly distinct but not separable. What it means to be a form is to form matter in a distinctive way, and what it means to be matter is to be open to formation. The two principles are truly distinct and one can attribute certain things to the formal or material sides, but one can never

---

can survive the death of the body. Our form or soul, however, longs to be re-united to a body in the resurrection of the body, and we are not fully human in the absence of our bodies. For more on the significance of the distinction between more pure and qualified hylomorphist, see Chap. 3.

[5] Substance is not, as Locke mocks it, that which 'we know not what,' *underlying* various qualities. Nor, contra Descartes, that which exists *by* itself. It is, for Aristotle, that which exists *in* itself, in contrast to accidents. '*In* itself' here does not refer to the kind of self-sufficient autonomy characteristic of Descartes's account of substance but, rather, the center of identity over time continuing through various types of (accidental) change.

[6] We should add the qualification that this is true only for what it means to be the form of a corporeal being. The case would be a bit different if there are pure forms—if, for example, there are divinities or angels who are developmental in some sense and lack matter, including any kind of 'spiritual matter.'

isolate and point to one principle separated from the other. Thus, one can *understand* the distinction, but not see or imagine it; what can be seen or imagined—that is, anything we can point to—is already a form-matter composite.

The hylomorphic tradition strongly emphasizes that we are a unity, a single individual, and not a couple of pieces stuck together. In the unity of the person, one can distinguish the formal and the material principles, but there was never a form or soul that was later added to a body. The two principles, however, have differing lawfulnesses. Each type of form, for example, has a set of goals toward which it is directed, which would count as mature or full development for that type of being and which distinguishes one species from another. That development cannot, however, occur except in and through matter. Similarly there is no bare matter; it is, rather, always formed in some way, as fragments of a leaf, or $H_2O$, or a liver cell. Thus, one cannot go on a search for pure matter or pure form.[7] They cannot be found except in a composite state. We can, nonetheless, distinguish within the composite each principle. Form is best recognized, however, by observing changes over time. Form indicates something closer to the temporal pattern of development than a static physical shape, while matter is the principle of potency, i.e., that in which the formation occurs.

## Matter

Thus far, the account is fairly straightforward. It is, however, misleading to think of human beings simply as the composite of our human soul and pure matter, as if the matter were a blank slate upon which the form is repeatedly stamped.[8] There are at least two difficulties with this account. First, such an image encourages us to think of the two principles as separable, like a hand hovering over the dough. Anything, however, that can be so separated is already an example of a form-matter composite. But, more importantly, such an image misses the ways in which our matter is itself

---

[7] Unless there are angels or divinities of some type, although one would not 'go on a search' for an angel in the same way one searches for a shoe or other sensible object.

[8] Fr. Norris Clarke makes the point: "The impression given by Aristotle and some textbook presentations of the doctrine is that every composition of form/matter is between a form exactly identical in every detail to every other in the species, united directly to pure formless primary matter with no intermediary levels. That is too simple a picture. In fact, though there is definitely one major, central organizing form that operates as the one fully autonomous and operative essential form, it organizes and controls lower levels of organized elements—cells, molecules, atoms, subatomic particles. These already have a certain formal structure of their own taken over and controlled by the central form to make them part of a higher whole; they are not purely indeterminate formless matter lacking any formal structure at all. They are rather subordinate levels of formal organization taken over and controlled or used by the higher central form for the goals of the organism as a whole, hence no longer operating autonomously" (*The One and the Many: A Contemporary Thomistic Metaphysics* [Notre Dame, IN: University of Notre Dame Press, 2001], 99). Fr. Clarke—in both his writings and conversation—has significantly influenced my understanding of the Aristotelian tradition.

already formed matter. Matter and form are, in certain ways, relational terms. On one level, the structure and pattern making something to be a cell can be contrasted with the matter of which it is composed. Cells are themselves, however, part of the matter composing a heart, and the heart itself is part of the matter composing the human organism, etc. Our matter is not simply prime matter (although it is ultimately prime matter) but secondary matter or formed matter, which is formed in and through the forming power of our own souls but also already formed to some degree by the formational work of another soul. Thus, the food we eat and form into our own bodies is not prime matter but quite particularly formed. So too—although this is a somewhat more controversial example—is the basic matter out of which human beings are formed (that is, each ovum and sperm) distinctly formed, carrying particular chromosomes and genetic material.[9] They are not prime matter but, rather, quite particularly formed matter. Each of these (as well as all secondary matter) can, however, be considered as material rather than formal insofar as they are open to further formation.

This way of articulating hylomorphism and the matter-form relation is not without its critics. There has been substantive and intense debate, particularly in the medieval period, about whether the relation of form and matter is a, more or less, direct relation between prime matter and a single substantial form or whether there are many substantial forms.[10] The scholastic monists defended a single substantial form; the scholastic pluralists defended the character of matter by positing many substantial forms, albeit hierarchically arranged. The account of hylomorphism I would like to defend here, by and large, follows that of Thomas Aquinas and the more Dominican emphasis on the unity of a being lying in its single substantial

---

[9] The question of the status of genetic material is a particularly interesting one and clearly not one Aristotle explicitly addresses. On one hand, genetic material seems to offer something more formal than material insofar as it offers prescriptions for our growth and development, determining eye and skin color, blood type, other physical attributes, and possibly contributing to the shaping of psychological traits as well. On the other hand, however, having a particular genotype does not, in all cases, require a particular phenotype. Nor does genetic material well account for elements critical to form: unity over time, a center of identity and unity of experience, etc. My leaning is to understand genetic material as heavily formed matter, but nonetheless material. We can then recognize how certain chromosomal patterns, for example, provide matter fit for human development, while other combinations are unfit for human development (accounting, for example, for some miscarriages). Although I am inclined to place genetic material on the material rather than formal side, the success of this general position does not depend on agreement with my leaning.

[10] For a very short summary of the debate, see Clarke, *The One and the Many*, pp. 143–145. For a more extended discussion of the history of the debate, see Daniel A. Callus, "The Origins of the Problem of the Unity of Form" in *The Dignity of Science: Studies in the Philosophy of Science presented to William Humbert Kane, O.P.*, ed. James A. Weisheipl (Washington, DC: The Thomist Press, 1961), 121–149, and the more brief discussion in Emily Michael's "Descartes and Gassendi on Matter and Mind: From Aristotelian Pluralism to Early Modern Dualism" in *Meeting of the Minds: The Relations between Medieval and Classical Modern European Philosophy*, ed. Stephen F. Brown (Turnhout: Brepols, 1998), 141–161. For discussion of a contemporary version of the debate, see John O'Callaghan's "The Plurality of Forms: Now and Then," *The Review of Metaphysics* 62, no. 1 (September 2008): 3–41.

form.[11] But the Franciscans' point that we must acknowledge the character of the matter involved is, I believe, critical. There are intermediate formal elements, not intermediate *substantial* forms, but secondary matter, which offers up to the human form conditioned matter.[12] This reading strikes me as fitting plausibly with Aristotle. He famously claims, for example, that the matter involved in the generation of a female is colder than that involved in the generation of a male.[13] We might not want to agree about the specifics of this idea, but it reveals a commitment to the differing character of secondary matter.[14]

Thus, in thinking of the hylomorphic matter-form relation, we ought to understand matter not simply as prime matter but also as secondary matter. We can, however, further distinguish differing types of secondary matter. Presumably—although this may be ambiguous—our genetic material (e.g., DNA, chromosomes, etc.) contributed by the ovum and sperm offer some kind of matter for our formation. Certainly the food we eat is matter taken in to be formed into bones, teeth, blood, etc. Although the matter may be differently involved in our formation, it is nonetheless, in all of these cases, offering conditions *in which* we develop as human beings and thus properly placed on the side of the material principle rather than the formal one (at least in the sense of our substantial form).

---

[11] Thomas sees it as critical that there is only one substantial form, although there are many formal dimensions to the individual. But without a single substantial form, there is no single, unified entity. And for Thomas, we can go no higher than organisms such as chipmunks, baboons, and human beings. No political group or company, for example, would be a higher level individual of which each person would be the matter, nor are physical events the matter composing God, as Whitehead argues. Thomas is not a process thinker. Nonetheless, below the level of substantial form, we can recognize various other form-matter composites. Thus, matter can be said analogously of anything with the flexibility and plasticity to enter into further formation

(by their power) [*virtute*]" in mixed bodies. See *De mixtione elementorum*, especially 15–18, in Joseph Bobik's *Aquinas on Matter and Form and the Elements: A Translation and Interpretation of the de Principiis Naturae and the De Mixtione Elementorum of St. Thomas Aquinas* (Notre Dame, IN: University of Notre Dame Press, 1998). See also Christopher Decaen's "Elemental Virtual Presence in St. Thomas," *The Thomist* 64 (2000): 271–300, for further discussion of the text. Steven Baldner summarizes Aquinas's position: "The elements are present by their powers in compounds. What does this mean? I think that Thomas means that the substantial forms of the elements corrupt when elements are made into compounds. When, in Thomas' terms, flesh and blood are made out of water, water actually ceases to exist and part of a human body begins to exist. He does not mean to say that the substantial form remains in any way in the compound. On the other hand, he does mean to say that the power or quality of the element does remain in the compound. ... the original power or quality of the element comes to exist in some altered way in the compound. ... but the exact nature of that character or quality is now determined by the new substantial form. Further, it is possible to extract the element from the compound, and when that happens, the element will retain its primitive qualities" ("An Argument for Substantial Form," *The Saint Anselm Journal* 5, no. 1 [Fall 2007]: 8–9, http://www.anselm.edu/library/saj/pdf/51Baldner.pdf [accessed January 28, 2009]).

[13] See, for example, *Generation of Animals* 4.1.766a15-25.

[14] Aristotle also discusses the elements in *Metaphysics* 5.3; *On Generation and Corruption* 2.1-8; and *On the Heavens* 3.3-8.

If we understand matter to include not just prime but also secondary matter, then the door is open for understanding matter in a way that is perhaps broader than is commonly done. Matter is that in and through which we become ourselves. Our development is not, however, just biological, and our capacities are not exclusively ones of physical growth. We also have 'higher' capacities to appreciate art, reason through complex situations, feel a whole range of conflicting emotions, etc. The friends we meet and the TV we watch provide matter for our higher formation. Not only do our bodies grow, we also develop abilities to cultivate and sustain friendships, to do calculus, and to negotiate complex political compromises. The matter involved in developing these capacities is not simply food but also the various examples of friendship we see in our lives, the particular mathematical equations and problems we worked through as children, and the successes and failures of our attempts to negotiate playground games. These elements are matter for our formation, which we—in an analogous sense—"take in" and through which we become ourselves. We do not take friends 'in' in the same way that we consume pizza, and thus there is an important dissimilarity between food and these more cultural and social kinds of matter.[15] Nonetheless, we can understand friends as material in the sense that it is through our friendships that we learn to be friends and thus actualize our capacities for certain kinds of relationship. (This is certainly not to claim that we engage in friendships simply for the sake of our development, or that interpersonal relationships are fundamentally about achieving some individual telos. Friendships may be both for the sake of the friendship itself and also thereby self-developmental.) Thus, when we talk of matter and the formed matter upon which our substantial form works and we become ourselves, I would like to include the whole range of social, linguistic, and historical influences as well as our more biological matter and the food we eat.

On one hand, we can draw a general distinction between form and matter. On the other, however, substantial form is not the only form involved. There are various types of secondary or formed matter involved. We can probably make numerous distinctions among the differing types; for this purpose, however, I would simply like to distinguish two broad types of secondary matter: (a) *biological matter* and (b) *environmental* and *cultural matter*.[16] The first, biological matter, refers simply to our various physical, biological features—our hormones, chromosomes, particular organs including reproductive organs, etc.—as well as the nutrition we take in for our physical growth and any hormones or drugs taken to change our physical state. The second, environmental and cultural matter, refers to the whole host of social,

---

[15] It is not clear, however, that all biological matter ought to be thought of on the model of pizza. DNA and our various organs (heart, lungs, etc.) are not 'taken in' like food either.

[16] I originally referred to this matter simply as 'cultural matter,' but Deborah Savage and Mary Lemmons objected to this choice as too misleading (University of St. Thomas, St. Paul, MN, October 23, 2008). I am grateful for their alternative suggestion of environmental matter.

historical, and linguistic influences relevant to the development of our more than merely biological capacities.[17]

My inclusion of environmental and cultural matter in this account of matter may seem to depart a bit from Aristotle's intentions. Cultural influences, for example, would seem to be formal rather than material. They are fundamental to the 'common good' toward which we aim, and thus would seem to be formal in the paradigmatic sense—i.e., that which *forms us* rather than that in which formation occurs.[18] It is surely true that, in some very profound sense, what I have termed 'environmental and cultural matter' forms us rather than acting simply as the matter for formation. But this is true of all secondary matter. Consistently eating fast food forms us (in one sense) quite differently than eating a balanced diet; possessing a double X chromosomal structure directs our development in a different way from possessing an XY chromosomal pattern; etc. Our matter is not simply unformed stuff, and the nature and quality of our secondary matter is not insignificant for the way in which our substantial form unfolds itself.

The fact that something forms us in some sense is not sufficient for placing it on the side of the formal rather than the material principle (at least insofar as the focus is on the formal and material principles of a substance). What makes something formal is that it characterizes *what* a thing is. Our cultural influences, although important, do not characterize *what* we are.[19] Whether an individual lives in a democracy, oligarchy, or anarchic state, she will be a human being if she has a human form. There are certain features or patterns characteristic of human development that are independent (in principle, not in fact) of social environment. This does not mean that the environment is insignificant for the development of those human patterns; but we evaluate the adequacy of that environment in comparison to the relatively invariant and deeply characteristic patterns marking human (in contrast to other types of) development.

influences, including the people around us, on the side of matter rather than form. Aristotle himself is not adverse to including living things, which are in their own right substances, on the side of another substance's material principle. He says, for example, in the *Politics*:

> as in the arts which have a definite sphere the workers must have their own proper instruments for the accomplishment of their work, so it is in the management of a household. Now instruments are of various sorts; some are living, others lifeless; in the rudder, the pilot of a ship has a lifeless, in the look-out man, a living instrument; for in the arts the servant is a kind of instrument.[20]

---

[17] For an alternative account of 'formed matter,' see Lonergan's discussion of conjugate forms and Allen's appropriation of that to questions of gender in Chap. 2 of her forthcoming Volume III of *The Concept of Woman*.

[18] I am grateful to Brendan Palla for taking the time, during his celebration of his former housemate's wedding reception, to make this critique.

[19] They may significantly shape our identity, but they are not essential to us *qua* human.

[20] *Politics* 1.4.1253b2626-30.

Similarly in his discussions of the virtue of friendship in the *Nicomachean Ethics*, Aristotle distinguishes different types of friendships and emphasizes the significance of friendships of the good over those of utility and pleasure. We cannot develop proper friendships or the virtues enabled by friendships of the good without having friends. Our friends are thus part of the matter by which we cultivate our capacities in these respects. Our friends do not lose their own status as themselves substances in becoming part of the matter through which we actualize our capacities, nor does the fact that they are material in any way undercut the truth that these friendships are deeply formative for the individual.

It is tempting to think of matter as simply inert stuff, something closer to food or construction materials rather than the influences exerted by our friends and family. But the Aristotelian understanding of matter is not the modern vision of dead matter in motion. Matter, for Aristotle, is a principle, not a thing. The temptation to think of matter on the model of things is precisely one of the temptations Aristotle's hylomorphism is meant to challenge. Thus, although perhaps not the common description, I nonetheless think that environmental and cultural influences are properly material, in an Aristotelian sense, rather than formal.

In making this distinction between biological matter and environmental and cultural matter, I am not claiming that these are separable. Differing kinds of secondary matter can be distinguished without claiming that we experience these in separation from each other, as if we could have a pure experience of biological matter in contrast to some pure experience of environmental and cultural influences. All of our experience includes elements of both. For example, a slice of pizza eaten for lunch is part of our biological material. But the fact that we eat pizza is not unrelated to significant environmental and cultural influences (including our understanding of tomatoes as not poisonous and our distinctive association, whether warranted or not, of pizza with Italian cuisine). So also our understanding of our own bodies is not unrelated to developments in the medical sciences and cultural influences prioritizing certain aspects of physical bodies. There are no *experiences* that are purely physical or biological. Nonetheless, a distinction can be made between the biological and the environmental and cultural. In making this distinction, I am in no way claiming that the one occurs in isolation of the other, but I am claiming that we can understand and distinguish that in the experience which belongs on the side of the biological (or functions according to biological lawfulness) and that which belongs on the side of the environmental and cultural. This does not mean that in every case we can accurately make such a distinction. There may be cases where the experience is highly ambiguous or we lack something necessary for rightly making the discrimination. But these difficult cases do not show that, in principle, such a distinction cannot be made.

If this is correct, then we can distinguish not only (substantial) form and matter, but also various types of secondary matter. Form is responsible for *what* we are; matter, however, is critical for *how* we develop. Aristotle understands the quality of our formation to be tied, in significant part, to the fitness of the matter involved for that formation. Insofar as our form is of the same kind, we will grow and develop in broadly the same ways, will all be of a common species, and will share basic capacities. Insofar, however, as the matter and conditions in which the form must actualize itself differ, we will be quite different. And some matter is simply better for human formation than other matter. For example, some books are just plain better for developing our capacities to think critically than others. Some stories develop our affective abilities and range more fully than others. Thus, the quality of our formation is not unrelated to the quality of the matter involved. But there is also a range of differing matter all of which might quite effectively help actualize our capacities. Children can eat tofu or oatmeal, curry chicken or black-eyed peas. So also we can read stories of Tom Sawyer or Harry Potter, play Mozart or Miles Davis. Not all matter is equally good for human formation, but there may be many different materials all of which may be equally good for human formation.

What is critical for the hylomorphist is, first, the claim that formation occurs in and through matter and, second, the commitment to a temporal structure of development and thus some kind of teleology common to all forms of the same type, even if actualized in and through quite differing matter. Thus, although our form is common, our matter is not. At the level of secondary matter (including both biological matter and environmental and cultural matter), we differ significantly. Further, for rational beings, such as human beings, we need to add the import of our freedom and choices for the development of form. I may choose not to go to the gym but rather read Jane Austen. In doing so, my intellectual and affective faculties may be further developed but at the expense of my physical and perhaps social faculties. Thus, in analyzing our development, we need to attend to secondary matter (in all its varieties), substantial form, and the import of our freedom and our choices.

## Form

Just as I made a number of distinctions among differing types of matter, so also I would like to clarify differing understandings of what might be meant by form and various capacities of form. Aristotle uses only one Greek word (δύναμις, and its variants) for a whole range of terms translated as *capacity, ability, potency, potentiality,* etc.[21] There are, however, subtle differences among these. Aristotle was not unaware of this, but he made the distinctions without employing distinct terms. I will try to use the term *capacity* to refer to a positive ability or power of the soul.[22] Thus, all beagles, for example, have a capacity allowing them to sniff out rabbits.[23]

[21] I am grateful to Alasdair MacIntyre for pointing this out and referring me to relevant texts.

[22] Although relevant, by and large, I will not be discussing Aristotle's account of our faculties or their relations. For a few very brief comments on the relevance of such a faculty psychology, see Chap. 3 below.

[23] The notion of a *potency* strikes me as broader than that of a *capacity*. All capacities are potencies of a being, but not all potencies need be capacities. I take a *potency* to refer to something possible for some being but without requiring (as in the case of capacities) a positive goal-directed-ness. It is possible, for example, for beagles to be bowled over by boulders. The beagle need not have any positive ability to be so acted upon, but it is nonetheless a potency of beagles. We could contrast

In the matter-form composite, however, certain capacities of form may not be able to be actualized. For example, it is a capacity of all human beings to engage in a walking motion. Someone lacking a leg, however, may not have the *ability* to realize that capacity. Thus, all human beings have the same capacities, but we do not—because of material differences[24]—have the same abilities. These differences are not indicative of different fundamental capacities but, rather, different present abilities to actualize those capacities. Some of these inabilities may be deep-seated and long-term; some may be temporary or superficial.

The claim here is that all human beings are identical at the level of capacities. There may be differences at the level of abilities, but these differences are due to matter (either biological or environmental and cultural), not form. On this view, however, there are, contra Aristotle himself, no differences of ability overall due specifically to female biological matter rather than male biological matter. Our sexually-differentiated biological conditions may influence or offer incentives to the development of our various capacities, but there is no reason, insofar as we are female or male, that the conditions be inferior.[25]

Critical to this position is the claim, first, that equality originates in our form and, second, that our biological matter as female, male, or intersex in no way undermines that equality of form. Our form is the seat of our common human capacities, and no human being lacks any of the human capacities, even though material conditions (or choices) may be such that a particular person lacks certain human abilities.

There are a number of challenges that these claims raise, and many of the challenges circle around the distinction between *capacities* and *abilities*. It is not at all obvious what counts as a capacity, how we ought to recognize capacities, or whether one can truly maintain this distinction between capacities and abilities. I would like to address three of these challenges.

First, how do we recognize capacities in contrast to abilities? Is, for example, the carrying of a child within one's body a capacity or an ability? By and large, pregnancy is not a common male experience. (There is, however, the case of Thomas Beatie giving birth to a little girl. Beatie had, however, formerly been biologically female and maintained his female reproductive system.[26]) In contrast, most adult

---

such a potency with the logical possibility that a beagle could sprout wings and fly over the boulder. Such a thing is not logically impossible, but it does not reflect any genuine potency of the beagle. Thus, a potency is not a mere logical possibility but is, rather, based in the structure of the being. Capacities, however, require the further element of being positively oriented toward their own full development and thus are distinctly teleological.

[24]These material differences should be understood broadly and may include chromosomal patterns, hormone levels, available food, social influences and role models, etc.

[25]For more defending this claim, see the discussion of Aristotle's position in Chaps. 4 and 5.

[26]A more interesting case would be the male pregnancy advertised by "RYT Hospital-Dwayne Medical Center" (see www.malepregnancy.com [accessed January 28, 2009]). The site advertises a medical center that has, they claim, successfully begun a pregnancy in a man without a female reproductive system. Although a striking website, it is no more than that yet. Were pregnancy in a male with an exclusively male reproductive system to become possible, significant medical intervention would be necessary.

women have an orientation to carry a child, even if, as in cases of infertility and advanced age, the material conditions may be such that a particular woman cannot do so. Thus, there seems to be an ability common to women that is regularly not present in men. If this ability originates in a capacity, then the commonality at the level of capacities would be eliminated.

I do not think, however, that we should understand capacities in this way. Rather, we should say that the capacity is *generation* or *reproduction*, not the particular material mechanism by which women and men contribute to the generation of a child. Both women and men equally have the basic capacity for generation, and each can contribute to the generation of either female or male children. Women can contribute to the generation of a child with a male reproductive system, just as men can contribute to the generation of a child with a female reproductive system. There is thus flexibility in the kind of reproductive systems we can ourselves help generate; therefore, our capacity does not seem to be simply to produce a child *like us*, but to produce a child with generative capacities. Thus, it seems to me better to describe the general generative functioning as the capacity and not the material specification of that. Thus, although women's and men's particular abilities in generation differ, their capacities for generation per se do not.

How, though, does one recognize our capacities? We never meet a soul or form running around by itself. Core to the hylomorphic account is the claim that form is the formation of matter. If so, then we can never get a clear-eyed vision of the form, independent of matter, and thus an unambiguous account of the capacities untainted by our material (and often hindering) conditions. We never meet, for example, the capacity to generate that is not specified in some way. All capacities must be distinguished through the abilities we see actualized around us. How then do we recognize which, of the abilities we encounter, express well common human capacities, and which are imperfect actualizations of a much richer capacity? This task is particularly important because our account of the human capacities — and thus the proper pattern of human development and ideal for full development — is the standard by which we judge what counts as healthy versus unhealthy, normal versus abnormal, good versus defective, etc. If we have an incorrect standard, our judgments will likewise be affected. And given the number of lives and the depth at which such judgments can affect lives, it is critical to judge well.[27]

---

[27] There is a temptation, given the risks, to think that we ought not to make such judgments at all. Why call anything 'defective,' 'abnormal,' or 'unhealthy'? Why not simply understand variations as 'differently healthed,' etc.? And yet this approach itself is already making judgments calls about what is appropriate or fit, and what is not; it is, after all, claiming that certain judgments are inappropriate to make, etc. It strikes me as impossible to get away from making such judgments, and the very attempt to do so is itself a variant of such a judgment. But further and perhaps more importantly, without some criteria regarding human nature, we would significantly hinder our development. We would have little way of judging that we should eat this but not that, do that but not this, etc. Our understanding of human nature and the human capacities may need to be much more nuanced and complex, articulated more in terms of ranges and spectrums, than has been traditionally done, but such changes would not involve getting rid of a concept of human nature or human capacities, but of improving on our understanding of it.

The general tack of Aristotle—and the tack that strikes me as the right one to take, even if it is not easy—is to identify capacities proper with what is common and marks our 'for the most part' development.[28] Thus, for example, it is common to women and men to reproduce but not to carry a child within a womb. Thus, the former but not the latter is a human capacity. And, for the most part, mature healthy human beings are able to reproduce. And thus, reproduction is a human capacity, even though a good number of human beings are not able to do so. There is no easy way to make these judgment calls in all situations. Given limited experience, one can make the wrong generalization, thinking some pattern marks proper human development when, in fact, it may not. Our judgments may erroneously focus simply on some specification of a capacity (focusing perhaps on male, rather than human, development) and thus not be representative of the full complexity of that human pattern.[29] Or they may overestimate the import of some material condition and thus mistake a pattern enabled by certain cultural conditions to be the *human* pattern per se. Such errors have occurred many, many times and have been the basis for much sexism and racism. Carol Gilligan, for example, points to one in her critique of Kohlberg's theory of moral development. Kohlberg thought that he had articulated a pattern of human development in moral reasoning. Gilligan argues that he drew, however, from too small a set of examples and ended up making inadequate judgments about what counts as the ideal pattern for developing one's moral reasoning. He overestimated experience conditioned as male and presumed that it represented *human* capacities and thus right human development, rather than simply one specification of that development.[30]

---

[28] In *Metaphysics* 11.8, Aristotle writes: "We say that everything either is always and of necessity …, or is for the most part, or is neither for the most part, nor always and of necessity, but merely as it chances….Now we have said what the accidental is, and it is obvious why there is no science of such a thing; for all science is of that which is always or for the most part, but the accidental is in neither of these classes" (1064b31-1065a5). Aristotle here claims that there can be a science of the 'for the most part.'

There are several ways in which study of the human form could be a science of the 'for the most part.' On the one hand, we could argue that, even if all of the capacities are necessarily a part of the species-form, they would nonetheless only be properly *expressed* 'for the most part.' Thus, study of human capacities is interested in what is necessary, but that is found only in 'for the most part' expressions. On the other hand, we might think that the capacities themselves are only present 'for the most part,' and thus argue that the essence or form is that which is within some statistical range of a certain pattern, accommodating evolutionary theory. Regardless, either version would require some degree of shift in our understanding of definitions away from Aristotle's emphasis on necessity and universality in his logical works to a 'for the most part' account, closer to that mentioned in the *Metaphysics*.

[29] For a brief discussion of such challenges, see *Generation of Animals* 3.10.

[30] A number of feminist critics, including Luce Irigaray, have criticized Aristotle for beginning his studies with *endoxa* [received or expert opinion], all of which was male (and upper class). Freeland notes: "I can't recall a single case of a woman expert being cited in any Aristotelian survey of *endoxa*" ("On Irigaray on Aristotle," 78–79). Although beginning with an analysis of expert opinion and historically accepted positions strikes me as laudable, critics are surely right that Aristotle's beginning points were likely limited, at least for the analysis of certain topics.

As far as I can tell, there is no way to avoid all such mistakes. If hylomorphism is right, such a risk is inevitable. But there are ways to find and correct those errors, and Gilligan again provides a great model. Gilligan does not advise getting rid of all models of what would count as appropriate and inappropriate moral development. Rather, she first points to the places where Kohlberg's model is limited and then articulates a second pattern of development. Both of the models Gilligan articulates are patterns of how we can develop as moral reasoners; both mark more and less advanced stages; both provide criteria for recognizing adequate and inadequate development. And thus Gilligan maintains a theory of *human* development, but she shows why an account more complex than that given by Kohlberg—one that can map a greater range of possibilities and take into account a fuller scope of conditions—is needed.

Might there be cases where the material conditions so qualify a capacity that very few human beings are able to actualize that capacity and thus enable us to recognize it as a human capacity? Might certain capacities be so consistently hindered by our material conditions that it is nearly impossible to recognize them as proper to human beings? First, it seems to me that, if hylomorphism is right, having material conditions per se could not be the problem. But our particular material conditions (perhaps due to the pervasiveness of some toxin or the persistence of a disease) may consistently be so far from ideal that they hinder us from recognizing certain truly human capacities. This strikes me as a real possibility. And as conditions change, we might so change our pattern of how certain capacities are developed that we barely recognize our ancestors as like ourselves. But the fact that we can do some kind of science of human beings and study of the patterns of our psychological, moral, emotional, biological, and spiritual development, and the fact that we can distinguish a set of beings recognizable as human (albeit not without occasions of significant disagreement and ambiguity but nonetheless for the most part), offer

of human beings.

I have claimed that the form is the principle of growth and development, functioning as the metaphorical 'seat' of our capacities. What precisely, however, is the form? Although I hope that this has been made clear already, it is nonetheless worth reiterating that form or soul in Aristotle's sense is *not* a Cartesian mind or the type of immaterial substance common to dualist conceptions.[31] It is a principle—not a thing-like item. It is closer to a 'life force' or principle of organization, than a chair or ghost. Nonetheless, there are differing leanings among Aristotle interpreters, understanding his account of form as leaning in more materialist directions, seeing the form as essentially the functioning of the organism, and more spiritual-leaning interpretations, seeing the form as closer to an immaterial power of organization

---

[31] I should qualify this slightly. There is debate about how to interpret certain sections of Aristotle, for example, his discussion in *Nicomachean Ethics* 10.7 and the discussion in the *Metaphysics* of *primary ousia*. I will not, however, be following lines of interpretation that understand substance as a non-composite form.

fitting well with the possibility of immortality.[32] I would like to leave the account presented here open to a range of leanings. Whatever (substantial) form is, however, it must (a) be a principle (although it need not be 'thingly') of organization 'articulating,' in some sense, the pattern by which an organism takes in matter and organizes it, (b) reveal itself in a thing's temporal development, and (c) account for how the organism is one entity with identity over time.

## An Aristotelian Account of Women and Men

### *On the Terms Sex and Gender*

This Aristotelian account of the distinction but inseparable interaction between a formal and material principle has great explanatory power for making intelligible the nature of, and difference between, sex and gender. Before turning to this, however, I would like to clarify my use of the terms 'sex' and 'gender.' Prudence Allen and Beatriz Vollmer de Marcellus both trace the origin of the distinction between the two terms to anthropology in the mid-1970s, and Allen places its introduction into philosophical discussion in the following decade.[33] In general, the distinction is made between *sex*, which is seen to be biological (e.g., female and male), and *gender*, which refers to our psychological self-understanding, behaviors, and meanings often associated with sex (e.g., femininity and masculinity). I find this broad distinction to be useful, but there are a number of oddities about the distinction, and some writers — including Allen — object to it. Among the oddities are the very words used. 'Gender' is linguistically related to terms that are explicitly tied to our biology, including 'generate,' 'generation,' and 'engender.' And yet the term 'gender' is now commonly used for that which is the less biological element.[34] Further — and a quite different type of concern — a sharp distinction between sex, on the one hand, and gender, on the other, may encourage us to think of our biology as one thing and the world of meanings as another. We are, however, *human* and all of our experience — including of our biological life — is meaningful experience, imbued with the categories, divisions, relations, comparisons, and distinctions arising through our

---

[32] Nussbaum provides an example of the former type of reading, while Thomas Aquinas leans toward the latter.

[33] See Beatriz Vollmer de Marcellus's *On the Ontological Differentiation of Human Gender: A Critique of the Philosophical Literature between 1965 and 1995* (Ph.D. dissertation, Pontificae Universitas Gregoriana, 2004), 13. See Prudence Allen's *The Concept of Woman: The Aristotelian Revolution, 750 B.C. – A.D. 1250* (Grand Rapids, MI: William B. Eerdmans, 1997), xx, citing Gayle Rubin, "The Traffic in Women: Notes on the 'Political Economy of Sex'" in *Towards an Anthropology of Women*, ed. Rayna R. Reiter (New York: Monthly Review Press, 1975), 157–210 and Sandra Harding, "Is Gender a Variable in Conceptions of Rationality? A Survey of Issues" in *Beyond Domination: New Perspectives on Women and Philosophy*, ed. Carol C. Gould (Lanham, MD: Rowman & Allanheld, 1984), 43–63.

[34] See Allen's discussion of this point on page xx of the above cited text.

communal lives.[35] In light of this, any attempt to partition sex off as unrelated to the world of meaning misses something fundamental to all human experience.

There are dangers in making too sharply the distinction between sex and gender, and part of the argument of this text is that sex and gender cannot be separated into unrelated spheres. Nonetheless, I think that a distinction can be made—albeit on the field of our meaningful life and not sharply opposing the biological and the meaningful.[36] Further, I think that it is useful to make the distinction in order to emphasize the differing degrees and kinds of malleability possible for differing aspects of our lives and identities. In making this distinction, however, I want in no way to *separate* the two. There is a distinction to be made between sex and gender, but this does not mean that we can understand the one in isolation from the other. Nor do I want to accept the common understanding of gender as (merely) socially constructed. Gender is social, but it cannot be reduced to a social construction nor separated from, even if distinguished from, our sex.

## Application to the Question of Sex

Aristotle's hylomorphism runs between the extremes of dualism and materialism (and all forms of monism). We are more than simply lumps of matter. We are marked by a second principle and not simply composed of a single type of thing. On the other hand, the two elements are not separable, occupying differing realms. We are each a single, unified being, but composed of two truly distinct but necessarily interrelated principles. Were one to apply Aristotle's distinctions, first, to the question of sex (in contrast to gender), she would have to say that our form is fundamentally a human one. It is, *qua form*, neither female nor male. Among the capacities of the form which may be developed are sexual and reproductive activities, but as a human formal principle, those activities are not specified beyond being sexual and reproductive. As embodied and developing in certain kinds of biological matter, the individual is female; when a human form develops in other material combinations, the individual is male.[37] *Qua form* or formal principle, all human beings are the same: human. *Qua* biological matter, however, we have a sex, and our sex is determined by our material principle.[38]

---

[35] This element is the basis of many criticisms of our sexual divisions, including, for example, Judith Butler's *Gender Trouble*.

[36] Allen understands the term 'gender' to include the notion of 'sex,' and thus she makes a distinction between the two insofar as 'gender' is a broader term than 'sex' (conversation, University of Notre Dame, February 14, 2009).

[37] This does not, of course, answer the question of *which* biological matter determines sex. For a brief statement affirming this understanding of the role of matter in sex, see Aristotle's *Metaphysics* 10.9.1058b21-25.

[38] Our *sex* will be determined by our biological matter, but this does not mean that our *sexual classification* will be so determined. In most cultures, only two sexes are distinguished: female and male. We do not, however, have to distinguish only two sexes. We might, instead, distinguish three:

All individuals are sexed, and there are no human beings who are not sexed in some way (but this does not mean all human beings are sexed as *either* female *or* male). One can distinguish within a particular human being that which is responsible for the humanity from that which is responsible for the sex, but the one is not what it is independent of the other. We are not human souls contained within a sexed body, but sexed human beings. Further, because our differences lie, not on the side of form, but of matter, our differences do not undermine our equality but, rather, point to differing conditions for the development of our common human capacities.

## *Application to the Question of Gender*

This position defends equality on the basis of commonality of form and accounts for difference through matter. Our sex is determined by our biological (in contrast to environmental and cultural) matter. Matter is likewise relevant to gender, but we need to distinguish the way in which matter affects gender from its effect on sex. By and large, the material principle involved in the determination of sex is biological matter. Environmental and cultural matter may be significant for how one values or relates to one's sex or how sexes are distinguished and classified, but the most significant feature in sex is biological matter. In the case of gender, in contrast, both biological matter and environmental and cultural matter play critical roles.

It is common to claim that sex is natural but gender is a social construct.[39] The view presented here agrees that sex is 'natural' in the sense that it is tied to our biological matter,[40] and it agrees that gender is a social construct, at least in part. But this final qualification is important. Gender is formed in relation to environmental and cultural matter—in part. But it is also formed in relation to biological matter as

female, male, and intersex. Or perhaps, following Anne Fausto-Sterling's perhaps less-than-serious suggestion, five. See "The Five Sexes: Why male and female are not enough," *The Sciences* (May/April 1993): 20–24 and "The Five Sexes, revisited," *The Sciences* 40, no. 4 (2000): 18–23. See also Fausto-Sterling's more considered position in Chap. 4 of *Sexing the Body*. My only claim here is that *sex* is determined by biological matter, not that any particular sexual classification system need be so determined.

[39] Marilyn J. Boxer, in a review essay on the state of women's studies, claims that "the social creation of gender is a basic assumption of women's studies" ("For and About Women: The Theory and Practice of Women's Studies in the United States," *Signs* 7, no. 3 [Spring 1982]: 687). As far as I can tell, this is still a dominant assumption nearly three decades later. There are, however, many things that "the social creation of gender" could mean, but it is often used to mean a largely arbitrary creation. I will agree that gender is a social creation, if what is meant is that gender is part of our social lives and arising because of our social interactions. It is unlikely that a purely private individual—i.e., one never encountering, referring to, or having any kind of relation with another person—would have a gender. But I am not sure gender is all such a person would lack, could she ever exist. But to claim that gender is an *arbitrary* social creation is, I believe, incorrect (even if I will grant that there is a great deal of flexibility in our understanding and cultivation of gender).

[40] Although gender too may be 'natural' in Aristotle's sense of cultivating or developing our nature.

well. We must grow and develop in the material conditions in which we find our-selves. We are free, but we choose among the options available to us and motivated by the various conditions influencing us. Our sex is something given quite early on[41]; gender, however, is something we must develop and is thus, like all of our development, something occurring in and through our material conditions. It strikes me that our differing biological matter offers to us differing *influences* for the devel-opment of our common capacities. Thus, an Aristotelian could say that women's common biological matter, differing from men's biological matter, offers different *incentives* for women's development in contrast to men's. Biological matter does not determine how the human capacities are developed, but sexually relevant bio-logical matter may offer a motivation making it intelligible why many women tend to develop certain of the human traits more quickly than many men, and vice versa. If this is right, then we can distinguish certain emphases among the human traits and describe them as more feminine and others as more masculine.

Thus, for example (my example here is simply intended as a possible illustration, not as a claim about what would actually be rightly considered 'feminine' or 'mas-culine'[42]): perhaps due to the comparatively lesser muscle to body mass ration, girls have a material condition that encourages the development of fine motor skills, while, due to greater muscle to body mass ratio, boys have a material condition that encourages the development of gross motor skills. I do not know whether this is actually true, but I simply want to suggest that it seems likely that common biologi-cal conditions would encourage common patterns of development.

I am not claiming here that common biological conditions *determine* common patterns of development. The process of actualizing one's capacities is not a simple process with a single explanation. One actualizes one's capacities in a particular order, with particular emphases, and to a particular degree for a variety of reasons, including the encouragement and opportunities of one's social environment as well

human capacities, and all of them take time and energy to develop. One must make choices among the various skills one might develop, and thus there is no reason to think that all girls will develop their fine motor skills in the same way, to the same degree, or boys their gross motor skills.

Further, the conditions under which we develop include more than merely female and male biological conditions. They also include the particularities of our own genetic material. Although all females share certain *general* biological features in common and all males others, they are only general features. The precise amount of estrogen or testosterone, for example, present in any particular female or male will

---

[41] This does not mean that it is thereby unchangeable, as sex-change operations reveal, nor that there is no development involved in our sex. It is simply to claim that, insofar as our chromosomal structure is relevant to sex, it is given quite a bit earlier than any gender formation.

[42] In no place in this text do I take a strong stand on the content of femininity and masculinity. It may be possible to articulate such content. But insofar as this text is interested in exploring the foundations of gender and not the content thereof, I have avoided making a strong commitment to any particular content.

differ from other females and males. And thus the commonalities of biological condition are only general and not exact or precise. This is particularly significant because there is competition for our developmental energies and time. Slight biological differences may provide a fairly strong motive not to put one's energy into something that is stereotypically feminine or masculine.

If this general picture is right, then it seems to me that we have an account of (i) the commonalities among all human beings, based in our common human soul or form, (ii) the general common characteristics of women and men, based in the common biological conditions for women's and men's development, and (iii) the true differences among individual women and individual men. Our particular material make-up is significant, as well as the particular families in which we grow up, all of the varied environmental conditions, and our free choices. Because all of our conditions differ to some degree, it is unsurprising that, although women might tend in certain directions, not all women need do so. And so also for men and intersexed individuals. For all kinds of reasons, particular individuals may develop various of the human capacities to different degrees and in differing directions.

Thus, it is possible to talk of feminine and masculine characteristics because of the similarities in our biological conditions and thus the motivation of those common conditions encouraging us to develop in particular ways, but we cannot claim that all women or all men will have all feminine or masculine traits in the same way or to the same degree. There will be, rightly, significant differences among individuals.

I would like to emphasize a few points regarding this account. First, some version of this claim was broadly Aristotle's tactic, but much to the detriment of women. He claimed that females develop in colder matter than males and thus have a harder time developing fully. I want absolutely and unequivocally to avoid any such suggestion. We can, it seems to me, accept Aristotle's general claim about different matter conditioning slightly different patterns of development without accepting that one of those patterns is superior to another. Difference need not mean inequities.[43]

Second, I would like to emphasize again: our biological matter offers an incentive for our development, not a determination of it. I would like to make this point strongly. The claim is not that our material conditions *qua female*, or *qua male*, determine the pattern of our human development but, rather, that they offer influences in combination with environmental and cultural matter encouraging our human development in certain ways rather than others. But we may—for all kinds of reasons—work against these incentives or have other, stronger incentives for heading different directions.

Third, we are rational beings, and not merely nutritive or sensitive souls. Critical to our rationality is freedom—that is, the ability (albeit not unlimited) to consider differing possibilities and patterns and choose among them. We have choices in what we want to emphasize, where we turn our attention, etc. And thus an account of *freedom* is crucial to any understanding of gender.

---

[43] Thus, I do not think that gender is well modeled on race.

Fourth, our individual biological matter, even that matter more relevant to sex, is not simply female or male but also individual variations on those patterns. Thus, even if we can articulate the feminine and masculine as characteristic tendencies intelligible given our differing biological matter, these groupings would only describe the biological motivations 'for the most part,' pointing only to general tendencies. Individuals will—and ought to—vary from those general patterns. Hylomorphists understand all of us as matter-form composites, and there are common general biological conditions for women which differ from those for men. These conditions are, however, merely general. The precise level of hormones, the precise chromosomal make-up, etc., will likely differ, perhaps even quite significantly. The general common biological make-up offers common conditions for the development of form. It may, for example, offer an encouragement for women to attend more to how human beings grow and develop than men; it might offer an incentive to develop certain of our human faculties prior to others. Thus, insofar as all women share certain common biological material features, women are inclined to develop certain of the human capacities more easily and quickly. Thus, we can talk of feminine traits. Insofar as all men share certain common biological material features, men are inclined to develop other, what may be considered, masculine traits. But the common biological features are merely 'for the most part,' and we ought to expect a corresponding flexibility in gender as well.[44]

Fifth and finally, the matter significant for our gender development is not simply biological; it is also environmental and cultural. Images and gendered ideals of our cultures—e.g., the behavior and attitudes of our parents, friends, and teachers, the particular toys we played with, etc.—will all be significant for our gender development. It is not unimportant for someone's understanding of femininity that, for example, all of the doctors she met as a child were male while the nurses were female, or that she ran to her mother for comfort while her father was the discipli-

involved is environmental and cultural as well as biological. And because of the significance of environmental and cultural matter, gender is malleable. We can change our understandings of the feminine and masculine; we can encourage girls to develop in ways that might be considered more traditionally masculine and boys in ways more traditionally feminine, etc.[45] The claim here is *not* that the social has

---

[44] What does this mean for gender ideals and symbols of femininity and masculinity? I am not yet sure. My inclination is to encourage the development of healthy gender symbols, images, and ideals. First, it is not clear to me that such ideals, symbols, and images can be eliminated. We are, after all, essentially material beings, working through the concrete and yet working toward something. On the other hand, I do not want women (or men) to be limited to just a few ideals (e.g., the Madonna or the whore). Thus, it will likely be critical to encourage the development of lots of differing feminine and masculine symbols and icons, rather than just a few. Providing a whole range of images of femininity and masculinity allows women and men to identify with those more relevant to their own situation and condition, and it acknowledges the flexibility (which is nonetheless not unlimited) of gender.

[45] Insofar as our goal is the development of all of the human capacities and not simply a few, such encouragement may often be desirable. See further discussion of this point and the import of sexed bodies even as fully actualized human beings in Chap. 3.

no role. I want to claim the opposite: it is absolutely central. But it is not the only factor. And thus there are limits to how much environmental and cultural matter can shape gender, even if it can do so to a very high degree.

Thus, the claim is that our biological matter does not determine our gender development, but it may make intelligible certain broad similarities among women in contrast to men and vice versa. And it may offer limits to the types of influence social factors may have. But our biological matter does not require that all women, or any particular woman, develop in characteristically feminine ways or men in characteristically masculine ways. Because of the significance of (i) cultural matter, (ii) our individual and distinct biological matter, and (iii) our freedom, biological matter offers only an influence and conditioning factor without being—as in the case of sex—a determining factor.

## Conclusion

This general schema strikes me as useful for understanding the persistence of gender stereotypes and categories and the difficulties of eliminating them simply by changing the social influences, and yet it also affirms that gender traits are truly, if not wholly, susceptible to social influences and thus capable of being affected and adapted by environmental influences. It also provides an account of our individual differences, the frequency with which individuals simply do not exhibit in any simple way the gender stereotypes, and affirms the critical role of human freedom. It can account for each of these without compromising in any way our commonality and thus basis for claims of true equality.

This model of gender also offers a way to run between the two extremes of biological determinism and social construction. One of the great fears of many feminists, one that is a legitimate fear, is that our societies will construe gender as a direct outgrowth of our sex.[46] That is, if you have a womb, you are expected to behave with a particular kind of passivity and limit your intellectual development and ambitions to what is relevant to keeping the domestic fires burning.[47] On the other extreme, in order to counter this biological determinism, gender is construed

---

[46] Contemporary U.S. society can rarely be accused of this failing, but we do not need to dig too far into our own history, or look too far from U.S. shores, to see examples, with varying degrees of seriousness, of this error.

[47] What is involved in such domestic work varies widely. There have been great changes in our societies regarding the ways in which political and societal power are distributed, the relation between home and work (the private and the public), and thus what is involved in limiting oneself to a "domestic sphere." See, for example, Christopher Lasch, "The Sexual Division of Labor, the Decline of Civic Culture, and the Rise of the Suburbs" in *Women and the Common Life*, ed. Elisabeth Lasch-Quinn (New York: W.W. Norton & Co., 1997), 93–120 and Alison Jagger's brief discussion at the beginning of *Feminist Politics and Human Nature*.

as unrelated to sex, as merely a social construction.[48] It strikes me that if some form of a broadly Aristotelian hylomorphism is right, then we can account for how gender is not simply the inevitable result of our particular reproductive organs, it is not 'natural' in the sense of the inevitable result of biology, but neither is it an arbitrary construct originating merely in various social influences.

If this account is broadly right, then we can claim that all human beings, female, male, and intersex, have the same basic human capacities, and thus the general goal of full human development is identical for all of us. We want to become fully human, developing all of our human capacities. And anything properly counting as a *capacity* would be present in all humans. Matter, however, including both biological matter and environmental and cultural matter, is significant. It provides various incentives for the ways in which the human capacities are developed, and the significance of the influence of biological matter would place limits on the malleability of gender, without denying the great flexibility possible in gender formation. Insofar as gender involves the development of our higher capacities, our social abilities, behaviors, and self-understanding, gender cannot be developed from biological matter alone. Gender development is also motivated by environmental and cultural matter—the various ways in which we are treated by others, the various images and examples we encounter, etc. Gender is thus socially malleable. Insofar as "traditional" understandings of gender attempted to read gender off of our biology, they missed the absolutely critical role of environmental and cultural matter, that is, various social influences. And contemporary feminists are absolutely right to attend to and critique deformed versions of such environmental and cultural matter. On the other hand, we engage our environment as human beings—as matter-form composites. Our biological matter—i.e., our bodies—are genuine aspects of how we engage the world, and our differing biological matter motivates and encourages (but does not determine) different patterns and ways of developing. If the more traditional

underemphasized it, focusing nearly exclusively on the role of environmental and cultural matter in gender formation. I think that we have to acknowledge the role of both.[49]

---

[48] For example, Nussbaum—although Aristotelian in certain respects—shies away from discussion of the import of differing biology in part because of this concern. See further discussion of both this critique and Nussbaum's form of 'Aristotelian feminism' in Chap. 1 above.

[49] "Classical philosophy lacks the exigent tone of modern intellectual work; its mode is one of patient reflection on and discussion of aims prior to action and change. Unlike modern philosophy, which makes human willing and choosing primary without being able to specify what it is best to will and choose and what the limits of human choice must be, classical philosophy recognizes human nature to have certain basic capacities—such as reason—with natural ends and excellences, and that the achievement of these ends is either helped or hindered by political circumstances. The intent of classical philosophizing, as I see it, is to speak about what would be the harmony of freedom and natural limitation, emotion and intelligence, equality and necessary hierarchy, desire and restraint, practice and theory, the subject and that which grounds the subject, male and female, as all of these manifest themselves in human life. A complete theory of human nature, expanded and fully inclusive of women, would ground the commonalities of men and women in such a way as to permit differences in masculine or feminine style or position to be acknowledged without the

We might make the point in more hermeneutic language. On the one hand, feminist critiques of traditionalism rightly argue that gender cannot simply be 'read off' of our bodies in an uninterpreted way. We have to acknowledge *our* role—and the role of society, culture, history, practices, and language—in our interpretation and understanding of ourselves as sexed beings. But, on the other hand, the dominant feminist approaches need to acknowledge that all interpretations (including bad ones) are interpretations of the real. They are not merely construction *ex nihilo*, but truly an understanding (or misunderstanding) *of* the real. And among the aspects of the real is the biological.[50]

---

imminent risk of devaluing or overvaluing one or the other, and thus dislodging one or the other from the realm of the fully human. A fuller account of male and female commonalities would also subdue the antagonism between the sexes, although, due to some ineliminable differences, there inevitably are elements of tension—and mystery—between women and men" (Tress, "Feminists and Their Discontents," 307).

[50] By and large I will present the position in a more metaphysical rather than a hermeneutical form, but one of the aspects brought out by the more hermeneutic formulation is that, although one can distinguish biological and environmental matter, they are not sharply separable. It is not as if we have an unmediated encounter with our biology. We understand our bodies through the language, practices, emphases, etc., of our culture and environment. Acknowledging such a point in no way reduces the biological to simply environmental or cultural forces. But it acknowledges that we make the distinction on the field of our experience—interpreted, mediated (but not thereby untrue) experience.

# Chapter 3
# Possibilities Beyond the Bare-Bones

The primary goal of this book is theoretical, articulating the broad structure of a substantial version of Aristotelian feminism. Although such a general version of this position might be useful in addressing certain issues of feminist concern (for example, the structure of university education, as discussed in Chap. 6), it cannot be put to significant use until developed in a bit more detail. My goal in this chapter is not to fill in the position, but simply to point to a few of the places where that filling in would need to occur and indicate briefly how different ways of answering certain questions would affect the general position.

## Summary of Position

The version of Aristotelian feminism presented here, in its simplest form, claims that we get equality from the commonality of our formal principle and difference from our material principle in combination with our choices. Because we share a common form, our faculties or capacities are also common. Thus, we cannot say (in terms of capacities) that women are emotional while men are rational, or women are relational while men are detached. *Qua* our capacities, we are—as humans—identical and equal. There are, however, genuine differences, which arise from the material principle and our self-conscious free choices. This position follows Aristotle in distinguishing formal, or structural, features guiding our development from material features, i.e., that in which and by means of which we develop our structure. Although not explicitly defended by Aristotle, I take matter or our material features to include anything by means of which we develop our human capacities, and thus the blocks we played with, the stories we read, and the friends we interacted with as children are as much a part of our matter as the pasta we ate last night.

This position takes commonalities to come from form, differences from matter. In form, we are all equally human; our matter, however, differs in a number of

© Springer International Publishing Switzerland 2016
S. Borden Sharkey, *An Aristotelian Feminism*, Historical-Analytical Studies on Nature, Mind and Action 1, DOI 10.1007/978-3-319-29847-4_3

respects. We get sexual difference from sexually-differentiated general biological matter and gender difference from the combination of sexually-differentiated general biological matter, environmental and cultural matter, and our self-understanding and choices in light of these features. We get individual differences from a combination of specific biological matter, environmental and cultural matter, and our self-understanding and choices. Because gender categories arise from matter (in its various senses) and not form, gender categories are always at best only 'for the most part.'[1] There will not be gender categories or descriptions that are true for all women, all men, or all intersex individuals. Gender is not exact, and our gender identity is qualified by (and filled out by) our individuality.

The material conditions relevant to gender include both biological and social conditions. Because of the significance of social conditions—that is, what I have been calling 'environmental and cultural matter'—an Aristotelian feminist can agree with much and take on board many versions of feminist critique, which look at, for example, problematic kinds of social formation, limiting gender stereotypes, unjust legal and familial structures, etc. Our legal, economic, educational, political, and cultural systems can and do regularly function in sexist ways, presenting—in various forms—feminine ideals that are damaging to the full humanity of women (as well as men). Virginia Woolf was right to criticize the "angel in the house" as a ghost of a person, and Betty Friedan's great classic *The Feminine Mystique* insightfully argues that, insofar as the feminine ideal is simply not a full human ideal, it limits and deforms women. Many models for women's lives have been and are models for less than fully human lives.

But this version of feminism does not think that environmental and social conditions are the only ones significant for gender: biological ones, including any differing sexual biology, matter too. Biological conditions are not irrelevant to our development. Because of the influence (among other things) of sexually-differentiated biology, we can be very particular... Thus, contrary to many views of gender, this view does not understand gender as occurring simply at the intersection of social environment and individual freedom. Biological matter also plays a key role, although it is certainly not determinative of gender. Thus, Aristotelian feminism of the sort I would like to defend (like Nussbaum's) focuses on capacities and our common human capacities, but (in contrast to Nussbaum's version) it also understands sexually-differentiated biology to play a role in our capacity development.

Making these claims does not yet, however, answer a tremendous number of questions. There are many ways and senses in which biology may 'play a role,' and how one answers certain more specific questions will substantially change one's understanding of gender and gender formation. I would like to dedicate this chapter

---

[1] This raises the question of what role gendered symbols or ideals ought to play in our societies. Are certain gendered images or examples appropriate insofar as some pattern of development is, for the most part, true for most girls, and thus it can aid many girls as they become more fully human? Or ought certain gendered ideals be eliminated insofar as there will be exceptions to the dominant pattern and thus individuals potentially harmed by the images?

to raising a few of these questions. Among the questions are things such as: How much of our matter is sexually differentiated? What kind of influence does sexually-differentiated biological matter have? And what capacities do we have and how are they related?

There are a number of different ways to answer these questions, and until one takes a stand on which is right, one will have, at best, only a very generalized account of gender. Furthermore, differing stances on these questions will lead to significantly different accounts of gender and the malleability of gender. For example, the claim that sexually-differentiated biological matter influences the pattern according to which all of our capacities are developed presents a much stronger notion of biologically-influenced gender differences than the weaker claim that only a few capacities are affected by our differing biologies and only in very limited ways. In the following, I would like to sketch out a few of the questions that need to be considered. I would like to show why these questions are important, but I will (generally) not try to answer the questions. My overall aim in this book is to articulate the general theoretical resources offered by a broadly Aristotelian understanding of gender. A full account would require addressing each of these questions in detail. My goal in this chapter is thus to sketch briefly the significance of each of these questions and the impact different answers will have on one's understanding of gender, but my focus here is on the questions and not on any particular answer to those questions.

I would like to divide the questions of this chapter into four groups: (1) general scientific, metaphysical, and methodological questions; (2) questions about what it means to *influence* and in what senses biology might influence development; (3) questions regarding the *way in which* biological matter might influence gender, looking at possibilities regarding the pattern of development, order of development, subjects toward which turned, and combination of faculties used; and (4) questions regarding *what* capacities we have and how they might be related. Once again, I am not interested here in providing answers to these questions, but simply in raising them and showing how there could be many different Aristotelian feminisms, depending on how one answers each of these questions.

## One: General Scientific, Metaphysical, and Methodological Questions

### *What of Our Biological Matter Is Sexually Differentiated?*

This is not a question best answered in a philosophical text. Although there are philosophical considerations relevant to answering this question, it is fundamentally a scientific, rather than philosophical, question.[2] It is a scientific question that needs

---

[2] For a few qualifications on this, see Chap. 1 above.

to be addressed in a methodologically adequate way, sensitive to the range of issues that can affect biological development, but it nonetheless strikes me as a question best addressed by philosophically astute scientists.[3] Although not fundamentally a philosophical question, how it is answered is critical for this account of gender. It is clear that, at certain levels of analysis, human bodies do not differ in very significant ways. Women, men, and intersex individuals all have the same average number of hydrogen atoms, oxygen molecules, subatomic particles, etc., in our bodies. In contrast, however, when analyzed at a chromosomal level, differences appear: women and men are generally distinguished by XX and XY chromosome combinations.[4] Similarly, at the level of chemical make-up, human beings differ in certain respects. Although the hormones in human beings do not differ (e.g., all of us generally produce some amount of testosterone and estrogen), the amounts and ratios of these hormones differ in the differing sexes. And at the level of organs and systems, there are differences—at minimum, in our sexual and reproductive systems.[5] Thus, although there is nothing like complete difference between human females and males, there are generally some differences—at minimum—in our chromosomal and hormonal make-up as well as certain of our systems.

We can ask, however, *how* much these difference matter, even at the biological level. It is clear that females, males, and intersex individuals all exhibit a range of estrogen and testosterone patterns, for example. There is no single or unchangeable hormone level that marks every female individual, for example, in contrast to each male. Thus, one question is *which* biological patterns, ranges, and combinations most commonly mark each sex. So also, we can ask how much our other hormones, patterns of physical development, and systems are affected by our sexually-differentiated chromosomes, hormones patterns, and reproductive systems. Is our brain structure or nervous system, for example, affected by sexually-differentiated matter, or are such differences comparatively limited? Should we think of the whole bodies?

Aristotle himself favored a fairly extensive understanding of sexual differentiation. He writes in *Generation of Animals*:

> Now as a matter of fact such parts are in the female the so-called uterus, in the male the testes and the penis, in all the sanguinea; for some of them have testes and others the corresponding passages. ... if in the sanguinea the parts concerned in copulation differ in their forms, we must observe that a small change in a first principle is usually attended by changes in many of the things depending on it. This is plain in the case of castrated animals; for, though only the generative part is disabled, yet pretty well the whole form of the animal changes in consequence so much that it seems to be female or not far short of it, and thus it is clear that an animal is not male or female in virtue of any random part or faculty. Clearly, then, the distinction of sex is a first principle; at any rate, when that which distinguishes

[3] See Chap. 1 for a discussion of some of the social issues that affect biological formation.
[4] They are generally so distinguished, but this is not universally the case, and when one considers the chromosomal structure of intersex individuals, a few further combinations appear.
[5] I am grateful to Prudence Allen for clearly making these points in *The Concept of Woman*, Vol. III, September 2007 draft of Chap. 2.

male and female suffers change, many other changes accompany it, as would be the case if a first principle is changed.[6]

Aristotle describes sexual difference as a 'first principle' in biology, and he takes sexual differences to have an impact on much of the rest of our biological development. It seems to me, however, that one might agree with Aristotle that our sexually-differentiated biological features are significant—and thus a 'first principle' of some sort—while still disagreeing (either with Aristotle or within the community of scientists) about how exactly our sex affects the rest of our biology. There is a broad range of positions, all of which could claim that sexual differences are among our critical biological differences.

One question—and a question best answered by biologists—is how much of our biological matter is sexually differentiated. Two related questions are *when* and *under what conditions* is our biological matter sexually differentiated. Although individuals possess their particular chromosomal structure from conception, for example, they do not develop in any way that is anatomically different until week six.[7] So also, children, although possessing distinct genitalia, do not exhibit distinct female and male bodies (e.g., developing breasts for females, deepening of voice and protrusion of Adam's apple for males) until puberty. These changes raise questions about the conditions under which and the times at which our biological matter is sexually differentiated. It is clear that certain environmental factors will affect the onset and nature of puberty, and our social and environmental conditions can thus affect our sexual differentiation. These features are not irrelevant to questions regarding how biological matter affects our gender development.

Thus, key questions for fully developing and filling out this account of gender are biological questions—questions about what differences count as sexual differences, when these differences appear, how much they influence other aspects of biological development, what conditions are essential for their appearance, etc. Were it to turn out that there are relatively few biological differences tied to our sex, then we would expect biological matter to have less significance for gender development than if there were more sexual differences. If it turns out that Aristotle is wrong, that sexual difference is not a first principle in any sense, then it is likely that the significance of biological matter for gender will be quite minimal. If, in contrast, there are quite a few differences tied to sex and these differences appear at critical points for capability development, then one would expect at least some biologically-motivated gender differences. Thus, the data of the sciences is not insignificant for judgments about how strongly sexual differences would be likely to influence gender development.

---

[6] *Generation of Animals* 1.2.716a32-716b12.
[7] See Fausto-Sterling, *Myths of Gender*, 78.

## *What Type of Hylomorphism Should Be Accepted?*

Among the key questions are biological ones about the nature of our sexual differentiation. A further, critical question is philosophical and metaphysical: What is our structure such that biological matter (sexually differentiated or otherwise) could affect our capacity development? Hylomorphists in general are committed to the formal principle, or soul, becoming itself through matter. Thus, all hylomorphists think that our material conditions—including our biological ones—matter. We can, however, contrast two broad types of hylomorphists: *strict hylomorphists*, who hold that all capacities of the soul must work through material conditions, and *qualified hylomorphists* (sometimes also referred to as *soft dualists*), who hold that most capacities must work in material media but that certain "higher" capacities can work in relative independence of matter.

Strict hylomorphism is a fairly straight-forward position, holding quite simply that *any* activity, any use of any capacity, works (quite directly) through or in our material conditions. Qualified hylomorphism, in contrast, claims that, although most capacities work directly through or in our matter, some of our capacities can function in relative independence from our material conditions. The claim regarding 'relative independence' is significant. Relative independence is not complete independence; it is not a pure encounter with no mediation. Thomas Aquinas claims that we can do activities such as higher mathematics in a way relatively independent of matter.[8] But if one had never studied mathematics—that is, if one never worked through two oranges plus three oranges equals five oranges, or never played with blocks—one would develop one's mathematical skills much less than if she played with many toys and took many courses in algebra, geometry, calculus, looking at many, many blackboards, writing out different types of problems in colored chalk,

oranges and colored blocks in our lives does not mean we do so with no relation to those fruits and wooden shapes. So also, we may be able to understand the general art of reasoning per se after watching Socrates reflect on justice and Crito on friendship, but one could not understand reasoning per se without having observed numerous, quite concrete examples. Thus, qualified hylomorphists think that we are capable of going beyond particular examples to a comparatively immaterial understanding of the structure of, for example, reasoning per se and of performing activities that do not function directly through our matter (e.g., doing higher mathematics). Crucial to an account of 'relative independence,' however, is the notion that "higher" faculties are built upon "lower" sense experiences; we are capable of coming to understand things that are not strictly material and of functioning in ways not strictly dependent on the material, but only because of and building upon our material experience. Thus, the independence of the more immaterial aspects is only a *relative* independence.

---

[8] Thomas does not speak of mathematics directly, but I take it to be an appropriate example, given what he claims in, for example, *Summa theologica* I, q. 88, a. 1–2.

Thus, we can make a distinction between strict hylomorphists, who understand the use of all of our capacities as intimately tied to our matter, and qualified hylomorphists, who claim some kind of relative independence (but not full independence) for the functioning of certain capacities. (Thomas Aquinas is certainly a qualified hylomorphist, although—in the way I have described the position here—Aristotle may have been as well.) It seems to me that, among other questions, whether we go with strict or qualified hylomorphism will significantly affect our understanding of gender. A strict hylomorphist would claim that all capacities function in some kind of fairly intimate relation to biological matter. If any significant amount of our biology is sexually differentiated, then this will have an impact on the functioning of all of our capacities.[9] A qualified hylomorphist, in contrast, even if agreeing that there is quite a bit of sexually-differentiated biological matter, could claim that certain capacities function in relative independence of biological conditions and are thus comparatively little affected by sexual differences. (All capacities would, however, experience some degree of influence because of the 'relative' dimension of 'relative independence.' A qualified hylomorphist could, however, distinguish among the more and less directly influenced capacities.) Given the same biological data, a strict hylomorphist would end up with a starker and more comprehensive account of the biologically-motivated aspects of gender than a qualified hylomorphist.

## Two: The Nature of Influence

### Is Biological Matter a Motive, Incentive, or Condition of Development?

I claimed in the previous chapter that sexually-differentiated biological matter, on this account, *influences* gender development, but does not determine it. There are a number of things, however, that this could mean. A broad distinction between 'determining' and 'influencing' is relatively easy to make. When an outcome is determined, there is a single factor (or set of factors) that requires or necessitates a particular outcome. When an outcome is influenced but not determined, the single factor (or factors) under discussion exert some role in the final outcome but that influencing factor is not sufficient in itself to necessitate any particular outcome and its presence at the outset may be compatible with a number of (quite different) outcomes. An influence may make some outcome intelligible without, however,

---

[9] Insofar as strict hylomoropbists are *hylomorphists* and not materialists, however, the position would affirm a marked distinction between the formal and material principle. Because of this distinction, even strict hylomorphists can affirm that the biological matter, although deeply influencing all of our activities, is nonetheless simply an influence and not a determination of development.

allowing the kind of exact predictability possible in the case of determinations.[10] This view claims that biology *influences* gender but does not determine it.

There are, however, a number of things that 'influence' could mean. I have used descriptions such as 'conditioning,' 'offering an incentive for development,' 'being a motive for,' etc. Each of these is subtly different. A promised chocolate dessert might be an incentive for doing something, for getting one moving, without conditioning that action or being the real reason or motive for that action. (For example, I may promise myself chocolate in order to 'kick start' myself on the process of grading a stack of papers, but I do not grade *for the sake of* getting chocolate.) In contrast, working with a prosthetic limb conditions a physical action without necessarily acting as an incentive or motive for that action. (That is, it shapes the way in which the action is done.) Finally, something might be a motive for an action—a reason for doing it—without being a conditioning factor in the way a prosthetic limb is or an incentive in the way chocolate cake might be.[11] One key question is: In what sense, does biological matter influence gender development—as an incentive, condition, motive, or in some other way?

The answer to this question will likely depend in part on *which* biological features one is considering and one's relation to those features. For example, one's chromosomes or hormones might influence development in a quite different way from one's reproductive system or bodily composition, even though both may count as sexually-differentiated biological matter. So also, one's consciousness of and particular understanding of one's hormones or reproductive system might importantly shape the degree to which either acts as an influence on some aspect of development, etc. Biological matter could act as a different type of influence at different stages of development, for differing individuals in varied social contexts, and for different aspects of biological matter.

It is also true that our awareness of our differing biology can influence our devel-

race and associate that girl's failure to finish with the other child's being a *girl*, rather than her being tired, or uninterested in racing, or some other factor unrelated to sex. This association may then become part of her own understanding of herself as a girl and what is involved in being a female and thus incline her to not finish her own races. Our awareness of our sexual differences can thus influence our development in ways that may be little related to genuine sexual differences.

Although there are surely such largely arbitrary associations, our biological differences may also influence our development in other, less accidental ways. It can surely act as a motive in certain cases. An intersex individual might, for example, become interested in genetics because of experiences of distinctive sexual

---

[10] This distinction loosely follows Husserl's and Stein's between *cause* and *motivation*. See, for example, section III of Husserl's *Ideas II*, trans. Richard Rojcewicz & André Schuwer (Boston: Kluwer, 1989) and Stein's "Sentient Causality" in *Philosophy of Psychology and the Humanities*, ed. Marianne Sawicki, trans. Mary Catharine Baseheart & Marianne Sawicki (Washington, DC: Institute of Carmelite Studies Publications, 2000).

[11] These are not intended to be exhaustive of the options.

development, and sexually-differentiated biology thus acts as a motive or reason for one kind of development. Or a 22-year old female's awareness that the years during which she is fertile are fewer than those of her male counterparts may act as an incentive to go directly into graduate school rather than taking more time to think through the decision or spending time traveling. The reasons for pursuing graduate work may not be biologically motivated, but her biology might offer an incentive for allowing those reasons to motivate her to act. Thus, our awareness of our sexually-differentiated biology may act as both a motive and an incentive for certain forms of development.

In addition, however, biological matter appears to act as a condition for various forms of development. Our differing biological matter would seem to act in a way at least somewhat analogous to a prosthetic limb or differing skeletal structures. Two individuals may perform the same type of act but do so differently insofar as they are conditioned differently. Kangaroos and frogs, for example, can both jump, but their differing skeletal make-up conditions their jumping so that it looks different. Analogously, women's and men's differing reproductive systems condition our reproductive life, even if both can reproduce. It strikes me that our differing biological matter can act as an incentive or motive for our development; it may also, however, condition our development, acting as a differing medium for our common acts and common capacities. Given Aristotle's hylomorphism and claims about the inseparability of matter and form, this role of conditioning would seem to be one of the critical types of influence sexually-differentiated biological matter would exert. Bodies are not merely external incentives, like chocolate cake. Influencing by *conditioning* development would be one critical role of sexually-differentiated biological matter.

There are, however, a number of things that conditioning might mean and how strongly a biological feature might condition development. We can contrast, for example, an *intrinsic condition* from an *extrinsic condition*.[12] A prosthetic leg might act as an intrinsic condition of someone's running, but an extrinsic condition of her pre-race imagining of the upcoming event. The limb might condition both, but it does so differently in each case. We can thus distinguish stronger and weaker types of conditioning. If we take our sexually-differentiated biologies to condition our development in the stronger sense, then we would end up with a sharper account of the influence of sexual biology on gender than if we affirm that they condition only in the weaker sense.

This general position affirms that sexually-differentiated biological matter influences our development and gender differences, although it does not determine or cause them. There are, however, a number of things such claims to influence might mean. Surely our awareness of our differences can act, at least occasionally, as a motive or incentive for certain kinds of development. In addition, Aristotelian hylomorphism inclines me to think it also acts as a conditioning feature of our

---

[12] I owe this particular language and set of distinctions to discussions with my husband of Lonergan's work.

development. How strongly such conditioning occurs (that is, intrinsically or extrinsically) will significantly affect one's final account.

## Aristotelian Causality, Re-Stating the Previous Question in More Aristotelian Language

I like the language of biological matter acting as a motive, incentive, and condition. A different way of articulating biological matter's role might be found if we change the categories slightly. In November of 2008, at a conference at the University of Notre Dame, a young man—and I am afraid I never learned the man's name—suggested that I consider employing Aristotle's four causes to account for the differing ways in which matter affects sex in contrast to gender. That is, he suggested avoiding talk of 'influencing' versus 'determining,' employing instead Aristotle's account of the four causes. This would allow the position to draw more fully from distinctively Aristotelian sources and might enable one to make useful distinctions. Were we to use Aristotelian terms, the best way to articulate the claim is to say that biological matter acts as part of the material cause of gender.

In a number of places (e.g., *Physics* 2.3 and *Metaphysics* 1), Aristotle distinguishes four causes or four types of explanation: efficient, material, formal, and final. In most discussions of causality since the early modern period, causality is limited to efficient causality. That is, what we commonly mean by a 'cause' is that which pushes or moves something about. The motion of the pool stick might be, for example, the cause of a billiard ball's movement, rolling into a pocket. Aristotle thinks, however, that this is only one among the four types of causality. Aristotle understands the efficient cause to be that which moves something, acting firstly as its principle of generation (e.g., the parents as the generators of a child or a sculptor as the generator of a statue) and secondly as the principle of motion (e.g., the museum curator moving the statue from one location to another). The material cause is that which a thing is materially made of (and presumably here, he has in mind 'physically made of'). Thus, for example, the same parents can generate one child composed of one kind of chromosomal combination and another with a different set. Or a sculptor can make the same basic statue first out of wood and then out of clay. In these cases, the efficient cause may be the same—and even the type of thing generated the same—but the material cause or explanation differs. Third, the formal cause is the pattern or type of thing something is. A sculptor may make many things: gargoyles, sarcophagi, and statues of Socrates. She may even sculpt many different things out of the same physical matter, using the same tools and general techniques. The items can be distinguished, however, by the *kind* of thing that they are, that is, by the pattern or form characterizing *what* they are. Finally, the final cause is the goal or ideal toward which the thing aims. Things which grow and develop aim to become something; there is something (or some range of things) that it means to be a mature, well-developed version of this type of thing. That ideal is the final cause, drawing—in some sense—the thing to become itself.

The distinction among these four types of causes might be employed to understand the way in which biological matter influences gender, in contrast to its influence on sex. Insofar as biological matter is on the side of matter rather than form for both sex and gender, it is a material cause of our development. (Insofar, however, as it is *formed* matter, it contributes to the formal cause, for example, although not the species-form.) Thus, biological matter as matter is neither a formal nor final cause of our *human* development. But if we are not asking about general human capacities but instead more specific patterns of how those human capacities are developed, for example, biological matter might play a more complicated role.

Given this qualification, we can nonetheless consider biological matter to act primarily as a material cause. Our sexually-differentiated biological matter is the primary material cause of our sex, while it is only one of the material causes of our gender. Such a material cause is not insignificant for the other three causes, and, although not properly a formal, final, or efficient cause, it plays a role in relation to these. A sculptor working with brass in contrast to stone must apply different tools and techniques to the task of forming the material into a statue of Socrates, even while the sculptor's primary formal, final, and efficient causes remain the same. So too, female, male, and intersex biological matter may each contribute differing material causes to gender development without requiring a different type of formal (i.e., human), final (i.e., fully developed human being), and efficient cause.

Even, however, if we accept these Aristotelian categories of causality to discuss biological matter and its influence on gender, there are further questions of whether biological matter as a material cause functions differently at various stages and levels of development. Biological matter—as a material principle—acts as a material cause. Biological matter at the level of chromosomes in very early sexual development (e.g., as early as a few hours from conception) may differ from hormones as material causes at 5 months from conception or 12 years from birth. Because of the increasing role of our conscious understanding and freedom and the increasing complexity of our biological development as we grow, biological matter—even when taken simply as a material cause—may play differing roles at different times. Depending on how one spells these out, one's picture of gender and the influence of biology on that could be quite different. Although Aristotle's notion of a material cause provides a useful tool for analyzing the place of biological matter, it does not yet answer the question of how strongly that matter conditions development. And given the role of environmental and cultural matter, there are a range of claims one could make about in what sense and in what ways sexually-differentiated biological matter is a material cause of our gendered development.

## Three: How Might Biological Matter Influence?

### *Does Biological Matter Influence the Pattern of How a Particular Faculty Is Developed?*

In *In a Different Voice*, Gilligan articulates two distinct patterns of moral development, articulating the places from which one begins and stages through which one
may go in order to become a mature moral reasoner for each of the two patterns.
Gilligan does not argue that men have moral capacities that women lack, but she
does claim that the common patterns by which those capacities are developed differ.
We might ask whether sexually-differentiated biological matter influences development at the level of the *pattern* of development, affecting the ways in which the
human form is developed for various of our capacities. If this is so, then we should
look for and expect to find at least two broad patterns for the development of at least
certain human faculties, and we could characterize certain patterns as broadly feminine and others as masculine. Accepting this notion need not commit one to saying
that *every* faculty is equally affected. Some faculties may be more conditioned by
sexually-differentiated biological matter than others. And, once again, one certainly
need not claim that every individual will follow the gendered patterns of development (given, once again, the role of environmental and cultural matter, individual
biological matter, and choice). But, if biological matter has an influence at the level
of pattern of development, one would expect to see an influence — probably appearing quite early on, although this may vary depending on the stage at which the patterns begin to differ. Thus, although the capacities would not differ nor need the
ideal of what the capacity looks like as fully developed differ, but the means by
which women and men get to that full development may differ.

girls and boys are trained may need to vary for at least some of our capabilities
(even if, once again, they do not in fact show up in all faculties equally). Given
hylomorphism's emphasis on the essential role of our matter for all development, if
there is very much sexually-relevant biological matter and if that relevance appears
early, then such marked influence on patterns of development seems plausible. I am
hesitant to accept too easily this type of significant conditioning, but there are reasons for testing for such significant influence.

### *Does Biological Matter Influence the Order in Which Our Faculties Are Developed?*

A second possibility is that biological matter does not affect the *pattern* according
to which a common faculty is developed, but it does influence the *order* in which
faculties are developed. The previous question suggested that the very stages
through which one must progress in order to develop a particular capacity might

differ for girls in contrast to boys. That is, our differing biological matter might offer such differing starting points or conditions so that the very pattern by which a common capacity—e.g., mathematical or moral reasoning—is developed is likely to be affected. This second possibility is a bit weaker. It might be the case that, when one develops one's moral reasoning, one does so in the same way whether one is biologically female, male, or intersex. So also, when one develops one's gross motor skills, one does it in an identical manner regardless of sexually-differentiated biological matter. But our differing biological matter might influence *when* and in which order we develop our faculties. Thus, perhaps females are likely, because of the influence of sexually-relevant biological matter, to develop their verbal capacities prior to their motor capacities, or vice versa. The *way* in which these are developed need not differ but the timing and priority in development may differ.

Because it takes time, effort, and resources to actualize each and every capacity, I suspect that small differences in conditions could play a fairly influential role in the order of development. Just as a smile and word of encouragement can motivate an infant to try something again, so also small biological differences may play a fairly critical role in encouraging a choice to make eye contact again or work to turn over. These early 'incentives' may then play a role in where future efforts are directed. Thus, it seems to me highly plausible that biological matter could offer some significant influence to the order in which capacities are developed.

## Does Biological Matter Influence the Subjects Toward Which Our Faculties Are Turned?

It is possible that sexually-differentiated biological matter is largely irrelevant to the pattern or order in which our common faculties are developed. It might, however, nonetheless have an influence on the subjects toward which some faculty is commonly turned. Presumably both John Coltrane and Wolfgang Mozart developed their musical capacities extremely highly (and it is even possible that they did so following the same general pattern of musical development), but each turned those abilities toward quite different types of music. One can consider two individuals both to have a fully actualized or developed version of the same capacity, but, nonetheless, find them turning that capacity toward strikingly different subjects. Perhaps something analogous occurs due to the conditioning of biological matter. All of us have, for example, capacities for thought and intellectual development. We can turn that faculty toward the understanding of relations among concepts, words, emotions, actions, etc. Although perhaps the capacity is common and the pattern of development and order in which it is developed is common, but the types of topics toward which it is most commonly turned may differ. If this is the point at which sexually-differentiated biological matter exhibits its most marked influence, then it would exhibit a fairly marked difference as individuals grow (consonant with other, non-biological influences on gender development). One might expect women

academics to be interested in slightly different questions than men, for example, or
female medical professionals to lean toward certain subspecialties. Because gender
is developed in combination with many factors, making general claims becomes
difficult, but there may be some cross-cultural and transhistorical commonalities in
the general types of subjects toward which more women gravitate, which could be
tied to the influence of differing biological matter.

## *Does Biological Matter Influence the Combination of Faculties Employed When Turning to a Common Subject?*

Perhaps none of these three options rightly articulates the influence of sexually-
differentiated biological matter. It may instead be that—at least as far as biological
matter is concerned—the patterns, order, and subjects are the same, but the particular combination of capacities commonly employed to address some common subject differ. Perhaps females are more liable to employ both intellectual and relational
capacities when working through mathematical problems, whereas males are more
liable to employ intellectual and physical capacities, etc. Thus, although the capacities may be developed in analogous ways and orders, they may nonetheless be utilized in differing common combinations.

Each of these possibilities is slightly different. I do not know whether any or, if
some, which, is the more likely way sexually-differentiated biological matter would
condition development. But each suggests possibilities for differing biologically-
motivated gender development. And attention to these possible differences is significant for the ways in which we train and help form women's and men's capacities.
If our educational systems favor masculine patterns of intellectual development, for
example, then women are likely to develop those capacities less fully. And given the
dependence of advanced versions of our capacities on our basic training in that area,
our early educational patterns are critical. So too, if the medical field, for example,
rewards those who work in the subspecialties favored by men over women, this will
have a long-term effect on women's control over their environment (if they pursue
what they are more inclined to) or satisfaction in their jobs (if they do not). Thus if
there are biologically-conditioned feminine and masculine patterns of development,
orders of development, subjects of interest, etc., recognition and understanding of
these is not unimportant for creating societies truly interested in developing the
human capacities of all of us.

# A Spectrum of Positions

Given the various possibilities laid out thus far, we could draw a spectrum of different types of Aristotelian feminist positions, ranging from those which take biological matter to play a relatively minor role in gender development to those which take a very strong view of the role of biological matter in gender development. On one extreme of the spectrum would be those who hold that all of our biological matter is sexually differentiated and thus relevant to gender development, that the differences are marked, appearing quite early and at critical stages of capacity development. It would affect not only the subjects toward which, but also the order and pattern by which, our capacities are developed, marking, for example, a feminine way in which moral reasoning is developed in contrast to a masculine way, as well as the combination in which our capacities are commonly used. The strongest version would hold to a strict hylomorphism, understanding biological matter to act as intrinsically conditioning gender. If this strong version is right, it might be possible to distinguish feminine mathematics in contrast to masculine, feminine and masculine literary theory, etc. And we could distinguish sharp gender distinctions in educational patterns based in the influence of biological matter, with those gender distinctions amenable to comparatively little manipulation, and only with great effort, by environmental and cultural matter.

On the other extreme, on the minimalist end, one would understand very little of our biological matter to be sexually differentiated. It is clear that some is, but a minimalist Aristotelian feminist would take relatively little to be differentiated in a way relevant to gender formation, perhaps even arguing that the differences relevant to gender formation do not show marked effects until puberty. Such a minimalist would need to be a qualified hylomorphist rather than a strict hylomorphist, and the kind of influence of our distinctive sexually-differentiated biological matter would have is minimal: it would not influence any particular pattern of development, the order in which our faculties are developed, or the number of faculties involved in any particular operation. Insofar as such a minimalist is still a hylomorphist, she needs to acknowledge some material influence. Probably the most minimal type of influence would be either one claiming that our biological matter offers an incentive only at the level of the subjects toward which certain capacities are turned, or one claiming influence in timing of the development of certain capacities. Thus, we might on this account still be able to distinguish some version of the feminine and masculine, but there would be relatively few disciplines or accounts of human development that could be distinguished into 'feminine' and 'masculine' approaches. Perhaps, for example, female literary critics might be more likely to attend quickly to certain aspects of a text, in contrast to their male or intersex counterparts, but *literary criticism* per se could not be considered feminine or masculine, and things like mathematics would be fully gender neutral. On this account, one might still be able to articulate some minimal gender differences based in biological matter, but gender would be open to greater influence by environmental and cultural matter, and there would also be a greater possibilities for gender neutral disciplines and activities.

These two extremes could both count as variants of Aristotelian feminism, but each would have a very different picture of how our gender differences develop in concrete situations. Both would, of course, acknowledge the import of environmental and cultural matter, in addition to biological matter, but they would give differing accounts of the degree to which sexually-differentiated biological matter sets limits on our gender formation. It is worth noting that no simple empirical observation of the behavior of individuals within a society could tell us which extreme (or where in between) to prefer. The minimalist account could be true, but a particular society may encourage such strong gender distinctions that the women and men develop in quite distinctively gendered ways.[13] Or the strong version might be true, but a particular society might so work to counter gender distinctions that they are little exhibited.[14]

## Four: Questions About the Human Capacities?

The previous sets of questions focus on what is meant by 'influence' and what kind of influence might be exerted by biological matter. Equally critical, however, are questions regarding what our capacities, in fact, are and how they are related. I would like to begin by looking at Nussbaum's list of ten capacities and explore briefly how differing lists of capacities and different accounts of their relation would affect one's account of gender.

### What Are Our Capacities?

however, that her list is neither exhaustive nor metaphysically ordered, articulating more and less core human capabilities in contrast to the more peripheral ones (except for the architectonic role of *practical reason* and *affiliation*). Questions of *which* capabilities or capacities mark the human form and the particular order and relation among them are not insignificant for developing more fully an Aristotelian account. The ten capabilities listed by Nussbaum in 2000 are, as noted in Chap. 1: (i) life, (ii) bodily health, (iii) bodily integrity, (iv) senses, imagination, and thought, (v) emotions, (vi) practical reason, (vii) affiliation, (viii) other species, (ix) play, and (x) control over one's environment (both political and material). Nussbaum takes each of these to be critical and non-negotiable.

We might ask, however, what happens when the list is articulated slightly differently. Lisa Cahill, for example, argues for *kinship* and *religion* as specific capabilities,

---

[13] Although in this case, gender would be more attributable to the influence of environmental and cultural rather than biological matter.

[14] Although it is likely that, in such a case, great cultural efforts were necessary in order to achieve this.

and not simply as subsets of bodily health, affiliation, or practical reason. If we take the first, *kinship*, as a separate capability, then relations of kinship would need to be distinguished from more general, consensual social relations, and one could not pursue close friendships while failing to pursue kinship relations and remain a flourishing person.[15] If kinship and affiliation are two different capabilities (and because all of the capabilities are non-negotiable), both would need to be pursued, and one could not substitute one for the other. In contrast, if we only have capabilities for affiliation and not also kinship, then familial relations might be one among a number of ways in which we function in our affiliative capacities.

There may be some reasons to agree with Cahill in understanding kinship as a separate capability. We might think of the bonds among family members which slave traders attempted to break. Although the enslaved individuals continued to have and cultivate substantive affiliations, it would be difficult to deny that the traders nonetheless did substantive damage to those individuals' relational capabilities.[16] So also, children separated from their parents early in life often continue to have a deep interest and, for some, even a seeming need to know their biological parents. And many adults feel a strong desire to have children and thus have not simply ties of affiliation, but ties of kinship.

Thus, on one hand, *what* capabilities are listed is critical. Whether there are simply these ten or additional capabilities (e.g., kinship) is not insignificant for our understanding of what conditions are and are not conducive for the development of each of us as full human beings. So also, the particular way in which we articulate or name the capacity is significant. Do we have a capacity, for example, for *sexual pleasure, sexual relations, pleasurable bodily experiences*, or *relations involving self-transcending love*?[17] All four descriptions could include sexual acts as one kind of use of that capacity, but the first two would *require* sexual activity in order to use and flourish in that capacity, while neither of the other two descriptions would do so. A child's joy in playing on a swing or merry-go-round could count as a pleasurable bodily experience, one fit to the child's stage of development, and that child could go on to cultivate a love of dance or aesthetic enjoyment of food rather than sexual relations of any sort and still fully develop the capacity. Or perhaps sexual relations ought not to be classed at all as an act actualizing a properly physical capacity. Perhaps it is, at base, a relational capacity, properly classed under affiliation. Some people may choose to actualize that affiliative capacity through sexual relations, whereas others—equally well—actualize it through certain forms of service to others (e.g., Mother Theresa's service to the poor). Determining which description properly articulates the core capacity and thus which types of activities or range of

---

[15] This is not precisely how Cahill articulates the significance of kinship. See her discussion on pages 59–60 of *Sex, Gender, and Christian Ethics*.

[16] One might argue that the damage occurred fundamentally in the violation of the individuals' capacities for practical reason, for deciding how they wanted to pursue their affiliations. If this is true, then this would not support kinship as a distinct capacity.

[17] Cahill asks the question of whether sexuality is properly placed under bodily health or affiliation. See *Sex, Gender, and Christian Ethics*, 60.

activities might actualize that capacity is not an easy task. Differing positions on these questions will, however, affect one's final account of what is necessary in order to set the conditions for women to actualize the full range of human capabilities. Nussbaum has done a great service in listing a set of capabilities. The adequacy of her list—both in terms of the description of each capability and the divisions among them—is critical for how her position works itself out in the concrete.

## *How Are Our Capacities Related?*

Thus, among the critical questions are: What capacities, or faculties, do we as humans have? And how ought each to be described? Equally significant is our account of the relation among the capacities. Nussbaum lists *senses, imagination, and thought* as a single capability. Is there, however, some significant relation among these? Aristotle—in contrast to Plato with his theory of recollection—understands sense experience to be essential to thought. That is, Aristotle thinks that thought or understanding is founded upon sense experience. We draw our imaginations and understandings out of the data provided through sense experience. If this is so, then the quality and kinds of sense experiences we have are not unrelated to our thoughts and imagination. Further, if sense experience is any way conditioned by sexually-differentiated matter, then our gendered sense experiences are not irrelevant to our imaginations and understandings.

On one hand, we can ask whether acts such as sensing, imagining, and thinking are importantly related, and whether our thinking—at least in terms of our understanding—is built, in some sense, upon our sensing or imagining. On the other, we can also ask what types of things are included under *sensing, imagining,* and *think-*

seems to limit sense to the five external senses: seeing, hearing, tasting, touching, and smelling. David Hume, in contrast, includes our affective experience in our basic impressions. We can ask, first, what occurs at the level of basic sensing or experiencing. Further, sense experience, as commonly understood by the early modern British empiricists, is taken to be a given, a brute, uninterpreted and isolatable datum. Should we so understand sensation, or is it always already interpreted, understood in terms of various categories, etc.? If there is some kind of foundational relation between sensing and understanding, then one critical question is: What

---

[18] In an article on Lonergan and Feminism, Paulette Kidder raises several possibilities: "Rather than speaking simply of 'women's experience,' feminists could use Lonergan's terminology in order to distinguish a whole range of feminine contributions to knowledge (that is, not only our experience but our images, questions, insights, and judgments)" ("Woman of Reason: Lonergan and Feminist Epistemology" in *Lonergan and Feminism*, ed. Cynthia S.W. Crysdale [Toronto: University of Toronto Press, 1994], 44).

types of experiences are included in sensing and in what ways might sexually-differentiated biological matter condition those sense experience?[19]

Once the nature of sense or basic experience is clarified, one can then ask what is built upon that basic sense experience. For an Aristotelian Thomist, understanding supervenes on sense experience, and one's judgments and decisions are built upon and grow out of one's understanding. If this is right, then our decisions and judgments, although perhaps not directly conditioned by sense experience (and biological matter) are indirectly so conditioned, and the nature and quality of our judgments cannot be fully separated from the nature and quality of our more sensory experiences. If one fails, for example, to cultivate one's sensible life and imagination and thus does not have a rich set of images and iconic influences, one may expect greater explicitness of information when making judgments; there might be a tendency to make lists of pros and cons and an interest in functioning primarily at the level of what is articulable. In contrast, if one has a richly developed sensory and imaginative life with a range of iconic images and symbols, then there may be a greater comfort remaining at the level of the symbolic and a lesser need to articulate one's motivations and influences explicitly. And if a highly developed imagination is coupled with a less developed understanding, then that person may hate lists and prefer to make judgments without explicated reasons. Thus, the nature of our sensory experience and the degree to which such "lower" level experiences have been developed is not insignificant for the ways in which we use or develop our other capabilities.

## A Note on Aristotle's and Nussbaum's Aristotelian Ideals

Nussbaum claims that the capabilities are non-negotiable. Conditions ought to be set for the development of each and every capacity for each and every human being. This need not mean that all individuals develop equally or fully each capacity, but she does think that we ought to set the conditions for each individual to have the opportunity to meet some basic "*threshold level*," a level "beneath which it is held that truly human functioning is not available."[20] Nussbaum does not specify precisely where that threshold lies, but she takes there to be some kind of minimum that counts as an appropriate and human use of each capacity.

This notion of a threshold means that each state ought to have available to each individual the resources necessary to reach that threshold—and these resources would include opportunities for development, the resources necessary to have the energy, health, safety and security to work on development, as well as resources

---

[19] For one analysis of how sexual difference might be significant, see Pia de Solenni's "St. Thomas Aquinas and the Feminine Genius," paper presented at *Mulieris Dignitatem and the Church's Social Vision: The Feminine Genius in the Pursuit of the Common Good*, University of St. Thomas, October 23, 2008.

[20] Nussbaum, *Women and Human Development*, 6.

specific to the capacity and encouragement to attend in the right kinds of ways in order to develop that capacity. Nussbaum does not require that all of us develop all of our capacities, but she does call our societies to the task of making development to some threshold level an option available for each of us.

Nussbaum thus does not advocate holistic development (i.e., development of *all* of the capabilities) for each individual, although she does think that the *conditions* for this ought to be the goal of governing states. In contrast, Aristotle makes such holistic development itself the ideal for each individual. That is, Aristotle seems to think that, not simply the opportunity, but the actual development of the full range of capacities, is the ideal.[21] As far as I can tell, Aristotle does not make Nussbaum's distinction between a basic threshold level of development of some capacity and higher-level development; he simply sets forward the excellent man—the fully, holistically developed man—as the ideal.

Aristotle and Nussbaum differ in terms of whether states ought to focus on actual holistic development or the opportunity, at least to a basic threshold level, for holistic development, but both make holistic development a core concern; such holism is part of what it means to be *human*. Part of the attraction for me of a broadly Aristotelian position is that this strikes me as right. Tremendous opportunities or resources dedicated to one area do not justify allowing scarcity in another, because we are oriented toward being *whole* human beings. Further, I think that Nussbaum's distinction between full development of a capacity versus some threshold level of development is a useful one, even if still vague. It is clear that none of us has either the time or energy to actualize to the highest extent possible *all* of our human capacities. Few of us can be a world-class athlete, an involved civil rights activist, a professional-level pianist, an intelligent and deep theorist, and a deeply-involved and interpersonal parent and friend. We often develop one capacity at the expense of others—and Aristotle's ideal of full development of all of our capacities is not the

resources.

Nonetheless, a focus on some version of holistic development seems more appropriately human, even as we specialize in our higher-level capacity development. Although we may not develop all of our capacities to an equally high level, some kind of genuinely holistic development can be combined with specialization. A mathematician can cultivate her intellectual, aesthetic, and interpersonal capacities, for example, in the way in which she pursues her work as a mathematician. She may also cultivate an avocation that uses her physical capacities and her capacities for involvement with the natural world.

---

[21] As he says in Book X of *Nicomachean Ethics*, Aristotle thinks that the point of politics is to encourage full development of (the free male) citizens. Thus, Nussbaum's emphasis is on the opportunity for development whereas Aristotle's is on active encouragement of development. These may, in the end, however, not be very far apart. Aristotle takes choice to be an essential aspect of developing virtue and thus the kind of encouragement appropriate for a political organization may be quite close to Nussbaum's notion of offering the opportunity for development.

Specialized development can be one-sided in problematic ways because the individual lacked the resources to develop even an adequate version of some of her other capacities, or she may have pursued her primary capacity to the exclusion of all else. But such one-sided development is not necessary, even among individuals extraordinarily well-developed in certain respects. Avoiding one-sidedness may require significant support — and it would surely require meeting some basic threshold in all areas — but it does not strike me as an impossible ideal.

There are a number of ways to spell out a concern for holistic development, but all versions of Aristotelian feminism should be committed to some form of holism. This does not require that all of us live our lives in the same way, or that we eliminate significant specialization, or that political groups *require* individuals to develop holistically. But it does mean that certain forms of life are ruled out as inappropriate for full human flourishing. Conditions that require or encourage one-sided development, societies that provide inadequate resources for holistic capacity development, ideals that discourage any form of holistic human development, etc., would all be problematic.

## Conclusion

The general claim that commonalities lie in our formal principle, in our capacities, and our differences in our material principle, including both biological and environmental and cultural matter, offers a powerful way to understand sex and gender. It does not, in itself, however, tell us *how* malleable or *how* biologically influenced gender is. Answering this requires considering a number of further questions — and the particular way in which these questions are answered may lead to very different positions. Thus, I see the debate and real work here as just beginning. But given the significance of gender for our lives and societies, it is, I believe, work well work doing.

# Chapter 4
# Why Aristotle Was Not a Feminist

Prudence Allen subtitles the first volume of her mammoth history of the concept of woman, covering 750 BC to AD 1250, "The Aristotelian Revolution." Aristotle's works came to dominate the universities in the high Middle Ages and early Renaissance periods, and his account of women "crushed," as Allen puts it, alternative Western understandings of women, some of which were more amenable to the full equality of women.[1] Aristotle and the dominance of Aristotelian ideas surely contributed much to the development of the West, not the least of which was the critical, although not uncomplicated, role of his thought in the rise of the empirical sciences. His influence on views of women, however, has been less sanguine.[2] Aristotle not only describes women as (as it were) deformed and misbegotten males; he also understands women as incapable of fully actualizing that feature most distinctive to human beings: our rationality.[3]

---

[1] See, for example, the Introduction to *The Concept of Woman: The Aristotelian Revolution 750 BC-AD 1250* (Grand Rapids, MI: Eerdmans, 1997), 22–23. This is not to claim, however, that Aristotle did not also give a more positive account of women than some of his predecessors. See Daryl McGowan Tress's "The Metaphysical Science of Aristotle's Generation of Animals and Its Feminist Critics" in *Feminism and Ancient Philosophy*, ed. Julie K. Ward (New York: Routledge, 1996), 31–50, for a brief critique of Allen's reading and some of Aristotle's improvements regarding the role of women in generation.

[2] For a very brief account of some of Aristotle's influence on medieval understandings of women, see the opening pages of Maryanne Cline Horowitz's "Aristotle and Women" in *Journal of the History of Biology*, 9, no. 2 (Fall 1976): 183–213. For a longer discussion, see Allen's work on the concept of woman.

[3] Mette Lebech points out that such a focus on the supposed inferior rational abilities of women is more significant in modern contexts than it may have been in previous eras. Where being a citizen in a state (rather than a member of a religious group or a part of the natural world, etc.) is so significant for one's identity, and where that membership is tied in some way to equality as *reasoning* beings, Aristotle's claims regarding women's lesser rational abilities take on an even greater importance. See *On the Problem of Human Dignity: A Hermeneutical and Phenomenological Investigation* (Würzburg: Königshausen & Neumann, 2009), esp. Chap. 3.

© Springer International Publishing Switzerland 2016
S. Borden Sharkey, *An Aristotelian Feminism*, Historical-Analytical Studies on Nature, Mind and Action 1, DOI 10.1007/978-3-319-29847-4_4

In light of this rather unambiguous criticism of women as incapable of full development as human beings, a key concern is whether, and how, one can appropriate Aristotle's thought without falling in subtle ways into his own denigration of women. Aristotle's critical comments about women are not simply limited to a few isolated passages here and there. Comments committing him to this understanding of women are present throughout his corpus and form a fairly consistent position regarding women. Further and more significantly, the very nature of hylomorphism requires him to raise questions which he answers in ways detrimental to women. I do not think that there is simply a little misogyny here and there which might easily be purged.[4] The concerns that led him to his view are more deeply rooted than that. This does not mean that a broadly Aristotelian hylomorphism cannot be used for feminist purposes, but care is needed, and study of exactly why Aristotle ended where he did—and how to avoid doing likewise—is necessary.

In the this chapter and the next, I would like to look, first, at what Aristotle says about women and some of the arguments and evidence he puts forward for his claims. Second, I would like to consider areas where Aristotle's positions will need to be modified in order to avoid his misunderstanding of women.[5] Some of these changes will be relatively straightforward and uncontroversial, updating, for example, his understanding of the role of each parent in human generation. Others may be more controversial, reconsidering, for example, some aspects of his understanding of the virtues. I think that all of these areas will need to be addressed in some form in order to make Aristotle's thought compatible with a true feminism, although I am not claiming that these are exhaustive of what needs to be addressed nor that all the points discussed are equally essential. I would like, however, to offer some account of how we can admire and be guided by Aristotle's hylomorphism without accepting his conclusions regarding the natural superiority of men and inferiority of women. The discussion of Aristotle's position will be divided into two chapters.

---

[4] I agree with Robert Mayhew's argument in *The Female in Aristotle's Biology* that Aristotle's understanding of women cannot be accounted for as simple ideological rationalization; it is not simply misogyny but an argued and intelligible position. Nonetheless, there may be ways in which it is, at least in part, ideological in another, more Marxist, sense. Although articulating precisely how these influenced Aristotle's explicit statements may be difficult, it strikes me as, nonetheless, highly likely, for example, that Aristotle's account of a life dedicated to leisure and the economic need, in order for some to have such a life, that others attend primarily to tasks related to sustaining our physical existence had some kind of impact on the way in which he handled and pursued the various arguments and evidence regarding women (as well as natural slaves).

[5] I am here asserting what I take to be a fairly uncontroversial claim: that Aristotle was wrong about the natural inferiority of women. Someone might ask whether my assertion here is well-evidenced; whether it is not motivated by ideology rather than argument and evidence; whether Aristotle might, in fact, despite the idea's unpopularity, be right; etc. It seems to me, first, that there is abundant, conclusive evidence, now rightly accepted by most people, that women are not naturally inferior and, second, that if I can show why Aristotle's conclusions need not follow from the evidence, there is then further reason not to accept such a view, even when one accepts much else from Aristotle's thought.

women and, in Chap. 5, focusing on where he went wrong and how to avoid his errors.

Aristotle articulates an account of the inferiority of women that ties together a particular understanding of generation, the tendencies of women in contrast to men, and the comparative inability of women to actualize their rational capacities fully. Although Aristotle does not think that women are less *human* than men,[6] he nonetheless takes them to be — in principle — incapable of full human development and thus less able to achieve a full version of the distinctively human ideal. In this chapter, I would like to look at three arguments or types of evidence by which Aristotle reaches these conclusions, including: (1) Aristotle's account of human generation and female natural tendencies, which I take to be correlated to his account of women's rationality and virtue, (2) Aristotle's response to the challenges of hylomorphism, and (3) the role of particular examples in Aristotle's epistemology.[7]

Before turning to each of these themes, however, I should note that, although Aristotle's position forms a fairly coherent whole, I am not sure which commitments came first. I do not know whether Aristotle first committed himself to a certain account of animal generation and then looked for other points of inferiority, whether he was already convinced from his experiences of inferiority regarding the virtues, for example, and then saw how that fit with a certain view of generation, or whether it was the broad hylomorphic account itself that motivated him to expect one of the expressions of the human form to be inferior and he then proceeded to search for confirming evidence. I would like to look at various relevant texts, showing how the claims fit together and form a fairly consistent account of women. I am interested in the logic of the claims and the ways in which the pieces each fit together. I am not, however, taking a position about the actual order in which Aristotle himself came to these positions.

## The Female in Human Generation, and Subsequent Tendencies in Females

### *Generation*

Some of Aristotle's most famous comments about women come from *Generation of Animals* 1.20 and 2.3. He writes: "the woman is as it were an impotent male, for it is through a certain incapacity that the female is female,"[8] and "the female is, as it

---

[6] See, for example, *Politics* 1.13.1259b27 and 34–35.

[7] I am focusing here on a limited but critical set of concerns leading Aristotle to his position. For a more thorough account of the various relevant factors, see (for the more biological) Mayhew's *The Female in Aristotle's Biology* and (for the more metaphysical) Chap. 2 of Allen's *The Concept of Woman*, vol. I.

[8] *Generation of Animals* (hereafter *GA*) 1.20.728a17-18.

were, a mutilated male."[9] These are fairly damning passages; they read a bit differently, however, in their larger context (although never ceasing to be quite damning). Aristotle's focus in *Generation of Animals* is, as the title indicates, reproduction and various forms of animal generation.[10] He is interested in this section in what he takes to be true of all animal generation and not simply human generation. He considers questions of whether semen originates from the whole of the body or only a part, what is responsible for the sex of the offspring, whether the female as well as the male contributes seed, etc. A central question in the section where these passages appear is what the male and female each contributes to generation. It is clear that human generation occurs within a female body and that male semen is essential. Aristotle takes male semen to contribute some kind of seed to generation (females do not, after all, reproduce without males). Do females, however, also contribute something analogous to semen?[11] Aristotle concludes (1) that both semen and menstrual fluid are necessary (and thus both men and women make a contribution), (2) that both semen and menstrual fluid come from the same source, i.e., both are blood 'worked over,' (3) that the differences between semen and menstrual fluid show that males have worked more on the blood, refining it more fully than females, and thus, (4) that males' contribution shows more activity.[12]

Aristotle is not interested in male versus female activity in the sexual act per se (there are, as Aristotle likes to point out, animals where the female enters the male), but rather male and female activity in the generation of a new being. After investigating semen and menstrual fluid, Aristotle concludes that the female's menstrual fluid acts as a material rather than an efficient cause of generation and thus is a passive rather than active cause, whereas the male contributes, or is in some way the source of, the efficient and formal (and final) causes of the offspring.[13] The matter is

---

[9] *GA* 2.3.737a27-28. Aristotle's concern in *Generation of Animals* is with animal reproduction or

will often describe Aristotle's claims, which are made of all animals, simply in terms of human beings.

[10] Tress argues that the term 'reproduction' is misleading. Aristotle is not interested in the mechanical process by which matter is rearranged and we thus get another production of the same type. His interest instead is in the causes of the coming into being of a new form-matter composite, a new being. Thus, his questions are about *generation* and the substantial change involved in generation, rather than the more modern and mechanistic notion of reproduction. See her "Aristotle Against the Hippocratics on Sexual Generation: A Reply to Coles," *Phronesis* 44, no. 3 (1999): 228–241 as well as the above cited "The Metaphysical Science of Aristotle's Generation of Animals and Its Feminist Critics." See also the further discussion of this point in the section on the challenges of hylomorphism.

[11] A further question is what precisely Aristotle means in the various passages by 'seed.' For a detailed discussion of 'seed' in differing passages and arguments that both female and male contribute seed, see Mayhew's *The Female in Aristotle's Biology: Reason or Rationalization* (Chicago: University of Chicago Press, 2004), Chap. 3.

[12] See *GA* 1.20.728a25-30, *GA* 1.19.727a3-15, *GA* 1.20.729a29-34, and *GA* 1.2.716a5-7.

[13] He writes: "It is clear then that the female contributes the material for generation, and that this is in the substance of the menstrual discharges, and that they are a residue" (*GA* 1.19.727b31-33) and "what the male contributes to generation is the form and the efficient cause, while the female contributes the material" (*GA* 1.20.729a9-11). See also *GA* 2.4.738b25-26.

an essential element and true cause of the child, and thus the mother and not simply the father is a true cause of the child, but the mother contributes a more passive, although genuine, cause.[14]

Although passive in comparison to the activity of the male cause, the female cause is not utterly passive or inert. First, insofar as matter for Aristotle is potency for formation, all material causes differ in significant ways from modern understandings of the passivity of matter.[15] Second, the matter involved is not utterly formless matter, but matter with particular types of potencies, e.g., to become a human being. Male semen cannot be mixed with any matter and one end up with a human child. Third, insofar as the material cause may thwart the intention of the male semen to create a male human being, directing the formation instead toward a female child and even one appearing like the mother (to be discussed more in the following), it is more than mere inactive 'stuff.'[16] Nonetheless, given this general account of generation, Aristotle understands the female — in comparison to the male in the case of generation — to be less capable, that is, less capable of working her fluid up to the state of perfection necessary to contribute an efficient or formal cause.

Thus, when Aristotle describes the female in *Generation of Animals* as "an impotent male," he is writing specifically in terms of her contribution to generation and comparing what he takes to be the male contribution to the more passive female contribution. This is fairly clear when the passage describing the female as "an impotent male" is seen in a slightly larger context:

> Now a boy is like a woman in form and the woman is as it were an impotent male, for it is through a certain incapacity that the female is female, being incapable of concocting the nutriment in its last stage into semen (and this is either blood or that which is analogous to it in animals which are bloodless) owing to the coldness of her nature.[17]

Given his account of generation, the female is, as it were, 'impotent,' that is, incapable of something of which the male is capable. The 'impotence' and 'incapacity' of the female are presented in this text as of a fairly limited kind, relevant only to generation.[18]

---

[14] The significance of this account of generation cannot be well appreciated outside of Aristotle's metaphysical concerns. For further discussion of the Aristotle's account of generation in light of his metaphysical questions, see the section below on the challenges of hylomorphism.

[15] See Chap. 2 for more about Aristotle on matter.

[16] For more on the latter two points, see Chap. 3 of Mayhew's *The Female in Aristotle's Biology*.

[17] *GA* 1.20.728a16-21.

[18] Tress offers a slightly different reading of the second key passage describing women as "mutilated males." She writes: "His comment here about deformity is intended to anticipate and counter an objection to this theory; his crude-sounding analogy is meant to show that females can and do produce male offspring because they do possess (potentially) the 'extra' male organs. But they themselves, as females, do not manifest them and so might be said, in this way only, to be like those who are deformed or underdeveloped in that they possess parts which are of no use to them" ("The Metaphysical Science of Aristotle's Generation of Animals and Its Feminist Critics," 47–48).

## A Qualification ("As It Were" Deformities)

Further, the phrase "as it were" is likely significant. In neither passage does Aristotle say simply that women are deformed or mutilated; in both cases, these claims are qualified in some way.[19] Presumably, an "as it were' deformity is not a deformity *simpliciter*; it is not a mutilation comparable to a human being lacking functioning eyes or legs. Those suffering from "as it were" deformities can function quite well and perhaps even as nature—in some sense—intends, but they nonetheless do so without the benefit of the best 'equipment' for their type of activity. Robert Mayhew, following Allan Gotthelf, draws on Aristotle's discussion of seals, saying "a seal is 'perfect' with respect to its nature and function; but when compared to normal quadrupeds, it is as it were a deformity or mutilation, i.e., its legs do not function the way a normal quadruped's do."[20] We can find other examples of what are presumably such "as it were" deformities in *History of Animals*. After discussing various terrestrial and aquatic animals, Aristotle points to some exceptions—animals that live in water but can breathe air (e.g., dolphins and whales) and animals that have gills and can take in water but can also walk on land (e.g., "the so-called water-newt"). He then says of the latter types: "In the case of all these animals their nature appears in some kind of a way to have got warped, just as some male animals get to resemble the female, and some female animals the male."[21] The comparison here is not precise; his analogy here is not with an animal that *is* female, but a male animal that resembles the female and vice versa. Nonetheless, I take these unusual cases with his description of them as "warped" to be comparable to the situation of females. They all function quite well and thus are not deformed in any simple manner, but the equipment with which they function is surprising and seemingly less than ideal in comparison with that of other related animals.

women as *simply* deformed or mutilated and that he qualifies his claims in some way, nonetheless, the comparison with other "as it were" deformities is less than perfectly reassuring. It might be true that Aristotle is not denying that females function quite well, even surprisingly well; nevertheless, his account of females and their deformities is quite different from account of other so-called "warped" beings. In the other cases (seals, water-newts, etc.), the species *as a whole* is described as a "monstrosity" or an "as it were" deformity. In the case of females, in contrast,

---

[19] Likewise, in *Poetics* 15, Aristotle says of women, she is "*perhaps* an inferior" (emphasis mine, 1454a20-21). Not all claims, however, are so qualified. See, for example, *Politics* 1.5.1254b12-15 and *Parts of Animals* 2.2.648a11-14.

[20] Mayhew *The Female in Aristotle's Biology*, 55. See also Allan Gotthelf's "Notes towards a Study of Substance and Essence in Aristotle's *Parts of Animals* ii-iv" in *Aristotle on Nature and Living Things: Philosophical and Historical Studies Present to David M. Balme on His Seventieth Birthday*, ed. Allan Gotthelf (Pittsburgh: Mathesis, 1985) and Cynthia A. Freeland's discussion of monstrosities (e.g., seals and lobsters) and other "as it were" deformities in "Nourishing Speculation," 172–174.

[21] *History of Animals* 8.2.589b27-29.

certain members of the species are ideal and the other members—with the very same species-form—are the "as it were" deformities. Thus, for females in contrast to other possible "as it were" deformities, there is a clear species ideal marking the proper development of females, which the females consistently fail to achieve. There is thus a clear way of marking and noting the deformity in the case of females that differs from how one would do so for any other "as it were" deformity. Although Aristotle's description of females as "as it were" deformities and not deformities *simpliciter* might seem to soften his claim a bit, nonetheless, it is unclear how strongly we should take this qualification, given the significant disanalogy between females and the other examples of such deformities.

Thus, Aristotle thinks that females are "as it were" deformities (although "as it were" deformities of an unusual type) because their contribution to generation is material rather than efficient or formal. One might ask, however, why this comparison is not made in the other direction. The male is not described as an, as it were, incapable female insofar as the male cannot contribute a material cause to generation but only an efficient and formal one.[22] Presumably, Aristotle does not, however, make the point in this opposing direction both (a) because he takes the material cause to be passive rather than active (and a result of lesser concoction of the blood) and (b) because he understands form to be superior to matter and thus that which is responsible for the efficient and formal causes to be more significant than that which is responsible for the material cause.[23]

## *The Female's Role in the Sex of the Offspring*

Perhaps even more significant than his claims regarding the role of the male and female in generation, however, is his related account of the origin of male and female offspring. Aristotle denies Anaxagoras's[24] theory that the differentiation of the sexes is due to the origin of the semen from the right or left testes and Democritus's[25] that the parent whose seed is dominant will determine the sex.[26]

---

[22] Aristotle makes this point clear in *GA* 1.22.

[23] For further discussion of both of these points, including Aristotle's account of contraries, privation, and the association of form with the male and matter with the female, see Chap. 5 below.

[24] Anaxagoras (500–428 BC) was one of the *pluralists* or *elementalists*, advocating a materialist account of reality. He was part of Pericles's intellectual circle, and, as Plato tells us in *Phaedo*, Socrates was originally highly attracted to Anaxagoras's account of *Nous*, until he saw it as too mechanistic to be fully explanatory.

[25] Like Anaxagoras, Democritus (c. 460–360 BC) was an *elementalist*, who famously named the basic elements 'atoms.'

[26] See *GA* 4.1. Allen notes: "It is important to reflect on the fact that Aristotle intentionally rejected previous theories of generation that had maintained the presence of female seed. … Parmenides, Empedocles, Democritus, Anaxagoras, and the Hippocratic writings all contained reference to some sort of contribution of female seed to the process of generation. Therefore, Aristotle's theory, which rejects all contributions of seed—or of formative element—by the mother, is a radical

Instead, Aristotle places the responsibility for the sex of the offspring on the side of the material cause. He claims that the matter with which a form works when a male child results is warmer than that when a female results. It is precisely the relative coldness of the matter that prevents proper and full reception of the form—and thus the resultant de-formation, or lack of formation, which leads to a female child.[27] Aristotle further claims that boys who look like their fathers had the warmest initial matter; boys who look like their mothers, a bit less so; girls who look like their fathers were conceived in cool matter, but not so cool as that of girls who look like their mothers, etc.[28] Thus, the material cause can, in some sense, hinder the work of the efficient and formal cause, and when such hindering occurs one ends up with a female or a child resembling in various ways the maternal line.

Aristotle thus argues that the particular matter 'receiving,' or activated by, the form is responsible for one's maleness or femaleness. It is worth emphasizing again that the claim is *not* that women are less fully human than men; both women and men share the same type of efficient, formal, final, and material cause—a human one—and thus both are equally human. But women are less fully *actualized* human beings. Because females struggle with worse material conditions, they are less able to actualize their genuinely (and fully) human capacities.

Aristotle's initial description of generation, separating the efficient and formal causes from the material cause, leads to a description of the female parent—at least in the process of generation—as less potent and less capable. Aristotle then ties this account to a theory regarding the origin of the sexes which places the responsibility for differentiation on the material, and more passive, cause. Thus, a woman's comparative 'incapacity' in the process of generation can be tied to her initial inferior conditions, of having been formed in colder matter to begin with, and thus struggling—simply because she is female—with more difficult material conditions.

Although there is debate on this point, Aristotle seems to take these inferior

---

departure from what was thought to be the case at the time he wrote" (*The Concept of Woman*, Vol. I, p. 97). More significantly, however, many of these views were materialist and mechanistic accounts and thus could not—in Aristotle's view—properly account for the generation of a hylomorphic being.

[27] *GA* 4.1.766a16-766b26. In *GA* 4.3.768b25-29 articulates two possibilities: either the semen is in some way deficient in power or the menstrual fluid is "too cold and in too great quantity." I take the first possibility here, a deficiency of power, to be related to the second. It would, after all, be deficient in power *in relation to* the particular coldness (and quantity) of the menstrual fluid.

[28] Aristotle draws this out through several generations. See especially *GA* 4.3.767b15-768a11. This description raises questions about whether Aristotle can adequately account for the ways in which children resemble their mothers and the maternal line, given that the formal cause comes exclusively from the father. While Aristotle understands the female as the privation of the male, it is not clear that an *individual* female is a privation of an individual male. This would seem to have to be the case, however, for children to resemble not simply a female in general but the specific mother or mother's side of the family, unless the female contributes to the formal cause in some sense. David Balme takes this latter route and summarizes Aristotle's position: "The male contributes the primary formal influence, while the female contribution is primarily material plus a secondary formal influence" ("Aristotle's Biology was not Essentialist," 292).

simply on the development of the organs and processes relevant to reproduction (which, for Aristotle, would include the heart).[29] This is an understandable move given, first, Aristotle's hylomorphism and related commitment to the unity of the individual and, second, the degree to which differences, in Aristotle's experience, between females and males expressed themselves in ways not limited to reproductive organs.[30] Nonetheless, any move to look for the influence of initial inferior conditions on the whole of women's lives, and not simply on some limited aspect, will create a fairly broad-reaching account of the general inferiority of women. I would like to look briefly at a few passages revealing Aristotle's broad-reaching, 'holistic' account of women's inferiority, beginning with his descriptions of female natural tendencies in *History of Animals* and then turning to his account of women's rationality and virtue.[31]

## Women's Natural Qualities

Our culpability and moral state are related to our choices, and all of the virtues proper are a result of choice.[32] But all of us also have tendencies and various conditions in which we make our choices and cultivate the various virtues. Aristotle does not claim that women are less *moral*, in the sense of consistently making worse choices for which they are culpable, but he does describe women's natural qualities

---

[29] He says: "This [the heart because it is the principle of heat], then, is the first principle and cause of male and female, and this is the part of the body in which it resides. But the animal becomes definitely female or male by the time when it possesses also the parts by which the female differs from the male, for it is not in virtue of any part you please that it is male or female, any more than it is able to see or hear by possessing any part you please" (*GA* 4.1.766b3-7).

[30] Aristotle writes, "The fact is that animals, if they be subjected to a modification in minute organs, are liable to immense modifications in their general configuration. This phenomenon may be observed in the case of gelded animals: only a minute organ of the animal is mutilated, and the creature passes from the male to the female form. We may infer, then, that if in the primary conformation of the embryo an infinitesimally minute but essential organ sustain a change of magnitude, the animal will in one case turn to male and in the other to female" (*History of Animals* 8.2.589b29-590a4).

[31] Spelman objects to the kind of parallelism I am suggesting here between Aristotle's biology and psychology. See especially footnote 32 in "Who's Who in the Polis" in *Engendering Origins: Critical Feminist Readings in Plato and Aristotle* ed. Bat-Ami Bar On (Albany, NY: State University of New York Press, 1994): 122–123. Although she is surely right that the parallels are made significantly more complicated by Aristotle's descriptions of natural slaves (who would follow more easily the biological patterns rather than the psychological ones), nonetheless, I take some version of these parallels to be true to Aristotle's work and helpful for illuminating his position.

[32] Aristotle says: "Excellence, then, is a state concerned with choice, lying in a mean relative to us, this being determined by reason and in the way in which the man of practical wisdom would determine it" (*Nicomachean Ethics* 2.6.1106b36-1107a2). Our non-chosen habituation is certainly relevant to virtue and can aid our attempts to become virtuous, but it can nonetheless be distinguished from virtuous acts per se.

and tendencies—that is, the conditions in which they make their choices—to be worse. Because their conditions are worse, women's possibilities for achieving a fully virtuous life are hindered.[33] Before turning to questions of the virtues appropriate to and reasonably achieved by women, I would like to look briefly at the natural qualities of women in contrast to men and thus the conditions under which women pursue their moral life.

Aristotle has various descriptions of women's differences from men, some of which are striking but likely have little impact on his understanding of the virtues achievable by women; others are less innocent. Among the more innocuous descriptions are his claims that women have fewer teeth and live shorter lives[34]; these may have some minor impact on the virtues achievable by women, but likely not a significant one. His account of their differing voices may have slightly more relevance (affecting perhaps the degree to which it was thought appropriate for women to give commands), and Aristotle certainly describes the differences with language of superiority and inferiority. He says:

> the depth [in contrast to loudness or softness] seems to belong to the nobler nature, and in songs the deep note is better than the high-pitched ones, the better lying in superiority, and depth of tone being a sort of superiority.[35]

More significant, however, are his descriptions of the impact of women's (and all females') initial material coldness on the broader development of their traits. He says:

> For females are weaker and colder in nature, and we must look upon the female character as being a sort of natural deficiency. Accordingly while it is within the mother it develops slowly because of its coldness (for development is concoction, and it is heat that concocts, and what is hotter is easily concocted); but after birth it quickly arrives at maturity and old age on account of its weakness, for all inferior things come sooner to their perfection, and as this is true of works of art so it is of what is formed by nature.[36]

If books eight through ten of *History of Animals* are authentic, then examples specifying this deficiency can be found there. He says:

---

[33] Virtue here is a result of choice, but not choice alone. There are standards for what counts as a fully virtuous life, and, although we are morally responsible for striving for such a life, we cannot be held fully culpable for failing to achieve such life if, as in the case of women, the conditions hinder that achievement.

[34] See *History of Animals* 22.3.501b20-24. Some commentators have accused Aristotle of bad research in making such claims; if he had counted, for example, he could have realized the falsity of the claim regarding teeth. I am not sure, however, that this is quite where the problem lies. It strikes me as highly plausible that, given the likely differing nutritional intake and physical burdens of women and men in ancient Greece, many of the women of Aristotle's acquaintance did, in fact, have fewer teeth and lived shorter lives.

[35] *GA* 5.7.786b29-787a2. Women and castrated males lack a certain tautness, and thus depth, in the voice because "the testes [are] attached to the seminal passages, and these again to the blood-vessel which takes its origin in the heart near the organ which sets the voice in motion" (*GA* 5.7.787b25-29).

[36] *GA* 4.6.775a14-21.

In all genera in which the distinction of male and female is found, nature makes a similar differentiation in the characteristics of the two sexes. This differentiation is the most obvious in the case of human kind and in that of the larger animals and the viviparous quadrupeds. For the female is softer in character, is the sooner tamed, admits more readily of caressing, is more apt in the way of learning; as, for instance, in the Laconian breed of dogs the female is cleverer than the male.[37]

These descriptions might initially appear to be fairly positive. The female is softer, learns more easily, and is cleverer. Such optimism is not, however, well supported. His reference to "is the sooner tamed" suggests that each of the traits should be read in reference to controlling or taming of an animal. Thus, 'softness' here seems plausibly understood as that which is helpful in taming.[38] Females (that is, all females, not just human ones) are softer in ways relevant to domestication.[39] So also, the traits of cleverness and being more apt to learn are likely intended not to refer to any kind of properly human intelligence or rationality (although it need not deny that female human beings have such properly human intelligence), but simply to the interest in obeying another insofar as that helps one gain pleasure and avoid pain — i.e., insofar as it is tied to the initial softness.

Aristotle continues his account of female natural tendencies, saying:

In all cases, excepting those of the bear and leopard, the female is less spirited than the male; in regard to the two exceptional cases, the superiority in courage rests with the female. With all other animals the female is softer in disposition, is more mischievous, less simple, more impulsive, and more attentive to the nurture of the young; the male, on the other hand, is more spirited, more savage, more simple and less cunning. The traces of these characteristics are more or less visible everywhere, but they are especially visible where character is the more developed, and most of all in man.

The fact is, the nature of man is the most rounded off and complete, and consequently in man the qualities above referred to are found most clearly. Hence woman is more compassionate than man, more easily moved to tears, at the same time is more jealous, more querulous, more apt to scold and to strike. She is, furthermore, more prone to despondency and less hopeful than the male, more void of shame, more false of speech, more deceptive, and of more retentive memory. She is also more wakeful, more shrinking, more difficult to rouse to action, and requires a smaller quantity of nutriment.

As was previously stated, the male is more courageous than the female, and more sympathetic in the way of standing by to help. Even in the case of cephalopods, when the

---

[37] *History of Animals* 9.1.608a18-26. See Horowitz's "Aristotle and Woman," pp. 210–211 and Mayhew's discussion of women's 'softness' and lesser spiritedness in *The Female in Aristotle's Biology*, Chap. 6.

[38] A number of commentators, including Horowitz and Mayhew, draw a helpful connection between this passage in *History of Animals* and the discussion of 'softness' in *Nicomachean Ethics* 7.7. In *Nicomachean Ethics*, Aristotle describes softness as a lesser ability to resist pleasures and pains; individuals who are soft are not necessarily sweeter but, rather, less able to say no to a desired pleasure or to withstand pain. Such softness might, in fact, greatly aid the process of taming a dog. See, for example, 7.1150b1-6 and 11–16.

[39] Harold L. Levy reads these descriptions as articulating a fairly positive account of women, including in terms of their rational abilities. See "Does Aristotle Exclude Women from Politics?" in *Review of Politics* 52, no. 3 (Summer 1990): 397–416, especially 399. I do not, however, find this reading overly persuasive. Nonetheless, Levy's overall interpretation of Aristotle on women is provocative, intriguing, and worth further investigation, even if not wholly convincing.

cuttlefish is struck with the trident the male stands by to help the female; but when the male
is struck the female runs away.[40]

Each of these descriptions is interesting, but particularly striking is the claim that
the female of most species is less spirited. Spirit—in contrast to appetite—has to do
with our emotions. Women are sensitive, or soft, regarding their appetites, but weak
in spirit; presumably, he means that women have a lesser degree of anger, desire for
revenge, etc. He emphasizes the point that the female tends to run away in the face
of danger, whereas the male is more "more sympathetic in the way of standing by to
help." Thus, women's emotional responses appear to be less able to sustain at least
certain types of action. Aristotle also, however, describes the female as tending
toward both jealousy and compassion—which would appear to be types of spiritedness. Given his earlier claim regarding women's lesser spiritedness, there are several ways this could be interpreted. He may understand women's jealousy and
compassion as a kind of impulsiveness tied to their greater softness regarding the
appetites, or he may simply think that, although women are less spirited in certain
senses, they feel other emotions quite fully.

Not all of these descriptions of the female are negative: women are, he says,
more compassionate, more easily moved to tears, and tending to care for the young.
These need not be read as problematic traits, but nonetheless the preponderance of
the traits describing females is negative.[41] These descriptions, once again, are not
about the moral culpability of women but about their 'starting point,' that is, the
various weaknesses with which women need to contend in pursuing a virtuous life.
And at least in regard to that starting point, women's natural tendencies are—
Aristotle thinks—inferior to those of men. Thus, women's incapacity at the level of
generation is paralleled by a lesser capacity for dealing appropriately with appetites,
a lesser spirit, and an overall weakness at the physiological and psychological
levels.

---

[40] *History of Animals* 9.1.608a32-608b19.

[41] Mayhew gives a striking summary of Aristotle's account of women's natural tendencies and
traits: "Aristotle's remarks in the biology about female character are consistent with what he says
elsewhere, and his overall conception of a woman's moral character reads like a list of history's
clichés about them: women are—again, in comparison with men—tamer, more delicate, and more
sensitive and yet Hell hath no fury like a woman scorned; they are more impetuous and emotional
but also much less capable of withstanding pain and discomfort; they tend to be less brave (except
for female bears and leopards); they tend to be scheming, dishonest, and bitchy; and yet they also,
by nature, make the best parents; and so on. Just as Aristotle regards females as generally physically inferior to males, so he sees them as 'psychologically' inferior: they are softer and less spirited—that is, the female is weaker than the male when it comes to her spirit and her soul's control
over her appetites" (*The Female in Aristotle's Biology*, 115).

## Women's Inferiority in Rationality

The various traits discussed in *History of Animals* are non-rational. Insofar as there is inferiority in female traits in contrast to male, this can, presumably, be attributed to females' inferior material conditions in the development of their sentient life. Aristotle makes analogous claims about human females' natural inferiority in the use of their rational capacities.[42] Aristotle defines human beings as rational animals, that is, as animals for whom (among other things) discernment of numerous possibilities and choice are distinctive.[43] We do not act exclusively on instinct, even highly sophisticated instinct but, rather, are rational animals.[44] Aristotle clearly thinks that, in regard to this key human ability, women are at a disadvantage in contrast to (non-slave) men.

In the first book of the *Politics*, Aristotle gives a demeaning account of women's ability to use their rationality; he writes of the "constitution of the soul":

---

[42] Aristc
*GA* 2.5,
soul, is
tive by
could b
structur
ticulars
emphas
materia
emphas
conditic
Womer
*and Ar*
latter p
19. Altl
are for
bodily
of sign

raise a bit of a puzzle. In
or nutritive aspect of the
and male), and the sensi-
whether the rational soul
patterns and intelligible
wing from material par-
and *GA* 2.3.27-29. If the
, then women's inferior
nality. If, in contrast, the
hen the inferior material
W. Modrak's "Aristotle:
*ninist Readings in Plato*
specially section I.) This
e, *On the Soul* 1.1.403a3-
es initiated in generation
l intellectual acts and our
es would have some kind
.

[43] See,

[44] Although Aristotle draws a distinction between rational and non-rational animals, nonetheless, the most sophisticated of the non-rational animals—we might think, for example, of dolphins and baboons—may function in ways that mimic or are very like human rationality. See, for example, the discussion in *GA* 1.23. Aristotle's account of the three general types of souls—nutritive, sensitive, and rational—can each be thought to contain a range or spectrum of distinct species-forms, moving from less to more complex and sophisticated versions of that general type. See, for example, *History of Animals* 8.1. Thus, we might think of a scale within each type, perhaps stretching within nutritive souls between plankton and Venus-fly traps, and within sensitive souls, between perhaps slugs and dolphins. The highest exemplars of nutritive functioning would be very like, although still different in kind, from sensitive souls, while the highest exemplars of sensitive functioning would be very like, although still different in kind, from rational souls. Thus, rationality, although different in kind from merely sensitive and nutritive functioning, is nonetheless not utterly different from very complex versions of sensitive functioning. Further, rational animals are animals and thus share in the nutritive and sensitive powers of the other souls, but they have, in addition to these, rational faculties.

in it one part naturally rules, and the other is subject .... Now, it is obvious that the same principle applies generally, and therefore almost all things rule and are ruled according to nature. But the kind of rule differs—the freeman rules over the slave after another manner from that in which the male rules over the female, or the man over the child; although the parts of the soul are present in all of them, they are present in different degrees. For the slave has no deliberative faculty at all; the woman has, but it is without authority, and the child has, but it is immature.[45]

Women can reason but, as he puts it, without authority. The way in which the freeman rules over a slave is, on Aristotle's account, analogous to the way in which the rational part of the soul rules over the appetites. That is, the rational part of the soul simply gives the order, demanding that the appetites follow, without expecting them to understand why the order is given. In contrast, a woman's rationality is sufficient to understand the orders, but not to give them.[46] Aristotle says here that women have the deliberative faculty (i.e., reason), unlike slaves, but in women it more properly obeys rather than gives orders.[47] Although better off than slaves, who—Aristotle thinks—lack the ability to reason, women can reason but less well than men, that is, in a way that lacks "authority."

This description leaves open the question of *why* women are less capable of using their deliberative faculty with authority. Is it that they lack sufficient power to make judgments, tending to 'freeze up' in the face of competing possibilities,[48] or that they, although capable of full reasoning, nonetheless regularly allow their emotions or their appetites to dominate their reason (perhaps because of the strength of

---

[45] *Politics* 1.13.1260a4-5 and 7–15.

[46] See, for example, Aristotle's discussion in *Nicomachean Ethics* 1.13.

Barbara Parsons points to a challenge this seems to raise: "By defining the human as a rational animal and then by taking the male of the species as the paragon of humans, the first professional logician in the Western world created a problem that his androcentrism apparently prevented him from perceiving. The problem resides in this fact: Aristotle held that it is the very constitution of the human soul that the rational part should naturally rule the irrational part, or, in other words, that the deliberative faculty should have authority over the nondeliberative faculty, and not vice versa; however, he also held that the deliberative faculty does not have authority in the souls of women and that because of this lack, women are by nature subject to the rule of men. Given what Aristotle said about the natural condition of the human soul, it is difficult to see how he could have reconciled that belief with what he had to say about the nature of women. Three options present themselves: He might have denied that women are human, but that would have wrought havoc with both his biological and ontological classifications; he might have proposed that women are by nature evil or corrupted beings, but that would have put him at odds with the ideas of freedom and responsibility that are central to his ethical teachings; or, finally, he simply might have said that women are naturally unnatural, and that statement, however philosophically embarrassing, might have proved the most illuminating decision he could have made" ("Aristotle on Women" in *Women's Studies Encyclopedia. Vol. III: History, Philosophy, and Religion*, ed. Helen Tierney (New York: Greenwood Press, 1991): 34–35).

[48] Among his descriptions of women in contrast to men in *History of Animals* 9.1, Aristotle says of the female that "[s]he is also more wakeful, more shrinking, more difficult to rouse to action" (608b12-13).

the one and comparative weakness of the other),[49] or is it that they tend to make bad judgments because they have limited theoretical understanding or lack a broad enough awareness of the relevant contexts?[50] Cynthia A. Freeland emphasizes the latter aspect and surmises that Aristotle means that "women are less able than men to attain theoretical wisdom and to formulate fully adequate conceptions of *eudaimonia* (happiness or flourishing) on which to ground their practical decision-making."[51] Prudence Allen, although agreeing that women are — on this account — less capable of practicing philosophy, puts the emphasis on the relative strength of the lower parts of the soul and the weakness of the rational part. She writes:

> What Aristotle appears to mean by this is that the lower part of the soul is not able to be ordered by the higher or deliberative faculty. Therefore, the rational powers of deliberation cannot rule or have authority over the lower functions of reason in women. Consequently, women cannot practise the necessary prerequisites for philosophy, namely deliberation and the exercise of reason in the activity of definition and syllogistic argument.[52]

Regardless of precisely why Aristotle makes the claim that women's reason is "without authority," it is clear that, in some way, women's rational capacities are impaired.

This does not mean that women ought not to rule in any respect; Aristotle grants that "the matters that befit a woman he [a husband] hands over to her."[53] That is, women ought to be giving orders about household management, for example. And there are also, in fact, situations where women rather than men exert the broadest

---

[49] He says, for example, in *Nicomachean Ethics*: "Therefore the irrational element also appears to be two-fold. For the vegetative element in no way shares in reason, but the appetitive and in general the desiring element in a sense shares in it, in so far as it listens to and obeys it; this is the sense in which we speak of paying heed to one's father or one's friends, not that in which we speak of 'the rational' in mathematics. That the irrational element is in some sense persuaded by reason is indicated also by the giving of advice and by all reproof and exhortation. And if this element also must be said to have reason, that which has reason also will be twofold, one subdivision having it in the strict sense and in itself, and the other having a tendency to obey as one does one's father" (1.13.1102b29-1103a3). Given the previous account of the appetites, it might then be understandable that Aristotle claims that women should only *obey* and not authoritatively use reason. This is the interpretation of Aristotle favored by Thomas Aquinas. See *Commentary on Aristotle's Politics* Book I, Lect. X, sec. 7. I am grateful to Shane Drefcinski for pointing me to this passage.

[50] Or is it, more simply, that Aristotle recommended marriage between older men and younger women, and thus in most husband/wife relations, the male was far more experienced? For further discussion of the possibilities for "without authority," see W.W. Fortenbaugh, "Aristotle on Slaves and Women" in *Articles on Aristotle, vol. 2: Ethics and Politics*, ed. Jonathan Barnes, Malcolm Schofield, & Richard Sorabji (London: Gerald Duckworth & Co., 1977), 135–139 and F. Sparshott, "Aristotle on Women" in *Philosophical Inquiry*, 7, no. 3–4 (1985): 177–200 in addition to the texts indicated in the following.

[51] "Nourishing Speculation: A Feminist Reading of Aristotelian Science" in *Engendering Origins: Critical Feminist Readings in Plato and Aristotle*, ed. Bat-Ami Bar On (Albany, NY: SUNY Press, 1994), 153. See also *Politics* 1.2.1252a31-33.

[52] *The Concept of Woman*, Vol. I, pp. 109–111. Compare this reading with W.W. Fortenbaugh's in "Aristotle on Slaves and Women" and Deborah Modrak's in "Aristotle: Women, Deliberation, and Nature," 210–213.

[53] *Nicomachean Ethics* 8.10.1160b35. See also *Nicomachean Ethics* 8.12.

rule, although these arise largely through situations of inheritance rather than merit. But, in general, Aristotle thinks that women overall ought to obey rather than rule men, that they are generally less fit for philosophy,[54] and that, connected to each of these, the ordering of their souls is imperfect.

## Women's Inferiority in Virtue

Tied to this imperfection in their ability to achieve the distinctive human function, are women's differences from men at the level of virtue. If virtue is functioning well and women, because they are women, cannot function well as human beings, they cannot achieve virtue in the same way that men can. This is certainly not to say that women cannot be virtuous, nor that they ought not to be trained in virtue.[55] Aristotle's claim that women cannot be virtuous like men can is not a claim that women tend to be immoral. The conditions under which women struggle—including the physical, psychological, and rational limitations—are different from those of (non-slave) males. And thus the virtues women can hope to achieve in acting toward "the right person, to the right extent, at the right time, with the right aim, and in the right way" differ slightly from what a man may achieve.[56] Aristotle writes, continuing the passage from *Politics* quoted previously:

> So it must necessarily be supposed to be with the excellences of character also; all should partake of them, but only in such manner and degree as is required by each for the fulfill-ment of his function. … Clearly, then, excellence of character belongs to all of them; but the temperance of a man and of a woman, or the courage and justice of a man and of a woman, are not, as Socrates maintained, the same; the courage of a man is shown in commanding, of a woman in obeying.[57]

age, temperance, justice, etc., he makes clear that because women's reason functions in a different context than men's and thus women's ability to achieve the human function differs from men's, the virtues will also look quite a bit different in women.[58] He says, for example:

> his justice, will not be one but will comprise distinct kinds, the one qualifying him to rule, the other to obey, and differing as the temperance and courage of men and women differ. For a man would be thought a coward if he had no more courage than a courageous woman,

---

[54] This impairment at the level of rational abilities is significant, regardless, in Aristotle's thought, but it becomes all the more so if we emphasize the comments in *Nicomachean Ethics* X about contemplation—and particularly a kind of non-embodied contemplation—as the ideal life.

[55] See *Politics* 1.13.1260b14-20.

[56] *Nicomachean Ethics* 2.9.1109a27-28. See also *Eudemian Ethics* 7.2.

[57] *Politics* 1.13.1260a15-17 and 19–22.

[58] In *Nicomachean Ethics* 8.11, Aristotle makes clear, for example, that a man can have a friendship with his wife (although it is a friendship of unequals); he cannot, however, have a friendship with a slave *qua* slave, although he can have a friendship with a slave *qua* man.

and a woman would be thought loquacious if she imposed no more restraint on her conversation than the good man; and indeed their part in the management of the household is different, for the duty of the one is to acquire, and of the other to preserve.[59]

The behaviors appropriate to women in achieving the virtues differ from those appropriate to men, and the realm in which those virtues ought to be exhibited differ. Women ought to aim toward household management and appropriate arrangement of practical affairs,[60] rather than the management of the state or any kind of understanding relevant to more significant ruling.[61] And the kind of temperance, courage, and justice women ought to develop is, presumably, fit to the more limited ruling and decision-making appropriate for women. Women can, in fact, decide and rule in certain ways, and they can develop the virtues; but their limited capacities suggest that a special emphasis ought to be placed on obedience and, in the best case, obedience to a virtuous man.[62] The ideal of the virtues coming to full flourishing in the magnanimous man would not, then, be an ideal appropriate for a woman, and she cannot become virtuous in the most fully human ways, although she certainly could have a type of temperance, courage, justice, etc.[63]

## Digressions on 'Natural Slaves' and Impressive Women

Although this will not be central to the discussion here, Aristotle thought—as is clear in a few of the quoted passages—that there were other groups who were also unable to actualize fully their human capacities. Natural slaves, for example, are not fully actualized human beings.[64] (Aristotle does not think that all who happen to be slaves are, in fact, natural slaves. Natural slaves are, rather, those who have, as he puts it, "no deliberative faculty at all." Those who are slaves because of war, or political or social humiliation of some group, would not fit into the descriptions

---

[59] *Politics* 3.4.1277b18-30.

[60] In *Politics* 2.5, Aristotle makes clear his assumption that women will tend to the house. He asks, in criticizing Plato's proposal of common wives in the *Republic*, "the men will see to the fields, but who will see to the house?" (1264b1-2).

[61] Tied to this, there is little reason women ought to enjoy a life with the leisure necessary for philosophy. A life of toil, therefore, is not hindering for women. See particularly *Politics* 7.14.1333a25-36 and *Rhetoric* 1.5.1361a6-12 as well as Eve Browning Cole's "Women, Slaves, and 'Love of Toil'" in *Engendering Origins: Critical Feminist Readings in Plato and Aristotle*, ed. Bat-Ami Bar On (Albany, NY: State University of New York Press, 1994): 127–144.

[62] This raises the question of *how* limited women's rationality is in relation to men's. Is it better, for example, to have a good woman rule than a bad man?

[63] Allen has an illuminating discussion of the possibilities for friendship between women and men. She claims that Aristotle would be open to friendships of virtue between the two but, because of the inequality in virtue, the woman should give to the man more honor and love him more than he loves her. See *The Concept of Woman*, Vol. I, pp. 114–117.

[64] See, for example, *Politics* 1.2 and 1.5 for brief discussions of natural slaves in contrast to (free) women.

Aristotle gives of slaves—and they should not be slaves, on Aristotle's view.) Non-slave women are in a better position, in terms of their ability to actualize the human capacities, than male slaves.[65] And thus non-slave women are in a middle position on Aristotle's account, between non-slave males and male natural slaves (with, presumably, female natural slaves at the bottom of Aristotle's hierarchy[66]). Like children or young teenagers, they are human but not fully mature human beings; unlike non-slave male children, however, women can never fully grow up.

Aristotle's claims regarding women are compatible with the existence of a few highly impressive women.[67] There could be some extraordinary women who, although struggling with the problematic conditions common to women in general, nonetheless so struggle and have such resources available (as well as perhaps unusually good matter for a woman[68]) that they become strikingly well developed, perhaps even better developed than the average man. Thus, Aristotle's position could acknowledge the occasional, exceptionally accomplished or talented woman. Being a woman—and the general inferior development of women—does not mean that every individual woman will actually be inferior to all men.[69] Men too can fail to become fully human, and having better biological material conditions does not mean that all conditions are thereby better, nor that each individual man will take advantage of those conditions to become who he ought to be. But, in general, women are in a significantly worse position than men—not because they are less human than men, but because their matter is in some way inferior and thus the conditions for full human development are compromised. (It is worth noting that few human

---

[65] See, for example. *Poetics* 15.1454a17-24. Elizabeth V. Spelman discusses the relations among

*Origins: Critical Feminist Readings in Plato and Aristotle*, ed. Bat-Ami Bar On (Albany, NY: SUNY Press, 1994), 99–125. Although perhaps a bit strong, her point in "Who's Who in the Polis" is nonetheless illuminating: "In a well-ordered city-state, women and slaves are not parts of the polis, but they are the conditions of it. Without their work, the polis could not exist, but they do not participate in the activities of the polis" (100).

[66] I am not wholly sure about this. Since 'natural slave' is a category based on abilities and not primarily a political or social category, Aristotle—were he to comment—might rank different types of natural slaves based on their various levels and kinds of abilities rather than their sex.

[67] See, for example, *Politics* 1.12.1259b2-4. I am not sure, however, that they are compatible with the notion that such an exceptional woman could be the equal of an exceptionally virtuous and actualized man.

[68] See *Rhetoric* 1.5.34-38 where Aristotle comments on the possibility of good birth coming from the female line. This may refer primarily to one's social position, but the comments in the previous section about people "distinguished for qualities that we admire" suggests a reading more fit to my claims here.

[69] Aristotle says quite explicitly in the *Politics*: "the male is by nature superior, and the female inferior; and the one rules, and the other is ruled; this principle, of necessity, extends to all mankind" (1.5.1254b13-15). I take him here to claim that by nature (i.e., because of initial material conditions) the male has the better conditions for development, but it is not a claim about what, in fact, actual men do achieve.

beings succeed in becoming fully developed; there are many ways and reasons to fail to become so, and not simply one.[70])

Aristotle's account of the respective roles of the female and male parent in generation is subtle, distinguishing the causal contribution of each both to generation and to the differentiation of the sexes. That account of generation has, it seems to me, significance for Aristotle's understanding of the natural tendencies of women in contrast to men, as well as the rationality and virtues of women and men. Although Aristotle does not explicitly state that his biological, psychological, and moral theses regarding women are directly connected, they nonetheless fit into a logical whole presenting an overall account of the general natural inferiority of women to men.

## The Challenges of Hylomorphism

Aristotle's account of biological generation feeds into an overall vision of the inferiority of women. So too, Aristotle's hylomorphism—in contrast to other metaphysical positions regarding human structure—raises distinct questions which may have led Aristotle to see women as inferior. Aristotelian hylomorphism is a response to the inadequacies of both materialism and dualism, accounting for our unity as an individual while also acknowledging our deep materiality. Hylomorphism can make sense of much in human experience, and yet the position also raises a number of difficult challenges. Two are particularly important for Aristotle's account of women. First, Aristotle needs to give an account of generation sufficient to account for a substantial, and not simply an accidental, change.[71] Second, the commitment to the fundamental unity of form and matter requires Aristotle to offer some account of the very different physical expressions of female and male human beings. I would like to look briefly at both of these.

---

[70] As Aristotle claims in the *Nicomachean Ethics*, "it is possible to fail in many ways (for evil belongs to the class of the unlimited, as the Pythagoreans conjectured, and good to that of the limited), while to succeed is possible only in one way" (2.6.1106b29-31).

[71] A substance is *what* a thing is, that is, the appropriate macro-level description of the thing (e.g., a *squirrel,* or *chipmunk,* or *human being*). It is not Locke's 'that which I know not what' underlying various qualities, nor can it be identified with any particular material part of a thing (Henrietta Lack's cells, after all, have her genetic material but are nonetheless not *her*). An accident, in contrast, is a feature, trait, or quality *of* the substance (e.g., skin-color, location in space at that moment, or current height). Aristotle does not think that accidents can simply be dispensed with (no human being lacks size in toto, even though our sizes may differ), but he does think that you can distinguish *substantial* and *accidental* changes—that is, changes which lead to the beginning or end of that thing in contrast to changes occurring *to* the thing.

## Generation as a Substantial Change

Aristotle's question is—as Daryl Tress points out—about human *generation*, not human *reproduction*.[72] That is, Aristotle is not interested simply in how bits of matter move about and enlarge in various ways. Objecting to such mechanistic pictures of human beings is central to Aristotle's rejection of his predecessors' views (e.g., Democritus's and Empedocles's accounts of seed). Aristotle is interested instead in how new human beings come into being. A new human being is not simply a new arrangement of matter, on Aristotle's account, but a new matter-form composite, an entirely new being which cannot be reduced to a new arrangement of pre-existing material.

Aristotle makes this point, in part, by distinguishing what he calls *accidental* and *substantial* changes.[73] In the first, there may be all sorts of change (e.g., location, color, size, state, etc.), but no new *being* or individual comes into existence. In the latter, however, there is a change at the level of *what* exists and not merely how this or that continues its existence. Mechanistic accounts of reproduction treat generation as, what Aristotle would term, an accidental change; they give accounts of how matter is moved about in certain situations.[74] This is not Aristotle's only concern; it is one concern, but does not yet address how the changes involved result in a *substantial change*, that is, the arrival of a new substance, a new matter-form composite. (It is worth noting that just as a mechanistic model does not yet address all of the questions Aristotle wants to consider, so also a dualistic account of the person would likewise limit the questions. Insofar as the body and soul are seen to function relatively independently of each other, the dualist can accept a mechanistic picture of reproduction as sufficient at the level of body while positing a different type of source in order to account for the introduction of soul or mind. Aristotle is in what

the relevant material changes *and* how those processes work toward not simply an accidental but a substantial change.)

---

[72] See especially Tress's "Aristotle Against the Hippocratics on Sexual Generation: A Reply to Coles," *Phronesis* 44, no. 3 (1999): 228–241 and "The Metaphysical Science of Aristotle's *Generation of Animals* and Its Feminist Critics" in *Feminism and Ancient Philosophy*, ed. Julie K. Ward (New York: Routledge, 1996), 31–50. On page 231 of the first article, Tress lays out a particularly clear account of two reasons Aristotle rejected pansomatism, one of the dominant materialist theories against which he was arguing.

[73] The terms 'accidental' and 'substantial' have quite different connotations in everyday language as well as modern philosophy (e.g., in Locke or Hume). Accidental, for Aristotle, does not mean 'in an unintentional way' nor is substance some underlying stuff, as noted in the footnote above.

[74] Most contemporary medical accounts of reproduction would similarly treat the changes in a limited manner, looking at the various material structures involved and the ways the movements of the relevant matter might be hindered (e.g., blocked fallopian tubes, uterine scar tissue, insufficient hormone levels). Aristotle would certainly not object to such analysis—it would be a necessary part of understanding generation—but he would not consider these analyses to be sufficient for understanding generation.

On Aristotle's account, neither the female nor the male parent contributes anything that is *actually* a child; both contribute elements that are potentially a child,
and the contributions actually become a new child only in combination. Aristotle
emphasizes that both parents are necessary and that the kind of thing they contribute
differs. In the opening lines of *Generation of Animals*, Aristotle refers to the four
causes and the need for an understanding of generation that accounts for all of the
relevant dimensions, i.e., the final, formal, material, and efficient causes. Thus,
Aristotle wants to give an adequate account not only of how semen and menstrual
fluid are moved about but also of *why*—given those changes—we get a new being.
Such a new being is itself a matter-form composite, itself growing and developing
toward its own telos.[75] There must thus be something capable of introducing a new
form, or motivating the arrival of a new substantial form.[76]

Aristotle achieves this, in part, by separating the efficient and material cause. No
efficient cause simply pushes some matter into a new location, nor is the material
cause alone able to create a new being. Rather, the unique way in which material
and efficient (and formal and final) causes relate sets the conditions for a substantial
change. Aristotle well recognizes that generation in the case of human beings
requires two sexually differentiated partners. Such sexual differentiation is not necessary for generation—there are entities (e.g., amoebas and many plants) which are
asexual and reproduce without two partners. Humans, however, cannot reproduce
alone. Aristotle thus has two sexes, both of which play some essential role in generation. Given his need to account for four causes of generation, and not simply one,
and given the close ties of efficient, formal, and final causality, Aristotle had essentially two broad types of causality in need of explanation: those associated with
form and that associated with matter. He has two sexes relevant to generation, and
he chose the simplest route of attributing one pair to each partner: formal (including
efficient, formal, and final) to the male, material to the female. And thus, Aristotle

---

[75] Tress says: "But according to Aristotle, the organism grows not because it takes in a quantity of
food, but rather the organism takes in food in order that it may grow in a specific way to actualize
its potential" ("Aristotle Against the Hippocratics on Sexual Generation: A Reply to Coles," 234).

[76] Addressing this challenge is part of why Aristotle emphasizes that semen differs from menstrual
fluid. Although semen is an analog of menstrual fluid and arising, like menstrual fluid, out of
blood, it is not blood. Its different nature (including its more foamy nature, connected to its greater
association with air rather than the heavy element of water) is significant for its distinctive role
bringing the matter of menstrual fluid to act as a new human being.

Some commentators have objected that Aristotle overlooks the possibilities for female sexual
fluids in his account of generation. (He does, however, discuss female sexual fluids in *History of
Animals* 10.2 and 3.) Insofar, however, as pregnancy can occur without significant observable
female fluid but not without (prior to modern medicine) male seminal fluid, Aristotle may have
made an intelligible decision in placing less emphasis on female sexual fluids, in contrast to menstrual fluid.

Tress interprets semen, for Aristotle, as different *in kind* from blood, insofar as semen can
contribute a moving principle to generation (see Tress, "Aristotle Against the Hippocratics on
Sexual Generation: A Reply to Coles," 235). Such an interpretation is plausible and would go a
long way in accounting for how generation involves a *substantial* change and not simply accidental
ones. See *GA* 4.1.765b9-14 and *GA* 2.3.737a28-29. Compare as well *Metaphysics*
8.4.1044a33-1044b2.

posited the relatively simple thesis that each parent contributes a different type of causality.

## *Differing Physical Expressions of a Common Form*

Hylomorphism requires Aristotle to give a different and more comprehensive account of the principles involved in generation than either mechanism or dualism do. This need makes it understandable why Aristotle thought it fitting to separate the formal and material causes. Second, there is a pressure inherent in hylomorphism to have something significant to say about differing material expressions.[77] Aristotle claims that each of us has, as our substantial form, an instance of the common human form. Were each of our substantial forms not human—that is, if women, for example, had a different type of substantial form than men—then we would be members of different species.[78] And yet women and men can come together and give birth to new human beings (both female and male) who can themselves procreate and give birth to further humans. Given this pattern, Aristotle could not claim that women and men possessed different species of soul. We must both have human souls and equally so.

Plato similarly claims that all humans have an identical type of soul, and he places the equality of women and men in our common soul.[79] Plato, however, is a dualist, understanding the soul—not as the form of the body—but as largely independent of the body. Plato thus does not need to account for differing bodies or explain how such differences fit with any claim of equality. Our bodies are largely irrelevant to our souls, and thus bodily differences offer no significant challenge to a claim of equality. Aristotle, in contrast, understands the soul as the *form* of the ~~body. Hylomorphism does not separate the soul and body, even if it distinguishes~~ them; bodies are, rather, an expression of soul. As such, physical differences are not as easily addressed by Aristotle. And there are clearly such physical differences between women and men. Were the differences merely a matter of accidental[80] features (height, weight, hair color, eye color, or skin tone), then perhaps he could have overlooked such differences. But the differences appear to go quite a bit deeper: we are, quite simply, built differently, possessing not simply differently colored or sized

---

[77] Allen well discusses this point in both her Introduction and "Aristotle's indirect rejection of Plato's theory of sex unity" in *The Concept of Woman*, vol. I, pages 1–7 and 88.

[78] See *Generation of Animals* 1.23.730b33-731a1 and *Metaphysics* 10.9. See also Matthews's on this point in "Gender and Essence in Aristotle," cited above.

[79] See Allen's *The Concept of Woman*, Vol. I, pp. 57–82, for a more nuanced account of the equality of women and men in Plato's thought.

[80] Here I mean 'accidental' using Aristotle's distinction between 'substantial' and 'accidental'—not in the sense of insignificant or occurring in some happenstance way.

bodies but different body parts and bodily organs.[81] Such differences are hard to attribute simply to an accident, but must instead indicate something significant at the level of substance.[82] There are, however, only two principles present at the level of substance: (substantial) form and matter. As argued above, the differences between women and men can hardly be attributed to form, for then we would be two distinct species. Thus matter must be the principle responsible for the differences. Matter, however, is fundamentally potency for formation. Form, in contrast, is the principle directing the formation. If the form is structurally the same, why is the matter formed so differently in the case of women in contrast to men?

I do not think that Aristotle's way of addressing this challenge is, by any means, the only way to do so; it is, however, an intelligible answer, fitting smoothly with other aspects of his thought. Aristotle regularly makes distinctions between well-formed and malformed versions of the human, that is, individuals who well express the human form and those who are, for various reasons including material ones, not able to express perfectly the human form. Given the quite distinctive and deeply rooted differences between females and males, Aristotle takes a similar tack in this case, describing one of the expressions as an appropriate development of the human form (the male) and the other as an, as it were, deformation (the female). Thus, he addresses the challenge of two differing bodily expressions of a single type of form by describing the one expression as superior to the other.

Aristotle describes the male as the better formation and the female as the (as it were) deformation. One might ask again, however: why not go the other way? Perhaps the hylomorphic account led him to accept one bodily formation as a more appropriate expression of form, but why choose the male? There are likely a number of answers to this. Aristotle ascribes the greater quantity as well as lesser quality of menstrual fluid (in comparison to semen) as an indication of a lesser ability of females to absorb nutrients and concoct the residue[83]; he ascribes the facts that blood vessels stand out less in women than men and that women are "rounder and

---

[81] Aristotle says, after discussing the case of castrated animals, "Clearly, then, the distinction of sex is a first principle; at any rate, when that which distinguishes male and female suffers change, many other changes accompany it, as would be the case if a first principle is changed" (*GA* 1.2.716b10-13). In *Metaphysics*, he writes: "this difference [of male and female] belongs to animal in virtue of its own nature, and not as whiteness or blackness does" (10.9.1058a31-33).

[82] In *Metaphysics* 6.30, Aristotle distinguishes two meanings of 'accident.' The differences between male and female are accidental in the second sense—"what attaches to each thing in virtue of itself but is not in its essence [the Ross translation in the two-volume Barnes edition renders the final word as 'substance'; I am following Ross's choice of 'essence' in the one-volume McKeon edition]" (1025a30-31)—but not the first. Allen has an excellent discussion of these two meanings of accident and their significance for Aristotle's understanding of women in *The Concept of Woman*, Vol. I, 105–106.

[83] He says, "since it is necessary that the weaker animal also should have a residue greater in quantity and less concocted, and that being of such a nature it should be a mass of sanguineous liquid, and since that which has by nature a smaller portion of heat is weaker, and since it has already been stated that such is the character of the female—it is necessary that the sanguineous matter discharged by the female is also a residue. And such is the discharge of the so-called menstrual fluid" (*GA* 1.19.726b30-727a2).

smoother" than men to the notion that women are less able to concoct their nutri-ents[84]; and he notes that eunuchs develop in more feminine ways than non-eunuchs, indicating that feminine traits show up in literally mutilated males.[85] His description of the female as passive in contrast to the male is surely in part tied to the role of each in sexual acts, although he does regularly return to an example of an insect where the female enters the male.[86] We might also add the general differences in strength[87] and height between females and males as a group.[88] Most significant, however, is likely his account of the male as contributing the active principle of efficient (and formal) causality in generation in contrast to the female's more pas-sive contribution of the material cause. All of these factors in combination likely led him to conclude that the human form in males had a better situation for development than the form in females.[89]

Given his hylomorphism, Aristotle needs to say something about such differing expressions of a common human form. His comparisons of women and men as well as the distinctive case of eunuchs, in combination with his understanding of genera-tion, all likely contributed to push him toward an account of women as the deformed version in contrast to the male as the more ideal development.

---

[84] He writes: "Further, the blood-vessels of women stand out less than those of men, and women with the menstrual discharge. We must suppose, too, that the same cause accounts for the fact that the bulk of the body is smaller in females than in males among the vivipara, since this is the only class in which menstrual fluids are discharged from the body. And in this class the fact is clearest in women, for the discharge is greater in women than in the other animals. That is why her pallor and the absence of prominent blood-vessels is always most conspicuous, and the deficient develop-ment of her body compared with a man's is obvious" (GA 1.19.727a16-25).

[85] See, for example, *History of Animals* 9.50. The case of eunuchs is particularly interesting and well discussed in Mayhew, Chap. 4. Eunuchs are relatively rare in contemporary societies, and we tend to observe less often the striking ways (for example, in hair patterns) in which castrated males take on more feminine physical traits.

[86] See also *History of Animals* 5.8.

[87] Aristotle understands males to be stronger in a number of senses, including sheer physical power, ability to tolerate pain, and living longer (see *On Length and Shortness of Life* 5.466b15-17).

[88] It is somewhat unclear whether physical differences such as height and strength are appropriate indicators of fitness for ruling or pursuit of a life of virtue. See Aristotle's comments in *Politics* 1.5 regarding the frequency with which "some have the souls and others have the bodies of freeman" (1254b32-33).

[89] He does not seem, however, to have considered any role differing nutrition and training as well as the social influences may have played in encouraging the degree to which such differences are present.

## Epistemology and Examples

On the one hand, Aristotle's account of generation plays a key role in his understanding of the natural inferiority of women. He has an account of how animal generation or reproduction occurs, which sees the male as contributing the more significant aspect to the new being. This 'natural inferiority' of the female is repeated in Aristotle's account of our sentient life, our natural tendencies, our rationality and our virtues. On the other, his broader hylomorphic commitments raise questions about change and how *substantial* changes can occur as well as why there can be differing physical expressions of the same form. Such questions are deep concerns if one is a hylomorphist, but are not likely to be raised (at least in the same way) if one is either a materialist or dualist. In addition, finally, Aristotle's epistemology likely played a key role in his account of the possibilities for women, in contrast to men.

Aristotle's epistemology, although differing substantially from early modern British empiricism, is nonetheless empiricist, beginning with particulars and moving to the universal.[90] Plato could discount the import of differing bodies in part because of his dualism, and Platonic epistemology—although acknowledging that sense particulars may initiate a journey of recollection[91]—nonetheless requires a significant move away from particulars. There is thus in Plato's account of knowledge, a justification for disregarding certain disparities between theory and reality. Women failing to engage in equal numbers with men in philosophical pursuits, for example, does not require as full an explanation in Platonic thought as in Aristotelian.[92] Plato did not come to his understanding of human beings by looking primarily at actual, living human beings; rather, he takes us to have insight into structures that can exist in separation from individual human beings. If one can recognize what belongs to a Form, whether our 'fallen' material world allows it true expression is somewhat incidental for Plato.

In contrast, Aristotle takes the form to be found precisely in particular, concrete examples. One certainly needs to distinguish, from among the examples, those that actualize well the form and those that do not, but the examples and individuals we encounter are central to our understanding of the human form. Thus, the kinds of lives lived by Aristotle's female contemporaries were critical for his broader account

---

[90] Much of early modern empiricism employs an inductive model, understanding general ideas to be built out of particular sense experiences; Aristotle's abstraction, in contrast, emphasizes the concomitant experiences of sensation (involving particulars) and intelligibility (involving universals). We do not, thus, come to understand a series of sense particulars and then group them according to general categories. To understand anything is already to understand it in terms of certain general categories. We may come to a better or worse understanding of some universal through experience of particulars, but there is—on Aristotle's account—no experience that could count as 'understanding' some bare particular.

[91] See, for example, *Phaedo* 75e.

[92] This comparison can be overdone. Compared to Aristotle, examples are less significant for Plato. They are not, however, utterly irrelevant.

of women. To continue the previous example, there were certainly a number of great ancient women philosophers—e.g., Aspasia and the women of the Pythagorean school—but not nearly as many as men, and Aristotle needs to account for any significant discrepancies between women's and men's involvement in theoretical pursuits. Aristotle's epistemology requires he, in some sense, begin with the women he knows and talks with, the stories and reports he had heard, and the descriptions of women given by others. Thus, the comparatively limited number of women involved in philosophical and more theoretical pursuits needs an accounting for Aristotle that it would not for Plato.[93]

## Ancient Women's Lives: Athens Versus Sparta

Aristotle does not frequently avert to particular women or articulate their role in providing a basis for his view, but he does reference a few groups of women. One of the most striking is his discussion of the women of Sparta and their role in the collapse of Spartan society. It is likely that the contrast between women's lives in Athens and in Sparta provided Aristotle with a dominant image and model from which to develop his theories about women. I would like to look both at Aristotle's comments about women's role in the collapse of Spartan society and the differences between Spartan and Athenian women, with an eye to the role those differences may have played in Aristotle's developing view of women.

In the *Politics*, Aristotle attributes the demise of Sparta, at least in part, to what he sees as the excessive involvement of women in the state. He says:

> This was exemplified among the Spartans in the days of their greatness; many things were managed by their women. But what difference does it make whether women rule, or the rulers are ruled by women? The result is the same… … … …regard to courage, which is of
> no use in daily life, and is needed only in war, the influence of the Lacedaemonian women has been most mischievous. The evil showed itself in the Theban invasion, when, unlike the women in other cities, they were utterly useless and caused more confusion than the enemy. This license of the Lacedaemonian women existed from the earliest times, and was only what might be expected. For, during the wars of the Lacedaemonians, first, against the Argives, and afterwards against the Arcadians and Messenians, the men were long away from home, and, on the return of peace, they gave themselves into the legislator's hand, already prepared by the discipline of a soldier's life (in which there are many elements of excellence), to receive his enactments. But, when Lycurgus, as tradition says, wanted to bring the women under his laws, they resisted, and he gave up the attempt. These then are the causes of what then happened, and this defect in the constitution is clearly to be attributed to them. We are not, however, considering what is or is not to be excused, but what is right or wrong, and the disorder of the women, as I have already said, not only gives an air

---

[93] First, as noted above, Aristotle's claims are compatible with a few exceptional women. Second, there is also the question of whether Aristotle appreciated theoretical work in its full range of expression. Although perhaps not a dominant approach to mothering (particularly given the physical demands involved, especially in a relatively poor region), I can imagine, however, that some mothers, sisters, aunts, and grandmothers may have approached child rearing with a fairly theoretical attitude.

of indecorum to the constitution considered in itself, but tends in a measure to foster avarice.[94]

Aristotle makes a number of harsh accusations here. He thinks, first, that the husbands were under "the dominion of their wives" in Sparta[95]; second, that the women were not easily ruled and resisted the law; third, that this lawlessness and female boldness contributed to the internal deterioration of the society; and, finally, that the power of women "tends in a measure to foster avarice."

Although the comments are harsh (and are made against the enemy of Athens in the nearly 30 years' Peloponnesian War), Aristotle is right to contrast sharply the customs of Athens and Sparta. Although the kinds of activities in which women engaged in the ancient world differed significantly based on their status and class, nonetheless, the dominant Athenian (and broader Greek) ideal was a highly domestic one. In both Semonides's "On Women," written during the sixth century B.C., and Xenophon's "Oeconomicus," written in the fourth, the bee was employed as a symbol for women. Xenophon describes the foresight of the bee, working to prepare the home, and Semonides describes women—in a bee-like fashion—as increasing one's property. Like bees, Athenian women were the busy caretakers of the domestic sphere.[96]

Thus, on the one hand, Aristotle had the dominant example of women's lives in Athens—lives that focused primarily on domestic pursuits (the 'bee') and limited the education and physical exercise of at least the most privileged women. On the other, in Sparta, women had more education and a state that focused more (comparatively) on women's development. Like Athens, male education and formation were primary, but, unlike in Athens, the type of male formation led the society to emphasize as well a broader female education.

Sparta made a much sharper distinction between the public and private spheres than Athens, and the ultimate source of cohesion and loyalty was the state, rather than the family. Sparta was known for its military prowess, and many of the practices of the state were developed in order to train that military. After a male child was born, it was inspected for its physical fitness, and, if deemed unlikely to grow to be a soldier, it was allowed to die. The mothers then raised the healthy sons until they were seven, when they were removed from the family and sent to live in barracks, where they received military training, including training to withstand significant physical hardship. At around twenty, the men joined collective mess halls, sharing their meals together and living in common barracks. Even after a man

---

[94] *Politics* 2.9.1269b30-1270a14.

[95] Ibid., 2.9.1269b25.

[96] See Sue Blundell's *Women in Ancient Greece* (Cambridge, MA: Harvard University Press, 1995), especially 140ff and Mary R. Lefkowitz & Maureen B. Fant's *Women's Life in Greece and Rome. A Source Book in Translations* (Baltimore: John Hopkins University, 1982), 15–16, for discussion of this comparison. See also Susan Walker, "Women and Housing in Classical Greece: The Archaeological Evidence" in *Images of Women in Antiquity*, ed. Averil Cameron & Amélie Kuhrt (Detroit: Wayne State University Press, 1983), 81–91, for more on the ways in which upper-class women were limited to the house in Athens.

married (around thirty or so), he continued to eat in his mess hall and maintained a fundamental commitment to this group. The boys were thus raised with a rigorous ethic centered around obedience, courage in battle, and a fundamental loyalty to their military group.[97]

Unlike in Athens, the females of Sparta as well as the males received education and were encouraged to engage in physical exercise. And unlike in Athens, women were not married off until they were adults, that is, likely not until eighteen. Xenophon summarizes the Spartan practice:

> Take for example—and it is well to begin at the beginning—the whole topic of the begetting and rearing of children. Throughout the rest of the world ... we, the rest of the Hellenes, are content that our girls should sit quietly and work wools. ...
> Lycurgus [the one thought to give Sparta its law] pursued a different path. ... Believing that the highest function of a free woman was the bearing of children, in the first place he insisted on the training of the body as incumbent no less on the female than the male; and in pursuit of the same idea instituted rival contests in running and feats of strength for women as for men. ...
> By a farther step in the same direction he refused to allow marriages to be contracted at any period of life according to the fancy of the parties concerned. Marriage, as he ordained it, must only take place in the prime of bodily vigour, this too being, as he believed, a condition conducive to the production of healthy offspring. Or again, to meet the case which might occur of an old man wedded to a young wife ... he made it incumbent on the aged husband to introduce some one whose qualities, physical and moral, he admired, to beget him children.[98]

Many of the practices giving greater freedom to women appear to be, as in the training of the males, for the sake of a strong military. So also, the Spartan practice of allowing women to own and control property may be tied, in part, to the frequent absences of men on military campaigns. Nonetheless, women appear to have had significantly more opportunity to develop their various capacities, more power, and

cant lacks in the rigor of their formation[99]), and the ideals for Spartan women, although still primarily domestic, included a far greater range.

Athens suffered its defeat at the hand of Sparta in 404 BC, ending the long Peloponnesian Wars. Sparta was then, however, strikingly unsuccessful at ruling its

---

[97] The 2007 film *300*, based on Frank Miller's graphic novel, although certainly a fantasy in certain respects, nonetheless indicates something of the fierceness of the Spartan warrior and the rigor of their military code. For a brief but clear account of Spartan life, see www.historynet.com/Sparta-the-fall-of-the-empire.htm (accessed February 12, 2009). See also Sue Blundell's *Women in Ancient Greece* (Cambridge, MA: Harvard University Press, 1995) and the chapters on both the women of Athens and Sparta in Verena Zinserling, *Women in Greece and Rome* (New York: Abner Schram, 1973), 22–33.

[98] Xenophon, "Constitution of the Spartans," quoted in W.T. Jones *The Classical Mind* (New York: Harcourt, Brace & World, Inc., 1969), 41. Jones cites H.G. Dakyns's translations of Xenophon from *Greek Historians,* Vol. II, ed. F.R.B. Godolphin (New York: Random House, 1942), 658ff.

[99] Aristotle emphasizes the way in which the women were "useless" during the attack, suggesting that—while the men were rigorously trained—the women were left with comparatively less preparation. Saxonhouse emphasizes this point in her interpretation; I am not sure, however, how heavily to weigh it. See particularly *Women in the History of Political Thought,* 78–80.

new territory, and it suffered a very humiliating defeat to Thebes in the Battle at Leuctra in 371. Sparta never quite regained its military or cultural influence. Athens, in contrast, although defeated, maintained a cultural influence, and continued to be a significant city-state in the region until Philip II of Macedonia (for whom Aristotle's father was physician) conquered all of Greece. The long-term failure of Sparta, despite its victory, and success of Athens, despite its defeat, may be part of why Aristotle criticizes the Spartan society so harshly. Sparta declined and ulti-mately fell because of internal problems and a societal fragility, likely tied in part to the weaker family life and an excessive focus on a rigid male military code (which allowed various forms of downward mobility but little upward mobility).

Aristotle seems quick to place a good portion of the blame on the women of Sparta and their inappropriate role, as he sees, in the society, and he places the blame on the women not insofar as they made bad decisions or failed in other all-too-common respects, but insofar as they were *women*. (That is, Aristotle attributes part of the problem to the fact that the men of Sparta allowed themselves to be ruled by women.) Nonetheless, given that this was likely his primary example of a society in which women were both given greater opportunity to develop their capacities and exerted considerable societal influence—and given that Sparta's demise can be tied in some significant part to the societal structures—it is perhaps unsurprising that he at least considered the possibility that the differing status of women in Sparta, in contrast to Athens, played some role in the outcome.[100]

In addition to these more striking cases, there were also the common ancient experiences of women, rather than men, taking primary responsibility for caring for the home and the needs of young children, while men rather than women were more involved in all forms of professional work. Presumably, tied to these differing foci, men of the ancient world discussed more frequently and in greater depth political topics, while women discussed more frequently and in greater depth topics related to the emotional, social, and physical development of children, etc. These differ-ences in behavior could not, unlike in the case of Plato, be overlooked.

If Aristotle were not looking carefully at the various forms of social influence encouraging certain forms of development for females in contrast to males, then he would likely miss the role of such influences and might reach, understandably, for other explanations.[101] Aristotle was certainly not unaware of the significance of our social environment, especially the role of friends, community, and the state in our development—those elements are, in fact, absolutely central to his discussions in, for example, *Nicomachean Ethics* and the *Politics*. But Aristotle does not seem to have made similar analyses regarding the impact such influences have for the

---

[100] Harold L. Levy suggests that Aristotle intends his critique of the women of Sparta, not to be a criticism of women's excessive involvement in politics but, rather, an implication "that women should be educated to share in warfare and political rule" ("Does Aristotle Exclude Women from Politics?," 400). Although this is a possible reading of Aristotle's texts, it does not strike me as the most plausible one.

[101] Mayhew discusses a number of such possible cases, including for example Aristotle's account of women's greater 'paleness.' See *The Female in Aristotle's Biology*, 75–78 (as well as the whole of the chapter for further examples).

differing development of women and men, particularly the differences such influences might have on the development of rational abilities. Aristotle acknowledges that all capacities must be developed; thus, no one's rational capacities are fully expressed without relevant experiences. Aristotle does not, however, investigate — as far as I know — differing educational opportunities for girls and boys or articulate the significance this might have on their comparative abilities to use well their rational capacities.[102] And without an account on hand offering a critical perspective on our experiences and thus attuning us to the inequitable ways in which most communities allocate food, education, and attention (especially when resources are scarce) as well as articulating the impact of social expectations, it may be easier to forget our own role in cultivating gender differences. And these common differences between women's and men's behavior, in addition to the observable physical differences mentioned in the previous section, provided Aristotle with significant empirical data for which he needed to account in his understanding of human beings.

## Conclusion

In summary, Aristotle's biology, metaphysics, and epistemology all motivate data and questions that need to be addressed — questions with which Plato, for example, did not have to contend, at least not in the same way. Aristotle's account of human generation and his responses to the metaphysical and epistemological questions all fit together to form a somewhat elegant account of natural male superiority and female inferiority. Further pieces — such as his association of the female with matter and male with form, his account of contraries with the male and female as contraries

may have had on the way he attended to the evidence — fill out the picture and create an account of woman that became so powerful in the West.

Although detailed discussion of this point is beyond the scope of this study, it is worth noting that Aristotle's account of women (and natural slaves) is not easily separable from his broader political theory. Aristotle understands all human action as teleological, aiming at the good, with the intermediate ends functioning for the sake of an ultimate good. For each individual, that ultimate 'for-the-sake-of-which' is happiness, but each individual's happiness needs to be seen in light of the larger good of the *polis* as a whole.[104] The good of the *polis* will be attained, however, only if there is the leisure (for some) necessary to pursue a truly contemplative life. Such leisure is not mere physical inaction accompanied by lots of thinking; it can be a highly physically active life, but it does require that there be time which is not

---

[102] See section IV of Eve Browning Cole's above cited essay.

[103] See the discussion of these two points in the next chapter.

[104] Aristotle says, "for though it is worth while to attain the end merely for one man, it is finer and more godlike to attain it for a nation or for city-states" (*Nicomachean Ethics* 1.2.1094b9-11).

dedicated merely to the tasks essential to physical survival. Aristotle envisioned the polity as an organic whole with some individuals pursuing theoretical tasks while others perform the tasks related to childcare, food preparation, the making and exchanging of products, military protection, etc.[105] This vision of leisure—and the economic division of labor seemingly necessary to achieve such a life in the *polis*—cannot have been utterly unrelated to Aristotle's willingness to see some individuals as more fit to menial tasks than others. Aristotle gives arguments and evidence for his claims about the natural inferiority of women and (natural) slaves, and thus I do not think that economic motives were Aristotle's primary reasons for concluding that women were inferior. But it is likely that these economic features played some role in the kinds of questions he did and did not ask, the kinds of evidence he was most interested in pursuing, his judgments regarding how much evidence was necessary in order to make a claim, etc. Thus, although Aristotle presents evidence and makes arguments for his claims regarding women, they nonetheless should not be seen in full separation from his political ideal and the economic divisions seemingly necessary to support that ideal.

---

[105] Femenías summarizes the point: "The happiness of all or of the majority, the good life, the attainment of the supreme objective of the *polis* (the whole), takes precedence over the happiness of one or some (part[s]) of its inhabitants" ("Women and Natural Hierarchy in Aristotle" in *Hypatia*, 9, no.1 [Winter 1994], 165). See also Okin's discussion of this aspect of Aristotle's account of women in her critique of MacIntyre's Aristotelianism in *Justice, Gender, and the Family*, Chap. 3.

# Chapter 5
# How Aristotle Might Have Become a Feminist

Aristotle's descriptions of women present a strikingly consistent account of the natural inferiority of women.[1] He approaches the issue from a number of different angles, affirming in each case his basic premise that females—because they are female rather than male—are less well actualized human beings. Nonetheless, there are at least four areas of significant trouble with his account of women: first, there is an internal tension between his descriptions of women and his general account of the way in which nature works; second, critical aspects of his embryology are fundamentally wrong; third, his responses to the challenges of hylomorphism are understandable but nonetheless unnecessary as well as highly problematic; and fourth, despite his own deep awareness in other areas of the significance of communal and social influences, he fails to appreciate fully their role in the differing development of women and men. In this chapter, I would like to address each of these four areas, showing how the claims Aristotle actually made were neither the only, nor the best, positions an Aristotelian could take. That is, were Aristotle more fully Aristotelian, he may not have made the mistakes that he, in fact, did and thus may have drawn a different conclusion regarding women.

In addition to correcting these four areas of error, there are also a few emphases that, were they revised, would make Aristotle's thought more equitable. I am most interested in the four areas where I think Aristotle makes errors, but it strikes me

---

[1] The overall account of women is strikingly consistent; this is not, however, to claim that all of his comments regarding women can be fit together in a consistent way. For example, he claims that soft skin is a mark of intelligence, and yet does not extend this mark to females, who in general have softer skin than males. See Cynthia A. Freeland, "Aristotle on the Sense of Touch" in *Essays on Aristotle's De Anima*, ed. Martha C. Nussbaum & Amélie Oksenberg Rorty (Oxford: Oxford University Press, 1992), 227–248 and Mayhew, 66–68. Other arguments appear a bit strained. For example, he claims in *Generation of Animals* 4.6 that males, although the more appropriate expression of the human form, are nonetheless also more likely to be born defective than females, which Aristotle attributes to their greater heat leading to greater activity in the womb and thus greater likelihood of injury. See also Paul Thom, "Stiff Cheese for Women" in *The Philosophical Forum* 8, no. 1 (Fall 1976), especially 101–107 for other points of tension.

© Springer International Publishing Switzerland 2016
S. Borden Sharkey, *An Aristotelian Feminism*, Historical-Analytical Studies on Nature, Mind and Action 1, DOI 10.1007/978-3-319-29847-4_5

that Aristotle is also insufficiently attentive to certain aspects of our common humanity that are often revealed more fully by women. A fully feminist Aristotle would need not only to correct his previous errors, but also to add new dimensions and emphases to his overall account. Thus, after discussing the four most significant problems, I would like to turn to a brief discussion of two other issues: (a) articulating a fuller account of human interpersonal capacities and (b) rehabilitating the notion of receptivity, in contrast to passivity. These two issues are not exhaustive of what a fully feminist Aristotle would need to avert to, but they indicate some oversights and areas of where a change in emphasis would make Aristotle's thought more fully equitable.[2]

## A Tension in Aristotle's Account

Although Aristotle's various claims regarding women fit together into a quite consistent whole, they also create at least one striking tension with his account of the teleological working of nature. There are, I believe, stronger responses to be made against Aristotle's position than simply that of pointing to an internal tension, but it is worth noting that Aristotle must accept at least one oddity in nature in order to preserve his account of the natural inferiority of women.

Aristotle is well aware that we cannot procreate without both females and males; thus, even though he understands women as a deformation (and a quite consistent one) of the human form, it is nonetheless a 'fortunate' deformation.[3] I take it that this is at least part of the reason he describes women as only "as it were" deformations and mutilations. Without nature consistently being so deformed that we get women, we could not continue to have a human species (or many other species).

the human form and (b) that this deviation is a necessary one for the species; in combination, these raise a unique situation. Nature, as Aristotle is fond of saying, aims at the good; it functions for the sake of what is good. If something is necessary for the well-functioning (not to mention survival) of a species, it would seem to be itself good. And yet Aristotle describes women as not good insofar as they are a deformation, or lack of full human physical formation. Thus, on one hand, Aristotle understands nature as teleological and aiming for the good. On the other hand, he

---

[2] One area of possible modification that I will not discuss, but am highly sympathetic to and think may contribute to a more feminist Aristotelianism, is a slight revision of the place of relationships in one's understanding of substance. 'Relation' is generally considered at the level of accident rather than substance by Aristotle, but there may be types or kinds of relations that ought to be considered at the level of substance and not merely an accident of a substance. That is, perhaps substance ought to be 'substance in relations' and not merely 'substance.' Articulating precisely what this would and would not mean is difficult, and I will not discuss this issue in this chapter.

[3] He says, "The first departure indeed is that the offspring should become female instead of male; this, however, is a natural necessity" (GA 4.3.767b7-9).

has to admit that nature's regular failure to achieve at least the optimum good is the condition of many animals continuing to exist.[4]

It might seem that, because Aristotle describes women as an "as it were" deformation and not a deformation *simpliciter*, he is not creating quite as problematic of a tension. Seals, water-newts, lobsters, and other 'monstrosities' are not deformations or something that ought not to be in any strong sense, and being a seal certainly cannot be compared, for example, with having a broken leg. One might argue that Aristotle's qualification of females as merely "as it were" deformations qualifies this tension. I am not convinced, however, that this quite solves the problem. As noted in the previous chapter, seals are full species, and there is no ideal of seal that actual individual seals are nonetheless failing to achieve. For females, in contrast, there is a species ideal—exemplified by male human beings—that females are failing to achieve. Further, given Aristotle's comparisons of women's and men's psychological traits, rational abilities, and virtues, there is a fairly strong notion of women as failures, in some real sense; they have not and cannot fully achieve what is proper to their own species-form and thus are deformations in a relatively strong sense.

Given Aristotle's description of nature as teleological, all deformations (even, I take it, females) ought to be understood to be, in some very real sense, tragedies or something that ought not to be. This does not mean that one cannot turn such a tragedy to good, nor that the tragic features may not themselves be the condition of finding or creating some truly worthwhile good. Thus, it seems appropriate that someone accepting Aristotle's broad view could nevertheless also speak, for example, of the 'gift' of a disability. Disabilities, deformations, and tragedies do not in themselves eliminate a person's value, nor her ability to create and live a life of value. But a disability or handicap, of whatever variety, presents particular challenges and difficulties and is—in some sense—something that ought not to be, even if an individual may find ways to turn that situation into a truly impressive good. Living and triumphing in and through one's disability is a human achievement, and to deny that that person has a disability is to deny at least part of the achievement.

Aristotle essentially claims that all women—simply because they are women—suffer from some situation that, in some sense, ought not to be. On Aristotle's account, slightly over half of the population suffers from some kind of, presumably tragic, deformation. And yet, it seems odd to describe the situation in this way. Women's 'deformation' is, after all, necessary for the sake of our survival. Were

---

[4] Cynthia Freeland articulates well the strangeness of these claims. She notes that, on the one hand, in *Generation of Animals* 4.3, Aristotle describes females as "defective and in every case accidental by-products of a natural process whose normal aim is male offspring" ("Nourishing Speculation: A Feminist Reading of Aristotelian Science," in *Engendering Origins: Critical Feminist Readings in Plato and Aristotle*, ed. Bat-Ami Bar On (Albany, NY: State University of New York Press, 1994), 174). On the other, he argues "that sexual reproduction and division of the sexes are themselves teleologically ordained" (Ibid., see *GA* 11.1.731b24-732a12). Freeland concludes: "This is the only case I know of in which Aristotle holds that something is both a good end-result in and of itself (rather than simply a 'making-do' with limited material resources) and a mere accident or by-product" (ibid.).

women not deformed, they would be men. Thus, Aristotle appears to be committed to the problematic position that some feature is both a deformation of the species and is absolutely necessary for the good of the survival of the species.

If Aristotle were a thorough-going Darwinian, this would not present a challenge. Mutations occur regularly; they are part of the adaptation and evolution of species; and, most significantly, nature is not thought to be teleological. Darwin accepts a fairly mechanistic picture of the natural world, and, on such an account, there would be no problem with describing something as a mutation or deformation (in one sense, although a Darwinian could not accept this description in Aristotle's sense) and at the same time to be an essential part of the survival of some species line. The difficulty with Aristotle's claim is that he is not a thorough-going Darwinian,[5] and thus his seemingly easy acceptance of some feature as both necessary and deformed is more problematic.

This internal tension strongly suggests that Aristotle ought to have claimed that females are not deformations in any sense but, rather, fully appropriate, although differing, expressions of the species-form. Aristotle's overall understanding of nature should, it seems to me, have pushed him toward an account of the species-form with at least two sexually differentiated expressions, rather than an account positing one of those expressions as a less well actualized version of the form. In failing to do so, he is left with a tension in his overall account which cannot be easily reconciled or eliminated.

## Problems with Aristotle's Account of Generation

The tension between Aristotle's descriptions of females and of nature in general

with Aristotle's account of women is that he is simply wrong about critical features of human generation. He knew nothing, understandably, of the female ovum, and certainly had no clear notion of DNA or chromosomes.[6] As is now abundantly clear, however, human reproduction occurs when a sperm, usually carrying simply an X or Y chromosome, fertilizes an ovum. Each parent contributes equally 23 chromosomes to the newly formed embryo, and the DNA of the offspring is a unique combination formed from the material from both parents.

Given this account of human reproduction, it is hard to support a theory of generation dividing so sharply the material and efficient causes. It is certainly true that Aristotle's questions differ slightly from contemporary questions, and the

---

[5] Aristotle explicitly argues in Book II the *Physics* against Empedocles' evolutionary-style theory, on these grounds. That is, Aristotle rejects mechanistic and evolutionary explanations because they fail to acknowledge the teleological nature of the physical world.

[6] There were ancient theories of female seed, and analogies could have been drawn between the eggs of birds and those of humans; but ancient biological dissection had not yet found empirical evidence of a female ovum.

contemporary scientific understanding may not yet answer all of Aristotle's questions. Nonetheless, such data is not irrelevant to Aristotle's concerns, and, given his strong empiricism, it cannot be ignored. One might say, because of the offspring's residence within its mother for its initial growth (at least for most mammals), the female contributes more material, in some sense, to generation than the male. And the male sperm, in some very limited way, acts (in most cases) as an efficient cause initiating key aspects of the process. Nonetheless, in the most relevant senses, both the female ovum with its genetic material and the male sperm with its genetic material act equally as efficient and material causes.[7] Certainly in any truly important sense in which either parent acts as a material cause (i.e., insofar as each contributes genetic material), they do so equally.[8] Given the equal role of female and male in the genetic make-up of the offspring, there is little biological basis for Aristotle's way of dividing up the female and male roles in generation.[9]

More significant, however, than even his account of the female and male parent in the initial generation of a human is Aristotle's understanding of the origin of each sex. Aristotle takes female offspring to result when the mother's matter is comparatively colder and thus resists the forming work of the male semen, whereas male children result when the matter is hotter and thus more developmentally appropriate. This claim, which certainly fits well with Aristotle's initial description of generation, is the more problematic one for feminists. It is also, however, unambiguously false. In large part, the chromosomes carried by the male sperm, rather than the condition of the female 'matter,' determine the initial sexual development.[10] Thus, insofar as Aristotle's account of the inferiority of women is tied to his understanding of the biological features of generation, it is also undermined by the errors in that description.

---

[7] It could further be pointed out that semen is not, as Aristotle thought, concocted out of blood and acting as the principle of efficient causality (there can be human generation without male semen, although not without male sperm). The difference between semen and sperm — and the similarities between sperm and ovum — creates a further point of conflict.

[8] See Chap. 2, footnote 9 for discussion of chromosomes and DNA as material.

[9] One might object to my placement of genetic data on the side of matter rather than form. But even if genetic data is understood as formal rather than material, the problem for Aristotle remains. Both parents would still contribute equally.

[10] First, as noted in the second chapter, there is some debate about whether chromosomes, hormones, or reproductive organs are the most significant features for determining sex. Insofar as the chromosomes are contributed prior to the development of sexually relevant hormones or organs, I am focusing on them; I am not, however, taking a strong stand on the more nuanced debate about what we should emphasize when all three elements are present. Second, in claiming that Aristotle's is unambiguously wrong about the heat or coldness of the female determining the sex of the child, I am not claiming that the condition of the female has *no significance* for which sperm is likely to reach and fertilize the ovum, or no influence on the hormone levels relevant to the sexual development of the offspring, etc. Given these factors, the female parent may have some role in the sex of the child; she does not, however, play the role Aristotle thought.

## *On Male and Female as Opposites*

Aristotle's account of biological generation not only divides the various causes between the two parents and attributes the origin of the sex of the child to the material condition of the female parent, it also develops the latter point through an analysis of the female and male as opposites. Although not central to the discussion in the previous chapter, I would like briefly to address Aristotle's comments about male and female as opposites and his association of the male with form and female with matter.

In *Generation of Animals*, Aristotle says:

> After these premises it will perhaps be now clearer for what reason one embryo becomes female and another male. For when the first principle does not bear sway and cannot concoct the nourishment through lack of heat nor bring it into its proper form, but is defeated in this respect, then must the material change into its opposite. Now the female is opposite to the male, and that in so far as the one is female and the other male. And since it differs in its faculty, its organ also is different, so that the embryo changes into this state. And as one part of first-rate importance changes, the whole system of the animal differs greatly in form along with it. This may be seen in the case of eunuchs, who, though mutilated in one part alone, depart so much from their original appearance and approximate closely to the female form. The reason of this is that some of the parts are principles, and when a principle is moved many of the parts that go along with it must change with it.[11]

I am particularly interested for the moment in Aristotle's claim here that the female is the opposite of the male. He claims that when "the first principle does not bear sway," the entity changes into its opposite, making clear that he understands the female to be the opposite of the male. There are, however, a number of senses of opposition in Aristotle. I would like to digress briefly from the main argument in order to look at possible ways in which male and female may be opposites, and the

form with the male and matter with the female.

There is some ambiguity in Aristotle's account of male and females as opposites.[12] Nonetheless, it strikes me as highly plausible, particularly given his biology, to understand the female as the opposite of the male in the sense of privation. In *Categories*, Aristotle lists four types of opposites: that which is opposite (i) "as relatives," (ii) "as contraries," (iii) "as privation and possession," and (iv) "as affirmation and negation." The second is an option. In *Metaphysics*, Aristotle says, for example, that things which "differ in *species* the extremes from which generation takes place are the contraries," indicating here that male and female, which are not different species, are nonetheless contraries within a species.[13] But the third

---

[11] *GA* 4.1.766a16-29. See also *GA* 4.3.767b15-768a11.

[12] See discussion of the ambiguities in Marguerite Deslauriers's "Sex and Essence in Aristotle's *Metaphysics* and Biology" in *Feminist Interpretations of Aristotle* ed. Cynthia A. Freeland (University Park, PA: The Pennsylvania State University Press, 1998), especially page 164, footnote 19. Deslauriers presents some reasons for hesitating about the interpretation I will give; nonetheless, I think that there is textual basis for some version of this account.

[13] *Metaphysics* 10.4.1055a7-8.

category—as privation and possession—also seems to fit particularly well with the meaning of opposite as used in *Generation of Animals*. He claims that if the efficient cause does not hold sway, it is defeated and turns into its opposite; such an opposition sounds like a privation, a failure to achieve fully what it intended. Combined with Aristotle's comments regarding women's lesser ability to concoct blood, lesser use of rational capacities, etc., the interpretation of opposite to mean 'privation of' is highly plausible. When Aristotle discusses such privative opposites in *Categories*, he gives the example of blindness and sight, with blindness as a privation of sight. If female and male are opposites in this sense, then the female is a privation of the male in some way analogous to blindness and sight.[14]

This claim is not, in itself, particularly different from what has been discussed thus far about the general inferiority of women. Aristotle, however, continues his use of the notion of opposition in order to associate the female with matter and the male with its opposite, form. And thus matter, which is the opposite of form and in some sense a privation of the activity of form, is the more feminine principle (and presumably women are more matter-like), while form is both the superior and the masculine principle.

Aristotle says, for example:

> For admitting that there is something divine, good, and desirable, we hold that there are two other principles, the one contrary to it, the other such as of its own nature to desire and yearn for it. ... The truth is that what desires the form is matter, as the female desires the male and the ugly the beautiful—only the ugly or the female not in itself but accidentally.[15]

Aristotle draws parallels here between the male and that which is more divine, more complete, and yearned for, while the female is associated with that which is defective, incomplete, and yearning. This association is reiterated in various places and appears to be closely tied to his biology.[16]

This association of form with the male and matter with the female raises questions about the suitability of hylomorphism for feminist purposes. If hylomorphism is itself already gendered—that is, if the distinction between form and matter itself already works to denigrate women—then simply correcting a few errors in explicit comment would not yet address the fundamental problem.[17] I am not convinced,

---

[14] See *Metaphysics* 5.22 for an account of the differing types of privation.

[15] *Physics* 1.9.192a16-23. The missing line reads: "But the consequence of their view is that the contrary desires its own extinction. Yet the form cannot desire itself, for it is not defective; nor can the contrary desire it, for contraries are mutually destructive." I take Aristotle here to be discussing the position of his opponents.

[16] See, for example, *GA* 2.1.73212-10. See also Irigaray's reading of Aristotle's *Physics* in "Place, Interval: A Reading of Aristotle, *Physics IV*" in *Feminist Interpretations of Aristotle* ed. Cynthia A. Freeland (University Park, PA: The Pennsylvania State University Press, 1998), 41–58 and Freeland's analysis in "On Irigaray on Aristotle," 59–92.

[17] Freeland says: "feminists can with some plausibility point out that there are important gendered concepts in Aristotle. A pair of gendered concepts lie at the heart of his metaphysics, namely, form and matter. Though these concepts seem like abstract components of a neutral reality, they bear strong gender associations. Form is active, superior, and intelligible; in humans it is associated with rationality. Matter is passive, chaotic, inferior, muddied, and unintelligible. Plato directly

however, that hylomorphism is so infected. There is no doubt that Aristotle made this association. But it is not clear that he should have done so. First, Aristotle's critical mistakes at the level of biology significantly weaken the association. Aristotle is simply wrong that females contribute the material cause while males contribute the efficient and formal causes. Although certain types of feminine and masculine symbols might still be appropriate, Aristotle's seeming notion that the male is to rule the female as the masculine form rules the feminine material is without biological basis. And without that basis, it becomes a merely arbitrary claim.

Further, the very hylomorphic account of human beings prevents any version of the association from being used literally. Charlotte Witt well points out that both female and male individuals are equally form-matter composites, and thus no actual man can be identified purely with form or actual woman with matter.[18] There are no human beings who are not both matter and form; whatever Aristotle meant by the association, he could not mean that men are literally form without matter or females matter without form.

Although it is surely true that Aristotle does, in some way, associate form with males and matter with females, his account of each of us as a form-matter composite raises questions of precisely how these associations are to be made. Witt writes:

> If we think of Aristotelian form as male and matter as female in a straightforward sense, then human beings turn out to be hermaphrodites, and not men and women after all. Moreover, given that hylomrophism is a perfectly general theory concerning the structure of all composite substances, whatever intuitive appeal gender associations with matter and form might have in the case of human beings is much weaker in the case of plants and birds, and disappears entirely with houses and brazen spheres. That is, there is a striking tension between Aristotle's theory of composite substances according to which all human beings (indeed all composite substances) are composites of matter and form, and the texts where sexual difference appears associated with matter and form. If all human beings are metaphysically identical, how can form and matter bear any gender associations?[19]

Witt, I think rightly, distinguishes hylomorphism as "a perfectly general theory" from Aristotle's sexual associations. First, the sexual associations are not "an intrinsic feature of hylomorphism."[20] One can agree that a formal and material principle can be distinguished without agreeing that the association of form with males or matter with females is particularly compelling. And, second, attempts to make those associations in a strong way (identifying form with actual men or matter with actual women, for example) create a tension with the more general hylomorphic theory. No actual women or actual man exhibits simply one of the principles. Insofar as

---

associates matter with the womb or uterus. And in the *Physics* Aristotle says that matter yearns for form, as the female for the male and the ugly for the beautiful (I,9,192a20-23)" ("On Irigaray on Aristotle," 65).

[18] Marguerite Deslauriers similarly points out: "while Aristotle is prepared to suggest that male and female as principles and as attributes of the genus animal are radically different, male and female animals, individuals qualified by those principles or attributes, are not radically different" ("Sex and Essence in Aristotle's *Metaphysics* and Biology," 143).

[19] Witt, "Form, Normativity and Gender in Aristotle," 122.

[20] Ibid., 126.

Aristotle associates males more with form because they contributed, he thought, the efficient and formal causes to generation while females contributed the material, he did so on a problematic basis.

Nonetheless, there may be other reasons or ways to associate females with the earth and that in which one is formed, while males are associated with transcendence and that which stands outside the formation process; but such associations are not uniquely Aristotelian. All earthly things are, Aristotle thinks, already composites, and thus an association with earth is not identical to an association with Aristotelian matter. The notion of matter as that in which or through which one is formed comes closer to an Aristotelian account of matter, but, once again, it is not at all obvious how these associations ought to be understood, given Aristotle's general hylomorphic theory.[21]

## A Range of Appropriate Expressions

The easiest ways to respond to Aristotle's account of women are to point to the internal tensions and to mistakes at the biological level, but addressing the challenges raised by the general hylomorphic position are critical. First, Aristotle's hylomorphism, with its related distinction between accidental and substantial change, requires answering a slightly broader set of questions regarding generation than either a materialist or dualist account, and second, the distinction but interrelated nature of form and matter requires a hylomorphist to have some account of differing material expressions of a single type of form. Aristotle's responses to both of these challenges moved him toward a view of women as naturally inferior to men. Although such a move is intelligible, it is not, however, the only—or even the best—way to respond to these challenges.

Aristotle's distinction among the four types of causality fits neatly with an account of generation, which separates the source of the causes most relevant to form from the source of the material cause. His division of the causes aids in his claim that the change taking place is a substantial one and not merely an accidental one. Further, it is not fully clear how contemporary accounts of reproduction would address all of Aristotle's questions regarding human generation. Contemporary biology can tell us what empirical data is relevant and the paths by which it is moved around, but it does not distinguish the differing types of explanation or itself articulate the difference between accidental and substantial change. Thus, on one hand, many of Aristotle's questions are still relevant ones and worthy of greater investigation, if a hylomorphic account is to be plausible. On the other hand, however, no acceptable answers to those questions can ignore the empirical data. Insofar

---

[21] It seems to me possible to have many different types of feminine and masculine symbols and associations. It is not clear, however, how these symbols do or ought to relate to individual women and men. I will leave aside the question of the appropriateness of these because adequate investigation would take us far from the main topic of this study.

as Aristotle's account of generation misconstrues or is missing relevant data, it is a mistaken answer. Thus, although contemporary biological accounts cannot themselves answer all of Aristotle's questions, they do show that Aristotle's answers—at least in the details regarding the female and male contributions—are mistaken. Further, although it might be elegant to posit the efficient and formal cause as arising from one parent while the material is contributed by another, such elegance is not necessary. One can affirm differing types of causality without positing that they are contributed by separate sources.

There is, however, a second challenge from hylomorphism: if male and female share in a common form, why do we not appear so very common? If form is taken to be responsible for our structure, how do we account for what certainly appear to be structural differences? Women and men have, after all, both 'static' structural differences (e.g., bodily differences) and temporal structural differences (e.g., differing developmental patterns). Such differences appear to be more than accidental ones, and yet they cannot be formal ones, compromising the commonality of our species-form. Aristotle's response to this question is, once again, simple and elegant. There is one form and one proper structural expression of that form. Males may vary at the level of accident without implying that one set of accidents is better than another, but anything that differs in a more than accidental way (e.g., natural slaves and females) counts as a deformation, a failure to develop in the way most proper to the form.

Although perhaps less elegant than Aristotle's account, I think that we must say, in contrast to Aristotle, that the human form expresses itself in a number of distinct physical ways—for example, in the female and male body—and not merely in one. This is not, however, simply an answer motivated by the desire to affirm the equality of all human beings while remaining an Aristotelian; it seems to me the better *Aristotelian* answer, the one that Aristotle himself should have accepted in order to

ply with one's current physical structure. Form includes the *temporal* pattern, with appropriate ranges for each type of thing, and not simply one's current shape. To focus primarily on one's physical shape encourages precisely the misunderstanding of form Aristotle set out to reject. (Aristotle criticizes Plato's view of Form, for example, for being overly static and failing to account for change, for our temporal being.) If form is a principle of development and not a static structure—and if species-forms all have a range of appropriate development—we can affirm even differing physical organs as part of what is fit to one species-form.

Furthermore, Aristotle had access to (and we have more evidence of) examples of individuals who, while remaining the same species, change their sex. Aristotle discusses the rumor, showing up among other places in Aesop's fables,[22] of hyenas that change their sex.[23] Although Aristotle rejects this in the case of hyenas (by,

---

[22] See fables 405 and 406. I am grateful to Nicole Hess for pointing these out to me.

[23] See *History of Animals* 579b15 and 594a31.

unfortunately, dissecting the wrong kind of hyena),[24] the predominance of this view shows that a natural change of sex was a commonly accepted possibility in the ancient world. We are now familiar with more examples of such sequential hermaphroditism among, for example, many fish, gastropods, and certain flowering plants.[25]

Given the number of species that can and do shift between female and male (and vice versa), it seems right to accept that species-form do not require one ideal expression of their physical sex. Aristotle is certainly in support of the notion that the human form is open to a range of ideal physical expressions. For example, he argues in the *Nicomachean Ethics* that the virtuous person aims at the mean, not the mean relative to the object but the mean relative to the person.[26] There is one thing that counts as acting virtuously for each situation, but precisely what that act is and how it is physically performed need not be the same for each individual. Because what it means to be virtuous in any particular situation takes into account features and elements distinctive to the individual herself, there are many expressions of each virtue. Thus, what is involved in a young child acting courageously will differ from what is involved in a warrior doing so, etc. A similar principle is true of differing physical manifestations of the human form. There is a range of possibilities, all of which are appropriate to the human form. A human being may be dark-skinned or light, five foot five or six foot one, asleep or awake. In each of these cases, we have a single virtue and a single type of form which are nonetheless appropriately expressed in quite different physical ways.

Aristotle certainly describes some expressions as deformations. For example, cowardice and rashness in the face of danger are inappropriate and thus deforming, rather than virtuous, ways to behave. Limbs of significantly different lengths count as mal- or de-formations rather than simply differences. In his account of form, Aristotle has criteria for determining what count as deformations, but in no way is all difference in expression thereby a deformation. Although his hylomorphism requires Aristotle to raise the question of whether any particular difference in expression is, in that case, simply a difference or a deformation, hylomorphism in no way requires him to answer this question in favor of deformation.

Aristotle might object to my argument by claiming that, in the case of the virtues, the differences are not structural ones per se[27] and, in the case of differing physical expressions of the human form, the differences are ones of accident (e.g., skin color,

---

[24] See Stephen E. Glickman et. al., "Mammalian sexual differentiation: lessons from the spotted hyena" in *Trends in Endocrinology and Metabolism*, 17:9 (September 2006): 349–356, available at http://courses.washington.edu/pbio509/Glickman_etal.pdf [accessed August 8, 2012], for a discussion both of why the ancients thought this and how Aristotle came to the right conclusion but with the wrong dissection.

[25] I am grateful to Robert Bishop for pointing me to this possibility.

[26] *Nicomachean Ethics* 2.6.

[27] There will be differences in the age or condition of the virtuous actor and differences in the situations faced by the differing actors, but the structure of what it means to be courageous per se will not differ in any significant way. In every case, it will involve acting for the right motive, out of a habituated character, in a way that is neither rash nor cowardly, etc.

height, and state). Insofar as the differences between female and male are structural and go beyond accidental differences, they are not accounted for as easily. I will agree that the differences between female and male bodily appearance and physical development include more than might traditionally be called accidental, it is nonetheless not obvious to me that they could not thereby fit within a legitimate range of appropriate expressions of the form. None of our bodies are identical. The particular number of cells or hair follicles each of us has differs, and an Aristotelian is not required to claim (and should not claim) that a particular number of cells is the ideal.[28] So also, an Aristotelian might claim that reproduction or generation is a part of the human form and thus having some functioning reproductive system may be part of the human ideal, but an Aristotelian is not required to claim that a particular set of such organs is the ideal.

Further, being structural is not the same thing as being part of the substantial form. There are many features of human beings that are both structural and material (at least in comparison to the species-form). Secondary matter is not utterly formless potency but, rather, formed matter open to further formation. Thus, noting that the differences between women and men go beyond accidental ones and include significant structural differences is not, in itself, sufficient for claiming that there are differences requiring us to call one structure a deviation from right formation.[29]

Insofar as Aristotle has placed a heavy emphasis on a certain easily visible physical expression of the form (as appears to be part of his account of the female as deformation), he has downplayed the role and import of interpretation, of recognizing true commonality among differing particulars and judging, in light of differing visible physical expressions, where there is a commonality of capacity and where there is not. Aristotle's epistemology is not naïve realist. He does not think that reality—and particularly form—is simply 'out there,' waiting to be grasped. Form is developmental and thus presents itself as a pattern: it requires a tremendous amount

our rational capacities in order to discern well the patterns marking a species-form. Thus, what is simply 'given' or what is most obvious, may or may not be relevant to recognizing the *capacities* (in contrast to the abilities) of the human form.[30] I think that Aristotle simply judged wrongly in the case of women. This wrong judgment was likely aided by some mistaken information and failures to appreciate the full import of differing social conditions. (For example, Aristotle mistakenly took females to be the shorter living of the sexes as well as the ones less capable of tolerating pain. Both of these claims were likely more influenced by the greater

---

[28] Although an Aristotelian might articulate some range that is appropriate for adult human beings.

[29] Aristotle's example of the eunuch presents a more interesting challenge. In that case, depriving the male of something leads to more feminine features. This example makes a stronger case for understanding the female as a male who has been deprived of something. Aristotle was, however, aware that there can be cases of "women of a masculine and men of a feminine appearance" (*GA* 2.7.747a1), and contemporary studies of the various relevant hormones and the ways in which both women and men can be made more masculine and feminine in appearance by the manipulation of estrogen and testosterone levels confirm this insight.

[30] See the discussion of this distinction in Chap. 2 above.

comparative hardships of women's lives than Aristotle realized.) There is nothing in his general theory, however, that requires Aristotle to say one physical expression is proper to the form and another not. In other features of human beings, Aristotle recognizes a legitimate range of appropriate expressions (while still judging certain things to be outside that range). In the case of human beings' sexual identity, he fails to do so. But it is not clear that this judgment is in any way necessitated by Aristotelian hylomorphism. Hylomorphism shows the difficulty of discerning what marks the form and what marks a deviation from right formation; but hylomorphism in no way requires that all differences be deemed deviations—in fact, it insists that commonality can only be found in and amid our differences, some of which are appropriate differences and some of which are deviations.

Claiming that both female and male bodies are fully legitimate and appropriate—although differing—expressions of the human form will require that we understand the human form to have greater appropriate flexibility than Aristotle himself did, at least in relation to physical growth and development. But it does not make the answer thereby non-Aristotelian. It is true to the flexibility he grants the form in the case of (at least free male) virtues. And, insofar as it maintains the key principles of Aristotelian hylomorphism, it does not do damage to Aristotle's overall metaphysical claim.

## The Role of Social Conditions

Aristotle is trying to account not simply for biological generation and questions raised by hylomorphism, but also for certain patterns of behavior. He claims—presumably based in part on his experiences of women and men—that men are more fully rational than women, that women tend to be more despondent than men,[31] that women ought to obey while men ought to rule, etc. These claims are surely based, in part, on the women and men of his experience. Aristotle, however, seems to have accepted this evidence in too uncritical a manner. As noted in the previous chapters, Aristotle cannot be accused of being unaware of the role of social conditioning in our formation. But he may, in his experiences with women, have been comparatively unattuned to quite relevant social conditioning.[32]

Fewer women than men were able to pursue advanced education in ancient Greece.[33] More women than men focused on the nurturing of children, especially in

---

[31] *History of Animals* 9.1.

[32] María Luisa Femenías connects this weakness to Aristotle's account of species-forms as static. She says: "Perhaps because of the static nature that generally characterizes his system, he considers the sociohistorical period in which he lived as if it were universally valid" ("Women and Natural Hierarchy in Aristotle" in *Hypatia*, 9, no.1 [Winter 1994]: 167). This may be right and would add a further reason to consider a more evolutionary account of form.

[33] Aristotle supports some kind of education for women, and thus he thought that women's capacities—as all human capacities—could be more fully actualized with relevant experience and training. See *Politics* 1.13.1260b12-20.

their early years, and thus relational and emotional skills were more critical for women than skills in political debate. Further, there were cultural expectations, as there are now, prescribing certain behaviors for women in contrast to men. There were likely high social costs to going against these expectations, and surely such elements were not insignificant for shaping the behavior of the women Aristotle knew. Once again, Aristotle was not unaware of the role of social conditioning nor the role of interpretation in our understanding; he emphasizes, after all, the critical dialectic between universal and particular. But he very likely failed to attend to all relevant aspects of social conditioning—and thus de-emphasized their import in his encounters with and thus understanding of women.

One example of such differing social conditions—one likely to have had an extremely significant impact on nearly all aspects of women's lives in the ancient world—was the food most women, in contrast to men, ate. In *Food and Society in Classical Antiquity*, Peter Garnsey outlines a number of differences between what females and males were encouraged to eat in ancient societies. The ancient medical community understood health to be a matter of the balance of humors in the body, and women were generally considered to be comparatively cold and wet.[34] They were thus encouraged to eat a diet which would help balance out their natural cold-ness and wetness. Although the details of such diets are unknown and likely varied from region to region, there were important commonalities in the recommendations. Rufus of Ephesus (first century AD) writes, for example, "one must … regulate and moderate their [women's] intake of food, and not let them touch meat at all, or other foods that are very nourishing."[35] Women were to eat a "simple diet," consisting of "the bare necessities."[36] Although it is difficult to know precisely which foods were recommended and which were not—and how rigorously the recommendations were followed[37]—the focus on women avoiding meat, fish, and other "nourishing foods," combined with a worry about women's excessive coldness and wetness, strongly

diet than men.

There was also a common assumption, one that can be seen in Aristotle's descriptions and showing up regularly in Greek literature, that women were strongly ruled by their appetites and thus should avoid foods encouraging such concupiscence, including meat and wine.[38] (Such a strong desire, especially for certain foods, would be unsurprising given a nutritionally deficient diet.) These features, combined with

---

[34] See Garnsey, *Food and Society in Classical Antiquity* (New York: Cambridge University Press, 1999), 105.

[35] Quoted Garnsey, 101.

[36] Garnsey, 102.

[37] See Garnsey's discussion, 103. This would be difficult to determine, but the fact that the doctors making the recommendations "were practicing doctors, not merely scholars sitting … producing their treatises" gives Garnsey confidence that the advice was not merely academic.

[38] For one example, see the discussion of Augustine's mother, Monica, and her 'inappropriate' love of wine in Book IX.8 of the *Confessions*.

the conviction that females require less food than males, created a more limited diet for women.

If women did, in fact, eat such a limited diet, this would have had a significant physical impact. First, there would likely to be a deficiency of vitamin A, found primarily in animal-based foods and green vegetables, which would lead to various eye diseases. Second, there would also be a vitamin D deficiency, which would affect the degree to which minerals can be absorbed, leading to higher incidents of rickets, dwarfism, and other physical deformities.[39] If we add to these features, the significant physical toll pregnancy, childbirth, and nursing would take on women already weakened by their diet, it would be little surprise if the women of Aristotle's experience were significantly weaker and less well formed than the men of his experience. Insofar as he failed to recognize the role of food, among other things, in this difference, Aristotle mistakenly attributed the differences to women's initial biological matter rather than the influence of environmental and cultural matter.[40]

As in his response to the challenge of hylomorphism, Aristotle appears to have failed to incorporate as fully as he could, and ought, his own insights regarding social formation and interpretation. Intelligible structures, including especially of human development, are not merely given; they are not simply there, present, but must be developed in and through our conditions. These conditions are environmental and cultural as well as biological. Insofar as Aristotle downplays the environmental and cultural influences in his interpretation of women's behavior and lives, he fails to draw on some of his own best insights.

Thus, the four major critiques I would like to make of Aristotle's account of women are, first, that that his position regarding female inferiority does not fit with his own teleological understanding of nature; second, that he needs to take more biological data into account (and then adjust his account in all the ways necessary when one does so); third, that hylomorphism allows for more flexibility in physical expression than Aristotle himself allowed, at least in the case of women and men; and, finally, that he needs to take material conditions, particularly environmental and cultural matter, more fully into account in his evaluation of women and women's tendencies. The two most significant points are the second and fourth critiques. In the second case, Aristotle did not have the biological data necessary for recognizing the role of ovum and sperm with their equal genetic material. The female ovum was not fully recognized until the eighteenth century, and its discovery was significantly aided by more modern and improved tools for dissection. And genetics was not developed until the nineteenth century, while the more precise knowledge we now have is owed to insights from the twentieth century. Aristotle simply did not have available all of the data we now do; nonetheless, perhaps Aristotle should have asked a few different questions, investigating more closely, for example, the observable ways in which children resemble not simply their fathers but also, and equally

---

[39] See Garnsey, 46–48.

[40] Although food per se is part of our biological matter, the particular foods we are able and choose to eat, and the reasons for so choosing, would be tied, at least in part, to our environmental and cultural matter.

so, their mothers. There were quite likely oversights and failures to pursue fully certain questions contributing to Aristotle's failures on this front, as well as simply not having enough data with which to work.

On the fourth point (that of de-emphasizing the import of interpretation and environmental and cultural matter in his evaluation of women's lives), Aristotle had the resources, in his own theory, for doing so. Although the approach I am favoring may place a heavier emphasis on the role of interpretation and what I have termed environmental and cultural matter than is common in certain interpretations of and texts of Aristotle, such emphases are certainly not absent from Aristotle's texts, and incorporating them in relation to sex and gender creates a position much more fit to the evidence we now have—including evidence regarding human biology and behavior, given changing social circumstances. These advantages are surely something Aristotle the empiricist would not find insignificant.

Finally, it is perhaps worth noting that Aristotle was not reaching for a radical idea when he posited the natural inferiority of women, although he was disagreeing with at least some of what his teacher and friend Plato had claimed. As a Macedonian outsider[41] trying to fit into Athenian society (and not always successfully, as his two self-imposed exiles reveal), it is perhaps unsurprising that Aristotle was less interested in disagreeing with dominant cultural ideas; it is, however, at the very least a tragedy that Aristotle had both the resources in his own thought and at least a partial example in his teacher for heading in a better direction.[42]

## Other Modifications

The previously discussed moves strike me as central to developing a more adequate, ever, I think that there are also a number of concerns and capacities that are more traditionally associated with women and which are underemphasized in Aristotle's thought. This then contributes to his failure to appreciate women's ability to achieve full human development. If one misunderstands the human ideal—if one overlooks or undersells certain features that may be a part of that ideal—then one is likely to measure wrongly to what degree and in what ways various individuals achieve that ideal.

Although it is perfectly compatible with hylomorphism to argue that there are a number of appropriate expressions of a single type of form, it may also be the case that certain material conditions bring out some aspects of that form more easily than others. For example, one can fully actualize one's musical capacities playing many types of music and on a whole range of instruments. Nonetheless, differing styles of music and instruments can contribute to that development in quite differing ways.

---

[41] Aristotle was Greek, although raised in Macedonia with strong ties to the Macedonian leadership.

[42] Plato's example was, however, significantly complicated by his dualism.

For example, the same basic chord can be played in different ways with differing fingerings on a guitar; there are, in contrast, relatively few ways to play a single chord on the piano. The skills and the particular way in which one's musical abilities are developed differ quite significantly if one is trained on the guitar rather than piano. So also, one can learn to hear musical harmonies by listening to Bach's fugues or Coltrane's jazz, and each will make certain aspects of that training easier than the other. Analogously, one can claim both that the biological conditions *qua* female and *qua* male are equally good for human development—that neither presents overall inferior conditions for the development of human capacities—and, at the same time, claim that those conditions may nonetheless be sufficiently different such that certain of the human patterns or traits are regularly more easily developed in the one, in contrast to the other. The only claim here is that female and male biological matter are both *equally good* for the development of the full range of human capacities, that both females and males may fully and equally actualize the human form—not that there are not differences, nor that some of those differences might make the tendency to focus on certain capacities rather than others understandable. But, overall, there are equal challenges on both sides, and neither sex is *qua sex* in a superior position regarding the actualization of the full range of the human capacities.[43] I have worries that Aristotle overemphasized those features of our human nature more easily developed by males and underemphasized those more easily developed by females.[44]

The general project of this book is to lay out the broad lines of an Aristotelian feminism, drawn from Aristotle's hylomorphism. Throughout I have focused less on the *content* of how biological matter might impact an individual's development (and thus what kinds of traits or tendencies might count as 'feminine' and 'masculine') and more on the broad theoretical lines of this position. Nonetheless, making Aristotle's thought fully feminist will require raising some questions of content. I do not think that we need simply to correct the points where Aristotle made problematic claims, but also to indicate oversights and mis-emphases in Aristotle's understanding of the human ideal. These oversights and mis-emphases resulted, I suspect, in part from his failure to attend as fully to female examples of human development and flourishing. All flourishing is *human* flourishing, and the general ideal—the full development of the full range of our human capacities—is identical for females and males, but some features may be more easily or quickly developed by women than men and vice versa. Insofar as Aristotle, because of his view of women as naturally inferior, failed to attend carefully enough to human flourishing as exemplified by

---

[43] Someone might object that, in acknowledging possible differences in development, I have thereby opened the door to claiming an overall inequality. That people may use the position in this way (as Aristotle himself did) is a risk, but (a) such inequality in no way follows from the claim regarding difference and (b) denying differences, if they exist, is itself a damaging proposition. For further discussion of this, see Chap. 1 above.

[44] We might also ask whether there are features of our human nature more easily developed by intersex individuals.

women, he likely downplayed certain aspects of human development, those exemplified more frequently or often more fully by women.

I would like briefly to discuss two such mis-emphases, including: (1) Aristotle's failure to discuss fully those capacities central to interpersonal development and (2) his de-emphasis on certain of the human virtues, including particularly the "virtues of acknowledged dependence." In each case, my claim will not be that Aristotle in no way attends to these features but, rather, that he underemphasizes or inadequately focuses on each of these. The precise ways in which these should be included will be left open, but I suspect that a fully feminist version of Aristotelianism would need to address at least these areas in some way. The following discussions will be brief and, once again, acceptance of the overall position is not dependent on agreement regarding these elements. Nonetheless, it is critical to go beyond simply responding to what Aristotle says in order to address what he fails to include or to emphasize sufficiently.

## Development of Interpersonal Abilities

There are a number of regions or types of human capacities that are not heavily emphasized by Aristotle. For example, although he acknowledges the excellence of the craftsperson, he does not often incorporate such manual labor into the ideal life. Such an oversight is surely important. I would like here, however, to focus on a slightly different group of capacities—those related to our interpersonal abilities. In so focusing, I am not claiming that this is the only set of capacities that need to be better incorporated into our understanding of the ideal, flourishing, and fully human life, but I think both (a) that they are among those that need to be better incorporated

Aristotle certainly focuses on our affective abilities and emotional responsiveness. He argues, for example, that there are virtues regarding anger, i.e., one ought to be angry to the right degree, toward the right person, for the right reason, etc. The feeling of anger is not a value-neutral experience but there are, rather, habits of affective response. Some of those affective developments are vicious whereas others are virtuous and reflective of a person who has cultivated a virtuous life.[46]

---

[45] Given the frequency with which women have traditionally cooked, cleaned, and attended to more domestic duties, the incorporation of the import of manual labor for human flourishing is surely also a feminist concern. Adequate discussion of this incorporation would, however, take us deep into questions of economic relations, the appropriate role of technology, etc.—questions that are surely important, but beyond the scope of this text.

[46] He says, for example: "things that are found in the soul are of three kinds—passions, faculties, states—excellence must be one of these. By passions I mean appetite, anger, fear, confidence, envy, joy, love, hatred, longing, emulation, pity, and in general the feelings that are accompanied by pleasure or pain; by faculties the things in virtue of which we said to be capable of feeling these, e.g. of becoming angry or being pained or feeling pity; by states the things in virtue of which we stand well or badly with reference to the passions, e.g. with reference to anger we stand badly if

Similarly, Aristotle discusses relation to our fears in chapter III of *Nicomachean Ethics*, understanding courage as a right relation to our fears. Aristotle cannot be accused of failing to focus on our emotions or emotional development, and his comments about anger, fear, and even the role of pleasure and pain in the raising of children[47] reveals an attention to features central to our personal development.

Nonetheless, I think that Aristotle's account of our affective abilities in interpersonal relations is underdeveloped. Although expecting Aristotle to provide a fully comprehensive listing of every one of our capacities is perhaps a bit much, Aristotle's failure to discuss those abilities developed more frequently and in greater depth by those who attend to young children and the most vulnerable in a society is a striking omission, revealing a failure to attend to the features of our common human nature that were likely developed more frequently and fully by the women of his society.

Empathy, for example, as the ability to recognize well another person's experience is a (presumably intellectual) human capacity, and there is a virtue of right empathy that involves rightly recognizing what another is experiencing. Tied to this are surely also moral virtues which run between the extremes of, on the one side, inattention to—or indifference to—another's experience and, on the other, an excessive interest in the experiences of another. Our empathetic capacities (including both the intellectual and moral components) are surely developed, in part, by working with young children, sick, and elderly family members, neighbors, etc., and particularly with those who lack the ability to speak or who have limited ways of expressing their needs and emotions. Such individuals (including all of us at various points in our lives) are often quite vulnerable, and rightly discerning what is being experienced is particularly important, especially in the cases where communication is a challenge.

Related to empathy is also a whole set of abilities, including the ability, not simply to understand another's experience, but to feel with others in their grief, their joy, and their fears[48]; appropriate judgments regarding when to express such co-feelings and compassion and when it is necessary to re-direct the behavior, curb or cultivate an emotion, etc., are necessary. Such 'emotional work' is essential for human development, and such interpersonal capacities are among the human capacities that all of us have and ought to develop in order truly to flourish as human beings. Thus, not only is the cultivation of such interpersonal abilities crucial for the

---

we feel it violently or too weakly, and well if we feel it moderately; and similarly with reference to other passions" (*Nicomachean Ethics* 2.5.1105b19-28). Aristotle then distinguishes the grounds on which we can be praised and blamed and the ways in which our passions are tied to our excellences.

[47] See, for example, *Nicomachean Ethics* 10.1.1172a19-23.

[48] In *Nicomachean Ethics* 9.11, Aristotle contrasts those "of a manly nature," who do not allow others to grieve with them, and women and "womanly men," who enjoy co-mourners. Aristotle is surely right that there is a vicious way of seeking attention in one's grief. But—particularly given the significance of the reiteration of our emotions in order both to know ourselves and to cultivate appropriate responses—there are crucial ways in which a "womanly" sharing of grief is essential. For a more detailed discussion of empathy and reiterated empathy, see Edith Stein's *The Problem of Empathy* (Washington, DC: Institute of Carmelite Studies Publications, 1989).

survival of our species (it enables us, after all, to survive our periods of extreme vulnerability and develop into more independent beings), it is also among our human capacities, and thus its cultivation is tied to truly *human* flourishing.

Attention to such interpersonal dimensions (and even their exemplification in women's lives) is not, once again, absent from Aristotle's thought. In *Nicomachean Ethics* 8.8, for example, Aristotle has a striking discussion of friendship between husband and wife. He opens the section by saying, "Most people seem, owing to ambition, to wish to be loved rather than to love."[49] Aristotle disagrees with most people, however, in prioritizing *loving* rather than *being loved*. He says:

> But it seems to lie in loving rather than in being loved, as is indicated by the delight mothers take in loving; for some mothers hand over their children to be brought up, and so long as they know their fate they love them and do not seek to be loved in return (if they cannot have both), but seem to be satisfied if they see them prospering; and they themselves love their children even if these owing to their ignorance give them nothing of a mother's due. Now since friendship depends more on loving, and it is those who love their friends that are praised, loving seems to be the characteristic excellence of friends, so that it is only those in whom this is found in due measure that are lasting friends, and only their friendship that endures.[50]

Aristotle praises here those who have cultivated a loving attitude toward others, even and perhaps especially when it is not adequately returned. And he explicitly points to the example of mothers in exhibiting such love.[51]

Our love can, however, be better or more poorly expressed. Expressing it well requires the cultivation of a whole set of interpersonal abilities. It requires the various feelings, insights, judgments, and actions relevant to attending well to another's experience, especially—although not exclusively—in its affective dimensions. Our abilities in these areas are developed in significant part through our interactions with literature and art, but also especially in friendships and parenting (in all of its forms).

acknowledgment of the import of loving another, such interpersonal abilities are critical in order to cultivate true friendships of the good. Aristotle's failure, however, to discuss these abilities in greater detail leaves a lacuna in his account. Although there are likely many reasons for this lacuna, his own example of such virtuous loving as exemplified by many mothers suggests that he may have been well served by allowing the example of women's lives to inform more fully his understanding of human flourishing.

---

[49] *Nicomachean Ethics* 8.8.1159a13-14.

[50] *Nicomachean Ethics* 8.8.1159a26-1159b1.

[51] We might also look at Aristotle's rejection of Plato's dissolution of the family for evidence of an interest in our interpersonal capacities developed in such familial settings.

## Virtues of 'Acknowledged Dependence' and Receptivity

Aristotle's ethics is centrally tied to the notion of virtue, that is, of becoming a certain kind of person, judging rightly about what is appropriate in various situations and being habituated so that one desires to act rightly in those situations. Among the virtues are such things as courage, justice, proper pride, liberality, and temperance. Aristotle discusses each of these in some detail, and his accounts are philosophically and phenomenologically detailed. Aristotle's analysis of certain virtues exhibits significant depth; he says comparatively little, however, about the virtues of "acknowledged dependence," as Alasdair MacIntyre names them. We are rational animals, that is, animals for whom rationality is distinctive. We are, however, *animals* and as animals are vulnerable and dependent in ways characteristic of all animals. There are thus virtues, MacIntyre argues, which acknowledge and grow—at least in part—out of features related to that animality and the particular types of vulnerability characteristic of us as rational animals.[52]

There may be a number of such virtues that ought to be more fully emphasized in a fully feminist (and more fully adequate) Aristotelianism.[53] I would like, however, to focus here on receptivity. Aristotle describes women as more *passive* in contrast to men, and he takes this passivity to be a privation of the activity more characteristic of men. Aristotle is not claiming that passivity is necessarily a vice; it might be appropriate to women, given their condition. But Aristotle nonetheless appears to understand passivity in contrast to activity and as a relatively simple absence of activity. It is worth noting that Aristotle's account of the passivity of matter, for example, is not simple inertness. Rather, he includes the notion of potency and longing for actualization. It is thus a fairly rich account of passivity, which cannot be reduced to a modern, more mechanistic account of mere inertness. Nonetheless, it could be even richer, and one can distinguish simple passivity from receptivity. There is a passivity that longs for actualization and a more active receptivity that prepares for another. Receptivity, although not active in precisely the way in which a primary efficient cause is, is not simple passivity either.

Thus, a distinction can be made between *passivity*—which may simply be an absence of activity—and *receptivity*, which strikes me as a genuine human virtue. To be receptive at the right time, towards the right things, to the right degree, etc., is neither easy nor simple. Proper receptivity involves a great deal of development, discernment, activity, and judgment. Someone receives a gift well, for example,

---

[52] MacIntyre summarizes his project: "I shall argue that the virtues of independent rational agency need for their adequate exercise to be accompanied by what I shall call the virtues of acknowledged dependence and that a failure to understand this is apt to obscure some features of rational agency" (*Dependent Rational Animals*, 8). MacIntyre discusses what he calls "virtues of receiving," which will be my main focus in the following, on pages 126–127.

[53] I am interested here in a few of the virtues that women have often exemplified to a particularly significant degree. This is not, however, to claim that attention to women's lives would be the only route to noticing such virtues. MacIntyre notes, for example, the import of Thomas Aquinas for his own attention to such virtues (*Dependent Rational Animals*, xi).

when she recognizes the significance (or insignificance) of the gift, accepts it with the appropriate combination of gratitude, sense of honor, joy, sense of her own worth in receiving the gift, etc., and—in expressing her gratitude—attends both to the one who gave the gift in all her individuality and the meaning of that gift for the future of that relationship. Judging rightly how to receive in each instance—in a way that is neither slovenly nor excessive—is difficult, and there are many ways to fail to receive well.[54]

Aristotle does not, however, acknowledge the centrality of receptivity insofar as he praises, for example, the properly proud man who "is the sort of man to confer benefits, but he is ashamed of receiving them" and is among those who will "remember any service they have done, but not those they have received."[55] In downplaying the significance of receiving, Aristotle seems to have overlooked something essential both to our animal vulnerability and our possibilities for truly human virtue.

There is room for a positive account of receptivity in Aristotle's thought. In her discussions of the proper attitude of the Aristotelian natural scientist, Freeland articulates some of the ways in which Aristotle's ideal for the scientific attitude differs from certain modern conceptions. She says that the scientist on Aristotle's account is "*passive* before the *agency* of nature which is seen as complexly purposive and efficiently organized."[56] Freeland here, like Aristotle in many places, emphasizes the contrast between the passivity of the one party and the activity of the other. Nonetheless, I think that the stance Freeland describes and attributes to Aristotle's ideal is better described as 'receptive' rather than 'passive.' If Freeland is right in her account of how the Aristotelian natural scientist ought to stand in relation to natural objects (and we understand that stand to be properly receptive), then Aristotelian science would itself present an example of the centrality of the virtue of receptivity—that is, a certain sort of prepared openness for something—necessary in order to have a truthful and objective engagement with reality.[57]

from Aristotle, and his focus on our animality, which involves related vulnerabilities, make such a concern for virtues of "acknowledged dependence," including receptivity, particularly fit. But these virtues of acknowledged dependence are nonetheless underemphasized in Aristotle's writings in comparison to the more clearly active and independent virtues such as courage, liberality, justice, etc.

Thus, there are certain of the human capacities that are emphasized less frequently by Aristotle, and among those are many that women have traditionally cultivated more fully than men. This tendency to emphasize capacities (and virtuous functioning of those capacities) exemplified most frequently, at least historically, by

---

[54] For more extensive discussions of receptivity and its centrality to human life (as well as all of being), see the work of W. Norris Clarke, especially his lovely *Person and Being* (Milwaukee: Marquette University Press, 1998).

[55] *Nicomachean Ethics* 4.3.1124b9-10 and 13–14.

[56] "Nourishing Speculations," 150.

[57] Aristotle's discussions of contemplation may offer another example of such proper receptivity.

men rather than women both impoverishes Aristotle's understanding of human nature and, likely, contributes to a devaluation of women's human development.

## Conclusion

Aristotelian thought offers tremendous resources for feminist purposes. Some of these have already been well exploited, and some are being utilized. I believe, however, that, in addition to what has already been done, Aristotle's metaphysics and particularly the hylomorphic account of the human individual can also be employed by feminists, although not without a few modifications. Many of these modifications strike me as even more true to Aristotle's thought than some of Aristotle's words. Others reach a bit further and include the incorporation of a broader set of capacities and virtues. None of the modifications, however, require jettisoning the core metaphysical claims. Thus, a truly Aristotelian feminism—one not adopting Aristotelian ideas in a piecemeal manner but, rather, adopting a substantive version of Aristotle's metaphysics—is both possible and, as I have argued, desirable. It can help articulate a coherent understanding of gender that avoids both biological determinism and full social constructionism; it can provide an account of how to incorporate bodily differences without in any way undermining equality; and it can do so without downplaying our individual differences and human freedom. I would like to turn, in the next chapter, to giving a little more 'meat' to these claims by looking at one way in which such an Aristotelian feminism might be used to address a contemporary concern.

As a final note before doing so, however, I would like to return briefly to the concluding comment of Chap. 4. I do not think that we can wholly separate Aristotle's account of the natural inferiority of women from his political theory or vision of the good life within the *polis*. The economic realities and pressures of his own day were surely not irrelevant to his understanding of some individuals as more fit to engage primarily in 'menial' tasks, while other people were properly fit for a contemplative life. This fairly sharp division of labor—and the economic situation contributing to Aristotle seeing that division as necessarily sharp—is not an unimportant feature of Aristotle's thoughts on women. We have, however, a wider range of economic options available to us today, and the great advances in technology (including certainly simpler things like contemporary cookware and indoor plumbing, as well as items like microwaves, sewing and laundry machines, and all the more complex technology and infrastructure involved in current work) have contributed to differences in how time is allotted to various tasks. This is not to claim that there are not still important inequalities and perhaps significant challenges to how those inequalities can be addressed. But it is not clear to me that we suffer from quite the same economic pressures that Aristotle did. It is now more possible to envision a life where contemplative, interpersonal, political, and manual labor, for example, can be combined in a single life—and a life that could be available not simply for a few, but for all. Contemporary societies have not yet done this well, but we have resources for doing so which were not available to Aristotle. Further, there are Aristotelian reasons for engaging in this task: his claims regarding human flourishing as functioning well, that is, actualizing the full range of the human capacities, and yet with an appreciation of our very particular material circumstances, hold the seed of a call to transform the structures of our societies so that they better set the conditions for all of us to become more fully human.

# Chapter 6
# Women and the Universities

In this final chapter, I would like to provide an example of what an Aristotelian feminism might look like in practice, that is, the way in which an Aristotelian feminist might critique and evaluate current structures. The position, as presented thus far, is simply intended as a broad sketch; it claims that an Aristotelian feminism emphasizes the significance of our capacities and the conditions for their development (without specifying what those capacities might be) and focuses on the import of material differences in that development (without saying which material differences are most significant and in what ways). This general account leaves many questions unanswered, questions which are significant for what kind of positions one takes on more specific issues. Nonetheless, even a very general version of the position can be used to illuminate certain inequalities. This last chapter is intended as an example or illustration of how this position might approach certain issues.

I would like to look at university education and its role in developing our capacities, but with an eye to our biological differences. It is a fitting test in part because Aristotle's writings and the early universities had a particularly tight relationship. The West's rediscovery of Aristotle's corpus and the development of the medieval universities coincided, and many of Aristotle's writings became the basic textbooks for university education. From the perspective of an Aristotelian feminist, however, the structure of university education that we have inherited is problematic.

All of us have a range of capabilities, and our societies ought to be set up to provide the conditions for developing each of them. It is not clear, however, that—given certain biological differences between women and men—our societies do so equally and in ways that allow both women and men to develop the full range of their capacities. Certain institutions (including universities) require choices among capacities and capacity-development of women that are not required of men in the same way. If one analyzes our university education from the perspective of an Aristotelian feminism, one will find that there are structural problems with our current systems. In this final chapter, I would like to sketch out these problems as an example of an Aristotelian feminist argument in favor of change to our current systems of higher education. I would like to begin with a few preliminary comments

© Springer International Publishing Switzerland 2016
S. Borden Sharkey, *An Aristotelian Feminism*, Historical-Analytical Studies on
Nature, Mind and Action 1, DOI 10.1007/978-3-319-29847-4_6

about our capacities and their cultivation, and then turn to a brief history of the university-model of education, the differences between women's and men's patterns of fertility, and the significance of these differences for the cultivation of the full range of our human capacities.

## Preliminary Comments on Our Capacities

As noted in Chap. 3, it is a critical question what counts as a capacity, or capability, and which are most central to us as human beings. Nussbaum, for example, does not list the development and use of our reproductive capacities as among the ten critical capabilities. Affiliation, however, is one of her ten, and the possibility of having children and substantive relations with our children would seem to be among our capacities as human beings. So also, however, we have capacities for intellectual and professional achievements. All of us as human beings are capable of developing skills that can be turned toward a professional career that can then contribute to our broader world.

Nussbaum makes a distinction between having a capability and using that capability. Nussbaum does not require that all of us *use* all of our capacities. Many individuals for all kinds of reasons may choose, for example, not to pursue any kind of professional activity. But this differs from either being unable to develop one's basic capacities to the point where this choice is a genuine choice or being prohibited from pursuing professional achievement by external or societal structures. Nussbaum calls us as societies to provide for the genuine option of using our capacities, but she does not require that each individual actually use all of her capacities.

I would like to adopt a version of this distinction. All of our capacities need to be

an option (although this threshold may differ in differing context). Thus, some significant holistic development, at least of our basic capacities, is part of the goal. Further, given the interrelatedness of all of our capacities, none can be well practiced without all being developed at least to a certain basic degree. But this concern for setting the conditions for holistic development does not prevent us from also acknowledging the import of specialization and various individuals' choices about how to develop more advanced versions of their capacities. For example, an artist—in contrast to an academic, a naturalist, or a child care specialist—may develop certain aspects of her imagination to a greater degree than the other three. All four individuals might use their imaginative capacity (as well as their capabilities for control over the environment, relation to other species, emotion, etc.), but some of these capacities may be more developed, dominating the overall approach in various ways or requiring more fine-tuned development. A naturalist, for example, must develop her senses and relations to other species to a degree that is less necessary for a child care specialist or historian, even though both would benefit from some development in these areas. Thus, although the general focus on capacities-development requires some attention to holistic development, it is not opposed to specialization in various forms. It would be fully compatible with this view to claim that all one's capacities ought to be developed to a certain threshold, while also acknowledging the import of opportunities for more specialized development.

Further, work in the Western world, among other places—with its important ties to control over one's environment and relations with others—has changed dramatically in the last several decades. There are still rewarding jobs (that is, challenging jobs requiring the cultivation and use of our distinctly human capacities) available without any form of higher education, but these are getting rarer and rarer. Increasingly, a college degree of some form is necessary, and, for many of the positions with more prestige, money, and—most significantly—human challenge, advanced degrees (e.g., an M.A., M.S., M.B.A., J.D., etc.) are expected. Getting hired to do work other than manual labor in most modern companies, for example, requires at least a bachelors degree, and promotion in certain fields (for example, teaching, finance, and law) is often tied to achieving more than a bachelors degree.[1]

Many feminists have focused on work/family challenges, with attention to various ways in which our workplaces can be made friendlier to those trying to juggle care of children and a career. There has been concern to provide more off and on ramps for various careers, better family leave packages, etc. But the challenges go beyond simply juggling the work and one's children. We need to think as well in terms of the patterns of how and when we pursue our various capacity development with an eye to biological differences. One common path, for example, is for students to enter college at 18, to focus full-time on their education for at least 4 years, and then to begin pursuing any advanced education within a couple of years of completing their bachelors degree. Generally, the greater rewards go to those who pursue education full-time, putting their focus nearly exclusively on schoolwork and any related work (e.g., working as a teaching or lab assistant, or as an intern in a related business, etc.), and many programs discourage those who are not willing to make such a commitment.[2] This pattern of education is not, however, particularly friendly to women, and, by and large, our dominant institutions for fostering the capacity development relevant to our careers have not been set up with an appreciation of women's biological development but, rather, men's. This inattention to the biological differences has great significance for women's lives and choices.

---

[1] There is certainly distinctively human physical development essential to many forms of manual labor, but physical labor and manufacture of physical items has changed substantially since the Industrial Revolution. The rise of the assembly line has made such distinctively human versions of manual labor rarer, and the less fully human versions more common.

[2] For a more personal example of this tension, see the discussion in *The New York Times's Motherlode* blog. See Lisa Belkin, "Choosing Not to Keep the Baby" (June 16, 2009) at http://parenting.blogs.nytimes.com/2009/06/16/choosing-not-to-keep-the-baby/ (accessed June 25, 2009).

# History of the Universities

## *The Medieval Heritage*

Prior to the founding of the universities, much education in Western Europe occurred in monastery and convent schools, or through private tutors and apprenticeships. The first universities were formed somewhere around the late eleventh and early twelfth centuries. Although putting a precise date on their founding is somewhat difficult since the educational activities and aspects of the structure often appeared prior to the charter establishing a university, recognizable degree-granting universities were playing an increasingly critical role in education beginning in the early twelfth and thirteenth centuries. Among the earliest Western universities were those in Bologna, Paris, Oxford, Cambridge, Salamanca, and Padua.[3] Of particular significance as models for further universities were the first two, the University of Bologna (known particularly for its medical and law faculties) and the University of Paris (known for its theology faculty).

The impetus for the development of universities in the high Middle Ages may have been humanistic; but, in practice, the spirit of education—at least for a significant majority of students—was quite practical.[4] As society became more urban, more specialized knowledge which prepared individuals to work in fields fit to the new societal needs was of great import. Having some financial resources was necessary to pursue university education, and part of the attraction to these new universities was, of course, the opportunity to gain the knowledge relevant to entering some of the more lucrative professions.

Prior to the rise of the universities, women had access to a number of educational resources, including convent schools and private tutors, that offered an education

aged sex-separated instruction; they were limited to families of some resources, although much monastery and convent education was offered free of charge; and, as is well known, education was not equally emphasized for women and men. Nonetheless, the convent schools and private tutoring offered at least some women access to the best in education. The medieval universities, in contrast, were largely closed to women.[5] A few women of particularly high rank and resource had limited

---

[3] There were previous official sites of learning (e.g., Plato's Academy and Aristotle's Lyceum), as well as degree-granting universities (e.g., University of Salerno). But the degree-granting universities founded in Europe in the high Middle Ages have played a particularly important role in our contemporary understanding of a university and the prominent role they play in advanced education.

[4] A.B. Cobban writes: "for the majority of students...the main priority was a speedy absorption of a selected area of learning in preparation for a chosen career" (*The Medieval Universities: Their Development and Organization* [Chatham, Great Britian: Methuen and Co., Ltd., 1975], 12).

[5] This certainly does not mean that women lacked access to all education or exerted no significant influence on various educational resources. See, for example, Susan Groag Bell's account of women's role in the production and reading of devotional texts, in "Medieval Women Book Owners" in

access to the universities. For example, there were a small percentage of both women and men of rank, who had had significant previous education through private tutors and who joined in university circles in order to supplement their education. Generally, these students of rank did not take a degree—to do so would be seen to diminish their rank—nor did they take exams or teach. Thus, some women living in university towns did interact with the universities.[6] But women were not allowed to be university students in the way that men could.

One hindrance to this was that men, so long as they were students, were granted a clerical status. As such, they were expected to dress like members of a minor order (which has since changed into contemporary academic regalia), keep the tonsure, and commit to a celibate life. There were a number of advantages to this status, including exemption from prosecution by secular courts, which ensured that an ecclesial authority rather than the more common secular authorities had jurisdiction over any complaint involving a student. (This was a privilege which the students could sometimes take great advantage of, leading to much 'town and gown' friction.)[7] The exact requirements with this clerical status differed in various regions. For example, in many northern universities, if a master married, he lost his position; this was not, however, as regularly enforced in the southern universities.[8] Nonetheless, whether there was an explicit and enforced prohibition for everyone, the medieval universities expected *students* to focus nearly exclusively on their studies without making commitments to attend to or financially support children—that is, university education was expected to be pursued in a way that did not include a family.

## Contemporary Universities

Contemporary universities, although differing in certain respects from their medieval fore-bearers, have maintained much from the original model. Our degrees (bachelors, masters, and doctorate) are medieval in origin, and the way in which they are to be broadly pursued, the general number of years necessary to complete the degrees, and the general ages at which the majority of students pursue these degrees have continued into modern universities. Some features have changed. For example, the sheer number of programs of study offered is quite different; the relation of the arts faculty to the rest of the university has subtly shifted in most colleges and universities; the involvement of the Catholic Church in sponsoring teaching

---

*Sisters and Workers in the Middle Ages*, ed. Judith M. Bennett, Elizabeth A. Clark, et. al. (Chicago: University of Chicago Press, 1976): 135–161.

[6] Schwinges, "Student Education, Student Life," 202.

[7] See, for example, Rashdall, vol. 3, 394.

[8] Rashdall, vol. 3, 396. See also Aleksander Gieysztor, "Management and Resources" in *A History of the University in Europe*. Vol. 1, ed. Hilde de Ridder-Symeons (Cambridge: Cambridge University Press, 1992), 109 and James W. Thompson & Edgar N. Johnson. *An Introduction to Medieval Europe* (New York: W.W. Norton & Company, 1937), 731.

licenses is nearly absent; and there has been significant introduction of part-time programs of study as well as programs explicitly oriented toward older students. Nonetheless, many aspects of the broad institutional structures marking at least the dominant contemporary universities originated in a model explicitly intended for male and not female students, committed—during the time of their education—to a child-free lifestyle.

In certain respects, contemporary changes to the medieval model have made universities even more markedly unfriendly to women. For example, it is significantly more common now for students to obtain at least a bachelors degree. Originally, nearly 50 % of medieval students only attended the university for 2 years or fewer; in contrast, the 'traditional path' now is to remain in school for 4 years.[9] In addition, significantly more students go on now to obtain masters and doctorates.

Thus, although differing in some significant respects, contemporary universities have preserved and even deepened a number of significant institutional structures originating in the medieval model: universities were intended to be, and continue to be, centers for capacity-development, and focused study in a university setting generally begins in the late teens and is expected to continue comparatively uninterrupted through its desired completion. These features, however, affect female students differently than male students. There are a number of different effects; one of the most marked shows up when we look at female and male fertility patterns.

## Differing Patterns of Fertility

Patterns for fertility differ for women and men, and these differences are relevant to the ways in which women and men can actualize their capacities for generation, or

capacity, simply that it *is* a human capacity (or sub-capacity) and thus full opportunity for women, as well as men, to actualize this capacity is among the things making a society truly feminist—as well as more fully human. This is certainly not to claim that all human beings do—or ought to—desire to have children. But arranging our

---

[9] Although still considered traditional, this path is not necessarily that of the majority of students.

[10] Someone might ask, of course, why the focus ought to be on generation. We have many capacities, some of which are more central to being human than others—and Nussbaum, for example, does not include generation among her list of ten critical human capabilities. (She does include 'affiliation' and 'bodily integrity,' both of which could, in differing ways, include our generative abilities. Generation or reproduction is not, however, included as its own category for consideration.) We might legitimately ask *how* central generation is to being fully human, actualizing truly human capacities, and thus how much we ought to emphasize the ability to have children in contrast to other abilities (such as artistic, intellectual, emotional, etc.). Nonetheless, it is clear (a) that generation is, in some form, among our capacities, (b) that the actualization of this capacity by some people is essential to the continuation of the human race, (c) that all of us were once children and thus owe a great deal to those who did, in fact, actualize this capacity, and (d) that many human beings have, at some point, a significant desire for children.

societies so that women who actualize this capacity face greater challenges for both their holistic and more specialized development than men who do so is not a fully fair society; it is not one in which women are truly equal and provided with comparable conditions for human flourishing. Thus, whether generation is or is not central to being human, it is certainly one place to test the degree to which a society can count as treating women equally, that is, as full human beings, and thus setting the conditions for women's as well as men's full human development.

## Environmental Influences on Fertility

Fertility involves significant environmental factors as well as biological ones. I would like briefly to look at some relevant environmental concerns before turning to the issue I take to be most critical: that the differences are biological as well as environmental, and the quite different biological conditions of women's in contrast to men's fertility has not well been taken into account in our educational and professional structures.

Environmental factors need to be acknowledged, and issues surrounding fertility are not unrelated to environmental and cultural matter. Although our fertility is more *biologically conditioned* than other things (e.g., than preference in toys or career choices), it is not unrelated to our environment. There are numerous environmental and cultural features that affect both women's and men's ability to reproduce, and these can differ significantly in differing regions of the world. For example, in Africa the overall percentage of infertility, measured by the percentage of women who are childless at the end of their childbearing years, is 10.1 %, whereas it stands at 3 % in the Middle East, and 6 % in North America.[11] These differences can be tied, in part, to the way sexually transmitted diseases are treated and the effect untreated disease can have on the ability to have children.[12] Thus, aspects of the differences in fertility rates between Africa and North America are tied to the convenience and availability of certain medicines and treatments (as well as family and work arrangements, etc.).[13]

---

[11] Frank, O. "The Demography of Fertility and Infertility" [Global Health Situation Assessment and Projections Unit, Division of Epidemiological Surveillance and Health Situation and Trend Assessment, World Health Organization], found at http://gfmer.ch/Books/Reproductive_health/The_demography_of_fertility_and_infertility.html (accessed March 12, 2009).

[12] These incidents would vary in differing regions of Africa. O. Frank places the level of infertility one would expect simply due to "inborn errors, congenital factors, and lifetime celibacy in women" at approximately 3 %.

[13] There are numerous environmental factors, and fertility cannot be discussed as simply a physical or medical issue. The environmental influences can be divided into a number of kinds, including those which influence someone's *choices* about having children and those which affect their physical *ability* to have children. In the first group are certainly societal expectations and approval for the age at which someone marries or begins thinking about having children; the social acceptability of bearing children outside of a marriage; options regarding education and work; the need for

Although there are significant debates about what causes infertility,[14] other environmental factors affecting male infertility include drug use, behaviors leading to excessive heat to the testes (e.g., saunas and tight underwear), disease (especially untreated sexually transmitted diseases), environmental toxins,[15] etc. So also, female fertility is significantly hindered by smoking,[16] disease, nutrition,[17] toxins in the environment, and lifestyle (e.g., frequency and kind of exercise, frequency of intercourse, etc.). These more environmental and cultural factors can have an effect on male sperm production (including both quality and quantity) and women's reproductive life, influencing the beginning and end of women's period of fertility, the structural condition of the reproductive organs, the quality and release of eggs, critical hormone levels and thus the ability of the body to sustain a pregnancy, etc. Such environmental factors can have significant effects on the reproductive health of both women and men, although given the greater physical involvement of women in pregnancy, the environmental factors can have a particularly significant impact on women's reproductive health.

There are likewise many environmental factors affecting the time invested in the having of a child. For example, the initial health of mother, whether she carries a single child or multiple, the resources available (food, prenatal care, etc.), the quality of care during pregnancy and delivery, etc., are each significant for how much time and energy any particular mother invests in each pregnancy. The time thus

---

children (e.g., to work land or to take care of one in old age); government policies encouraging or discouraging children; the availability, education regarding, and social acceptability of various of contraception (both natural and artificial) and family planning services; financial situation; religious values; availability of health care; etc. Each of these contributes to the conditions under which we make our choices and thus acts as a significant part of the environmental and cultural matter in which we develop our generative capacities.

refers, in a fairly generic way, to the inability to have children. In demography, however, 'fertility' and 'infertility' refer to the actual 'output,' that is, whether one does or does not have children, regardless of the reason. 'Fecundity' and 'sterility' are then used to refer to the underlying physical ability (or inability) to have children. In most medical circles, the terms 'fertility' and 'infertility' are more common than 'fecundity' and 'sterility,' and being infertile is generally defined as the failure to become pregnant after a year of sexual intercourse without the use of any contraceptives.

[15] See especially Theo Colburn, Dianne Dumanoski, and John Peterson Myers's *Our Stolen Future: Are We Threatening our Fertility, Intelligence, and Survival?—A Scientific Detective Story* (New York: Dutton Book, 1996), which traces the influences of many toxins on both male and female fertility.

[16] The American Society for Reproductive Medicine estimates that 13 % of female infertility is tied to cigarette smoking, and smoking can have a particularly detrimental effect on ovarian reserve, one of the most significant age-related causes of female infertility. See "Stats and Facts" regarding "What is Infertility?," available at http://www.Protectyourfertility.org/infertility_stats.html (accessed March 12, 2009).

[17] A Harvard Center for Population Studies article places the necessary body fat ratio for the onset of menses as 17 %. See http://www.ncbi.nlm.nih.gov/pubmed/3117838 (accessed March 11, 2009). Excessive exercise and malnutrition will likewise quicken the onset of menopause as well as affecting fecundity during the years in between. In contrast, obesity has been connected to an earlier onset of menses.

invested can differ significantly among differing regions of the world, differing economic classes, from individual woman to woman, and even among pregnancies for the same woman. If we add to the time investment in *having* each child, the very differing time investment involved in breast feeding versus wet nursing versus pumping versus formula (and all the factors relevant to which method is used and for how long it is used), the time investment in having and sustaining a child for the initial months and/or years of that child's life can be quite varied.

Despite these variations, however, it is undisputed that women make a greater physical and time investment in the initial development of each child than men. This does not mean that men could not end up making a greater overall physical and time investment once the children are born. Some initial greater investment by women is, however, non-negotiable. Women cannot have their own biological children without making such an investment,[18] and no one can have children at all without some women being willing to make such an investment.

## *Biological Considerations Affecting Fertility*

Thus, on one hand, environmental factors are critical, and one cannot draw a simple portrait of human fertility that fails to acknowledge the environmental features contributing to the ways in which we have children. Nonetheless, there is also an absolutely critical biological component that, although amenable to influence by various environmental factors, is not perfectly malleable. None of us can have children at any particular time that we want. The ability to reproduce, like all of our abilities, must be developed, and, like all of our biologically-conditioned abilities, will mature within a certain age range and then reduce over time as our bodies get older. What is particularly striking, however, is *how* these biological patterns regarding fertility differ for women in contrast to men. Both certainly have peak years of fertility, and both decline over time. Women, however, have a shorter period of peak fertility, and women's fertility is more susceptible to biological and environmental changes. This is perhaps no great surprise; given women's greater physical investment in carrying a child, there are more factors relevant for women in contrast to men. Taking such differences into account, however, strikes me as a truly *feminist* concern.

Among the key patterns is, first, that men do become less fertile as they grow older. Men over 50 have a 23–38 % drop in pregnancy rates. Further, there are risks for the children of older fathers. For example, children of men over 50 are 5.75 times more likely to have an autism spectrum disorder than the children of men under 30.

---

[18] An exception to this would be cases of gestational surrogacy. Generally, however, women turn to a surrogate when they have proven unable to carry their own children, and some (generally young) woman must be willing to make the time and energy investment in order for this to be a possibility for another woman.

But the drop in fertility is more marked in women. Peak fertility for women is in their late teens and early twenties.[19] The American Society of Reproductive Medicine report on age-related infertility places the infertility rate for women between 20 and 24 at 7 %. (By infertile is generally meant that a woman will not get pregnant after a year of at least twice-weekly non-contraceptive sex.) It jumps to 9 % between the ages of 25 and 29.[20] During this period in the later twenties, biological conditions for pregnancy begin to decline. Energy levels drop and metabolism slows down. More significantly, the ability to absorb and replenish the calcium supply (which babies take directly from their mothers' bones and teeth) begins to drop off. Rates of infertility are particularly significant for women thirty and over. For women 30–34, infertility is 15 %; for women 35–39, infertility is 30 %; and for women 40–44, infertility is 64 %.[21] (In any given month, a healthy 30-year old woman has a 20 % chance of getting pregnant. By the time she is 40, her chances are 5 %.[22]) There are some disagreements in infertility numbers, part of which arises from differing ways of marking infertility (e.g., is it marked by a lack of confirmed pregnancy or a failure of live birth?) and by looking at differing populations.[23] All studies, however, clearly indicate that the ability to have children is significantly affected by age.[24] Although no individual is guaranteed that she will be able to have her own biological children, it is clear that women's ability to do so begins dropping off at a fairly steep rate beginning in the late twenties and increasingly

---

[19] Nancy Klein summarizes the point: "Compared to other major organ systems, the female reproductive system ages to the point of failure at a relatively young age," and she points to studies confirming that "the fecundity of the couple is much more dependent upon the age of the female than the male" (see "Prevention of Infertility Source Document: The Impact of Age on Female

protectyourfertility.org/docs/age_femalefertility.doc, accessed March 12, 2009).

[20] Ibid., 2.

[21] Klein, 2. In the American Society for Reproductive Medicine's "Age and Fertility: A Guide for Patients," the numbers are cited slightly differently, associating the numbers given by Klein as not for infertility but for childlessness. (They cite slightly lower numbers for infertility.)

[22] American Society for Reproductive Medicine, "Age and Fertility: A Guide for Patients," p. 3, available at http://www.asrm.org/Patients/patientbooklets/agefertility.pdf (accessed March 12, 2009).

[23] I suspect that this data may also be affected by whether one is looking at first time mothers, having their first children in their thirties, versus women who have already had children while in they were in their twenties and continued trying to have children into their thirties.

[24] The most significant effect appears to be on the quality of the eggs, but age also affects particularly the uterus, which may impact women's ability to both carry a pregnancy to term and successfully deliver a child without significant complications, and with age, endometriosis (which affects 30 % to 50 % of infertile women) worsens. See Klein, 3, and American Society for Reproductive Medicine, "Age and Fertility: A Guide for Patients," 7 and American Society for Reproductive Medicine, "Patient Fact Sheet. Endometriosis and Infertility: Can Surgery Help" (2008).

sharply through the thirties.[25] Although menopause does not usually set in until the early fifties, for most women infertility has set in at least a decade before menopause.[26]

In addition to increased infertility, with a mother's age comes the greater likelihood of miscarriages[27] and greater risks for various abnormalities. For example, if the child is born to a 25-year old mother, the chances of having a child with Downs Syndrome are 1 in 1,250, but by 35, the chances jump to 1 in 378; by 40 to 1 in 106; and by 45 to 1 in 30.[28] So also the risk of other chromosomal abnormalities among newborns rises: for a 25-year old mother, the chances of chromosomal abnormalities are 1 in 476; at 30, 1 in 385; at 35, 1 in 192; at 40, 1 in 66; at 45, 1 in 21; and at 49, 1 in 8.[29] (It is worth noting that these statistics need to acknowledge the role of both sperm and egg quality, and not all of these can be directly attributed to the age of the mother's eggs. Usually older mothers are correlated with older fathers. But the marked rise in genetic abnormalities with the age of the parents is significant.)

Women's bodies become increasingly less able to carry a child healthily to term with age,[30] and the medical breakthroughs in the areas of fertility treatment (for those for whom these are available and financially possible) do not solve age-related fertility problems, if the mother's eggs are used. Fertility treatment can address a tremendous number of fertility-related challenges; they cannot, however, overcome the specifically age-related challenges (e.g., drop in egg and sperm quality). For example, only approximately 8% of in vitro fertilizations in 39-year-old women are

---

[25] Further evidence for age-related decline in women's fertility can be seen in older women's responses to ovarian stimulation (generally performed as part of infertility treatment). Older women produce fewer eggs than younger women in response to stimulation, despite higher doses of gonadotropins (the stimulating drugs), and the quality of the embryos is similarly lower, leading to lower implantation rates. See Klein, 2.

[26] Hewlett claims that "over a ten-year period (1989–1999) fewer than 200 American women over 50 succeeded in having a baby" (*Creating a Life*, 216).

[27] Women between 15 and 29 have an approximately 10% chance of a miscarriage of a recognized pregnancy. Between 30 and 34, that moves to 12%. Between 35 and 39, it is 18%; between 40 and 44, it jumps significantly to 34%; and after 45, it is over 50% (53%). See American Society for Reproductive Medicine, "Age and Fertility: A Guide for Patients," p. 7.

[28] See American Society for Reproductive Medicine, "Age and Fertility: A Guide for Patients," p. 6. Klein writes: "the rate of clinically significant cytogenetic abnormalities in live births rises from about 1/500 for women under 30, to 1/270 at age 30, 1/80 at age 35, 1/60 at age 40, and 1/20 at age 45" (3, citing E. Hook, "Rates of chromosomal abnormalities at different maternal ages" in *Obstet Gynecol* 58 (1981): 282.

[29] American Society for Reproductive Medicine, "Age and Fertility: A Guide for Patients," p. 6.

[30] In addition to challenges for the child, there are additional risks for the mother, including gestational diabetes and high blood pressure, which become significantly more common among pregnant women over 35.

successful and a mere 3 % for women 44 or over,[31] whereas the success rate with women under 35 is closer to 40 %.[32]

(There have been a significant number of older women successfully having children; even the onset of menopause need not be a hindrance to carrying a child to term, given enough medical intervention. Generally, however, these successful older pregnancies occur through donor eggs coming from younger women. Donor eggs are relatively expensive, although not as expensive as surrogacy, and if a woman uses donor eggs, a significant number of the fertility problems I have mentioned here can be eliminated.)

## Having Children and Developing One's Other Capacities

The years of peak female fertility coincide with the key years of traditional university study, and given the more limited years of fertility for women, in contrast to men, expecting university life to be child-free will have a different impact on women in contrast to men. In the early years of the universities, this was not a major issue, since women were rarely allowed into the universities. There were a few well-known women university students prior to the nineteenth and twentieth centuries,[33] but most universities did not offer unqualified matriculation into degree-granting programs to women until comparatively recently. (For example, Russian universities began opening their doors in 1906, and Oxford and Cambridge began allowing women to take degrees following World War I.[34]) Women have, however, responded quickly and enthusiastically. In the first three decades of the twentieth century,

---

[31] Hewlett, *Creating a Life*, 219. Klein cites a study of 431 in vitro fertilization cycles looking at women 41 and older. Of these, no woman 44 or over successfully delivered a child, and delivery rates for the women between 41 and 43 was between 2 % and 7 %. See Klein, 2, citing R. Ron-El, A. Raziel, D. Strassburger, M. Schachter, E. Dasterstein, & S. Friedler, "Outcome of assisted reproductive technology in women over the age of 41" in *Fertility and Sterility*, 74 (2000): 471–475. Similarly, success rates for artificial insemination (intrauterine insemination) are comparatively low for older women. For example, the American Society for Reproductive Medicine places the success rate of superovulation with timed intrauterine insemination (artificial insemination combined with ovary stimulating drugs) at 10 % per cycle for women 35 to 40 and less than 5 % for women over 40. See "Age and Fertility," 9.

[32] Success rates can, once again, be measured differently. One can ask about implantation rates per embryo transferred or simply per cycle (ignoring the number of embryos transferred); one can look at overall pregnancy rates based on detected fetal heart movement; or one can consider live birth rates. Each of these can lead to slightly different statistics. Further, differing clinics use various methods, transferring embryos at different stages of development, using assisted hatching techniques, etc.

[33] For example, "In Utrecht … Anna Maria van Schurmann was granted permission to follow university lectures, on condition that she stay concealed behind a curtain. At Padua, in 1678, Elena Lucrezia Cornaro Piscopia…obtained a doctorate in theology" (Rüegg, vol. 2, p. 296).

[34] Rüegg, vol. 3, 247–248. Other universities follow a similar pattern.

women's enrollment jumped from 17% to 26% in Great Britain and from 8% to 18% in Germany.

The trend toward greater female enrollment has continued. By and large and worldwide, women have embraced the opportunity to pursue higher education.[35] Between 1999 and 2005, women throughout the world have increased their enrollment in tertiary education (tertiary education encompasses all post-secondary education, including both university and vocational schooling). In 1999, 18% of women worldwide had enrolled in tertiary education[36]; in 2005, the number jumped to 25%. The jump is particularly marked in central and Eastern Europe (moving from 43% in 1999 to 63% in 2005) and North America and Western Europe (moving from 68% to 80%). But nearly all regions show some notable increase in the percentage of women involved in tertiary education.[37]

Many women enroll in a college or university the year they graduate from high school. For example, nearly 70% of women in the United States who entered in 2003 enrolled immediately into a college program, and women made up 57% of university enrollments that year.[38] Women similarly show a marked presence in graduate education. Overall, men made only 42% of graduate enrollment in 2003–2004, although the percentage of men versus women can vary significantly by degree program. The American Council on Education report cites, for example:

> Men still are the majority in theology (77 percent), MBA (59 percent), noneducation doctorate (55 percent), law (54 percent), and master's of science (52 percent) programs. Women hold the largest majorities in education programs (80 percent at the master's level and 64 percent at the doctoral level), but also have made strides in traditionally male fields. Women now have a slight majority in enrollment in medicine (51 percent) and other health science professional programs (53 percent).[39]

Neil Gilbert—citing data from the US Census Bureau Statistical Abstract of the United States for 2000 and 2006—notes: "Between 1970 and 2002 the proportion of medical degrees awarded to women increased by almost 529%; law, 888%;

---

[35] The increasing numbers of U.S. women pursuing university education has been sufficiently marked and notably higher than the number of males enrolled, so much so that the American Council on Education put out a book entitled *Gender Equity in Higher Education: Are Male Students at a Disadvantage?* (2000).

[36] Much of the following data comes from Joni Seager, *The Penguin Atlas of Women in the World*, 4th ed. (New York: Penguin Books, 2009). Seager titles the section cited here, "Women enrolled in tertiary education as a percentage of all women 1999–2005 by region." I take her to refer here to the percentage of women who were at that time, or had at some time, enrolled in tertiary education.

[37] See also the UNESCO Global Education Digest. Available at http://www.uis.unesco.org/template/pdf/ged/2007/EN_web2.pdf (accessed August 18, 2009).

[38] See Jacqueline E. King, *Gender Equity in Higher Education 2006* (Washington, DC: American Council on Education, 2006), http://www.acenet.edu/bookstore/pdf/Gender_Equity_6_23.pdf, Sects. 3.6 and 3.7 (accessed August 18, 2009). Women, however, make up a larger percentage of the 25 and older group of undergraduates. See Sect. 3.9 of the same text.

[39] Ibid., Sect. 3.7 (page 15).

business, more than 1,000%; and dentistry, 4,277%."[40] Women have steadily
increased in numbers, especially in the last several decades, not only in associate
and bachelor programs, but also in masters and doctoral programs.[41]

At the same time that women have embraced advanced educational opportunities, however, they have also delayed marriage, which is a strong indicator of a delay
in child-bearing as well. The average age at which women first married in 1980 in
contrast to 2000 has increased worldwide. For example, in Sweden, the average age
for a first marriage for women in 1980 was 26; in 2000, it was 31. In Bulgaria, the
average age moved from 22 (in 1980) to 25 (in 2000); and in both Germany and the
United Kingdom, it moved from 23 to 28.[42] There is clear data that in the United
States, college-educated women have increasingly delayed the age at which they
have children. In 1970, approximately 73% of women who had been college-
educated had had their first child by the time they were 30 years old. In 2000, that
percentage had dropped precipitously to 36%.[43] The American Society for
Reproductive Medicine claims that 20% of U.S. women wait until after they are 35
to begin having children.[44]

The average number of childbirths per woman has declined worldwide in a similar period.[45] In much of the industrial world (including the United States, most of
Europe, Kazakhstan, Russia, China, Iran, Australia, Chile, and Japan), the number
of children born is below replacement levels, that is, below 2.1.[46] In much of Latin
and South America, the levels are between 2.2 and 4. This level is comparable to
that in many countries in both northern and southern Africa, most of the Arabian
Peninsula, Turkey, Syria, Pakistan, India, Philippines, Malaysia, and Indonesia. The
central African countries have a higher rate of childbirth per woman, at 4.1 to 6 or

*A Mother's Work: How Feminism, the Market, and Policy Shape Family Life* (New Haven, CT:
Yale University Press, 2008), 22.

[41] See also King, *Gender Equity*, Sect. 3.15 for U.S. figures. King emphasizes that these trends are
not limited to the U.S. See Sect. 3.19, page 27. This data can be compared with that presented by
the National Center for Education Statistics, available at http://nces.ed.gov/programs/coe/2008/
section3/indicator27.asp (accessed August 18, 2009).

[42] Cited in Seager, *The Penguin Atlas*, 21.

[43] Cited in Mary Ann Mason & Eve Mason Ekman, *Mothers on the Fast Track: How a New
Generation can balance Family and Careers* (New York: Oxford University Press, 2007), 4, citing
*Vital Statistics of the United States: Natality 1970: Births: Final Data for 2000*, NCHS, 2002.

[44] See "Age and Fertility: A Guide for Patients," p. 3, available at http://www.asrm.org/Patients/
patientbooklets/agefertility.pdf (accessed March 12, 2009).

[45] Seager writes: The "average number of births per woman dropped at least half *between early
1970s and early 2000s*" for many nations, including Mexico, Peru, Brazil, Colombia, Libya,
China, Spain, Turkey, Iran, Romania, and Algeria. See *The Penguin Altas*, 35.

[46] We can see similar trends by looking at the number of women who are childless in their early
forties. In 2002, nearly 20% of U.S. women were childless by the time they hit their mid-40s,
which is nearly double the percentage from 1979. Similarly, the number of children each woman
has, has dropped markedly: those with three or more children has dropped by 50%. See Gilbert, *A
Mother's Work*, 23–24.

so, but these countries are also among those with the greatest number of children dying before they reach the age of five.[47]

Although it is clear that women have been both having children later and having fewer children, it is not obvious that this is how all women would like things to be. Data on women's satisfaction with the number of children they have is somewhat limited, but there are some studies suggesting that women are less satisfied with the current trends than men. For example, in a 2007 summary of a study of University of California faculty, Mary Ann Mason reports that "women faculty were more than twice as likely as men faculty to indicate they wished they could have had more children": 38% of women in comparison to 18% of men.[48] And Sylvia Ann Hewlett's *Creating a Life: Professional Women and the Quest for Children* is dedicated to studying the fairly significant number of high-achieving women who, nonetheless, have remained—but had not intended to be—childless.

In order for women to cultivate and use their capacities for intellectual development and broad social involvement and control (for example, in the economic and political life of a country), they have had to do so dominantly through the medium of the contemporary universities. And universities have, in many ways and particularly recently, been quite hospitable places for women. But the university model—with its origins in a male celibate and child-free model of life—has not been particularly friendly to women's capacities development in other respects. Rather than re-thinking or re-envisioning the whole structure of university education in order to include women (which would certainly not have been an easy task), the universities of the early twentieth century simply threw open their doors to allow women to partake in university life *as it was*. Since then, there has been some attempt to adapt here and there. But the dominant model for university education (and the related transition into the more advanced professional careers) remains one that is not particularly feminine or attentive to female patterns of biological development in contrast to male ones.

---

[47] See Seager, 33. See also the 2007/08 Human Development Report on fertility rates worldwide, available at http://hdrstats.undp.org/en/indicators/335.html (accessed August 18, 2009).

[48] See http://www.aps.org/programs/women/workshops/gender-equity/upload/Mason_Mary_Ann_APS_Gender_Equity_Conference.pdf (accessed August 18, 2009). In her book, citing similar data Mason places men's dissatisfaction at 11% rather than 18%. See *Mothers on the Fast Track*, p. 32 (she refers here to Mary Ann Mason & Marc Goulden, "Marriage and Baby Blues: Redefining Gender Equity in the Academy," *Annals of the American Academy of Political and Social Science*, November 2004, p. 98).

## *Impact of This Tension*

There are numerous options for having children. Not all women have children by simply having sex and then getting pregnant and carrying the child to term. Some women undergo various forms of fertility treatment[49]; they might choose surrogacy; or they may follow the path of adoption. Although these are options and can often have good results, it is not clear that we ought to arrange our societies so that these are the most attractive options for women. Fertility treatment, for example, can be expensive and is out of the reach of many women, both because of the lesser availability of such treatment in differing parts of the world and because of the expense of such treatment—and fertility treatment cannot address all age-related infertility issues.[50]

But perhaps more significant, if generation or reproduction is a *human* capacity, then setting up our societies so that women have significantly less opportunity to use this capacity than men, if they choose to develop other central human capacities, is not a fully equitable society. Many women may decide not to have children; some may be unable to for reasons independent of societal arrangements; but not using our reproductive capacities should be either an individual decision to self-limit or some kind of inability not created by the societal structures intended to *develop* our human capacities. Certainly, if university education is set up in such a way that infertility treatment, surrogacy, and adoption are among the standard options for women who want to develop both their professional abilities and have children, it is an inadequately feminist structure.

Given present models, women regularly face choices that are not faced in the same way by men. Women can pursue higher education and advanced careers paths in 'traditional' ways, but, if they do so, they usually have the question of how they

education completed and job secured while still having time to fit children in? Or will they delay professional development in order to focus on family, but do so with significant questions about whether, when they return to—or begin—their education and careers, they will be accepted and encouraged in their pursuits? Many

---

[49] For the vast majority of people undergoing fertility treatment, this involves diagnostic tests and the use of fertility drugs (e.g., Clomid) or surgery. Artificial insemination and artificial reproduction technology (ART), although much more expensive, are also by far less needed or common forms of fertility treatment. The American Society for Reproductive Medicine estimates that only 5 % of fertility treatment involves in vitro fertilization or similar treatments. See "Stats and Facts" regarding "What is Infertility?," available at http://www.protectyourfertility.org/infertility_stats.html (accessed March 12, 2009).

[50] Although various forms of surrogacy and donor eggs can address some of the age-related questions, both require that there be younger women who are willing to contribute in some significant way to another woman's child, and both raise numerous emotional, legal, and moral challenges. Similarly, adoption requires that some woman be willing to physically invest in and carry a child to term. These things may be good and thus rightly supported by our governments and societies, but none of these options should be ideals around which we organize and structure our societies.

women have negotiated this impressively; there is no doubt that a tremendous number of women have succeeded in pursuing both professional and familial development. Nonetheless, the set-up was not meant for women, and we are now trying to jerry-rig women in but without making significant structural changes. This is not an ideal scenario for achieving equality.[51]

## Conclusion

It is certainly true (a) that the window to actualize reproductive or generative capacities is more limited for women than for men and (b) that the physical, emotional, and time investment of women in the generative process is greater. Generation is a human capacity, and thus something that should be valued and conditions set so that it is a possibility for all of us. (The claim is not that everyone should have children but, rather, that there should be conditions enabling this possibility, with society allowing individuals to decide regarding their own self-limitation on this front. Self-limitation should not be required because of our societal structures or pressures.) An Aristotelian feminism requires us to re-think, for example, our educational structures in order to find ways for there to be both equally and differently patterned human development.

This view does not advocate that women begin having children in their early to mid-teens. Dedicating time and energy to taking care of children when the parents are themselves at such a young age will have significant implications for the development of other of the parents' human capacities. But it does advocate that we have structures—and particularly patterns for higher education—that acknowledge the biological differences between women and men, that provide equal and legitimate tracks for women to pursue both the development of their intellectual and professional capacities and their reproductive ones.

Thus, the point is not that women should get out of school and the workplace and begin having children. Quite the opposite! It is time to *change* our schools and workplaces so that women can do both as men have been able to do, at least to a much greater degree. That we have societies where there is a tension between education and family, professional development and children, is—I think—evidence of the sexist structure of our society. We have developed patterns of how intellectual, social, political development and actualization ought to occur that favor male biology. Insofar as the original universities modeled education on a celibate monk's life rather than a father's life, they were not especially attentive to the development of

---

[51] If this education/family tension is not addressed, hard-fought ground providing a greater place for women in the academy, politics, business, etc., may be lost. If women are not regularly making full use of their degrees, for example, will schools increasing deny slots or funding to women? (22 % of U.S. mothers with graduate degrees are at home, and 33 % with MBAs do not work full-time. See Gilbert's *A Mother's Work*, 13.) Although not often happening currently, it is not difficult to imagine a time when financial or other resources are even scarcer, when nations are besieged in various ways, and additional pressures require us to make difficult and unpleasant choices.

either female or male reproductive capacities. But the model is particularly unsuited for women and women's ability to develop the full range of their human capacities. Because males have a longer period of relatively reliable fertility, combining the medieval university model with fatherhood is possible. It is not so easily done by women.

I am not advocating getting rid of universities, overthrowing the whole of the university system, or tracking people so that some are educated and some are parents. None of these strike me as attractive ideas. Although it is true that all of us self-limit in certain ways, developing some of our capacities more fully than others, the Aristotelian ideal—and the Aristotelian ideal for each individual—is some significant holistic development, including the full range of capacities. Aristotle himself thought that some people were not able to so develop (that is, women and natural slaves), and thus he felt comfortable with a hierarchical society in which some enjoy the benefit of better conditions for full development than others. If some *could not* become fully human, then they ought to aid the development of those who could. But Aristotle does not argue that those who *could* become fully human nonetheless should not be allowed to become so. He thinks that non-natural slaves (i.e., those who happen to be slaves but are able to be more), for example, should not be kept as slaves.

If Aristotle is wrong in his claim that there are large classes of people unable to develop fully—that is, if he is wrong about women and natural slaves—then he ought to accept the claim that the conditions ought to be set for everyone to develop their capacities. In a rather odd way, contemporary societies have rejected Aristotle's notion of natural human hierarchies but have not accepted the Aristotelian implication of such a rejection: that we must then change our societies in order to reflect this equality of abilities. We have expanded access to university education. We have made it available to more and more people, including certainly more women. And

capacities more fully. This strikes me as right progress. Our societies have also changed so that such advanced education is critical for more and more of the jobs and essential for the careers providing the greatest economic and social security, as well as (frequently) the most humanly rewarding types of work. Now, however, we need to find ways to celebrate and encourage these advances while also enabling the development of other of our human capacities, particularly those involving the having and raising of children as well as the related interpersonal capacities often developed in context of such relationships.[52]

---

[52] Someone might argue that, women—because of their significant role in child-bearing—simply have to make a choice that men do not. Women need to face up to the demands involved in higher education and either commit themselves to pursuing that education or commit themselves to having children, but it is a pipe dream to think that women can do both well. It might be unfair, a choice women (but not men) have to face, but nature is unfair. One might be sorry that life has to be this way, but such choices are simply among the hard facts of life. One simply cannot try to do everything, and attempting to do so will necessarily end up watering something down; either the training, which must necessarily be intense in order to live up to the standards of some field, or having children, which requires a great deal of time and energy, must be compromised. I will grant

Full acknowledgement of our biological differences and their impact on our capacity-development would require no small set of changes. The changes will likely take time, but we are—it seems to me—on a collision course involving our dominant models for advanced education, the need for such education in our global society, and the opportunity for each of us to pursue full *human* development, including especially (although certainly not exclusively) women's generative capacities.

Creative interactions with Aristotle and Aristotelian thought played an important role in the early universities; it was work carried out by scholars from diverse cultural and religious traditions; and it required a monumental effort to make Aristotle speak the language of the day. It strikes me that Aristotelian feminism might offer resources for calling for another such re-birth in our universities. Its attention not simply to environmental and cultural conditions for our development but also biological ones, without reducing gender to biological features, offers resources for examining again the structures of our societies and noticing places where deep inequities persist.

---

to the objectors that there might be a few fields and areas of specialization which require extremely intense training that simply cannot be patterned differently while still achieving the goals. Although this might be true in special cases, I suspect that the particular way in which the training is pursued often grows more out of tradition and convenience than necessity. I suspect that, at times, this objection is raised to justify maintaining the current system and structures (which have worked well for many years and for many men) rather than as an opportunity to think creatively and well about alternatives that would cultivate women equally with men. For many, many years, nearly all academics were single, and most early universities were dominated by monks and priests, who had dedicated their lives to an intellectual life. They did not have children and did not attempt to mix family and an academic life. The breadth of learning as well as the depth of learning possible in this single-focused life is something that cannot be repeated by those—both men and women— who attempt to mix having a family and pursuing an academic life. There are things that single priests and nuns can pursue that no individual, male or female, can have, if they turn their attention in any degree to children, or even to a spouse or significant partner. There is certainly something that has been lost in moving away from universities taught purely by celibate religious, or at least by single individuals dedicated exclusively to the scholarly life. But something has also been gained by doing so, not the least of which is the greater access to university life now granted to both men and women, secular and religious. The opening up of university teaching has led to certain kinds of narrower education. Few Ph.D.'s can now claim the kind of thorough training (which often involved numerous languages and near fluency in Latin) that was common in earlier generations, but with this narrowing down, there is also the opportunity to mix an academic life with the possibility of having children. The greater humanization of the academic world may inspire less awe from students, but it provides them a different model of what a full human life might look like, one involving the development of a range of human capacities (even while specializing and gaining true expertise in some area) rather than the more exclusive focus of earlier generations of academics.

# Bibliography

Achtenberg, Deborah. "Aristotelian Resources for Feminist Thinking" in *Feminism and Ancient Philosophy*, ed. Julie K. Ward (New York: Routledge, 1996), 95–117.

Agonito, Rosemary. *History of Ideas on Woman: A Source Book* (New York: G.P. Putnam's Sons, 1977).

Alanen, Lilli & Charlotte Witt (eds.). *Feminist Reflections on the History of Philosophy* (Boston: Kluwer Academic Publishers, 2004).

Allen, (Mary) Prudence (also Christine Allen, Christine Garside, and Christine Garside-Allen). *The Concept of Woman: The Aristotelian Revolution 750 BC-AD 1250* (Grand Rapids, MI: Eerdmans, 1997).

_____.*The Concept of Woman: The Early Humanist Reformation, 1250–1500* (Grand Rapids, MI: Eerdmans, 2001).

_____."Integral Sex Complementarity and the Theology of Communion," *Communio: International Catholic Review* 17 (Winter 1990): 523–544.

_____."Metaphysics of Form, Matter, and Gender," *Lonergan Workshop*, Volume 12, ed. Fred Lawrence (Boston, MA: Boston College, 1996): 1–23.

_____."Sex and Gender Differentiation in Hildegard of Bingen and Edith Stein" in *Communio* 20 (Summer 1993): 389–414.

_____."Sex Unity, Polarity, or Complementarity?," *International Journal of Women's Studies* 6:4 (September/October 1983): 311–325.

_____."A Woman and a Man as Prime Analogical Beings" in *American Catholic Philosophical Quarterly* 66:4 (Autumn 1992): 465–482.

_____."Woman's Liberation Movement: Some Effects on Women, Men, and Children," in *Configurations*, ed. Raymond Prince (Lexington and Toronto: D.C. Heath and Co., 1974), 103–113.

Aristotle. *Categories, Eudemian Ethics, Generation of Animals, History of Animals, Metaphysics, Nicomachean Ethics, On Length and Shortness of Life, On the Soul, Parts of Animals, Physics, Poetics, Politics, Posterior Analytic, Rhetoric* in *The Complete Works of Aristotle: The Revised Oxford Translation*. Two volumes, ed. Jonathan Barnes (Princeton, NJ: Princeton University Press, 1984).

Arnhart, Larry. *Darwinian Natural Right: The Biological Ethics of Human Nature* (Albany, NY: State University of New York Press, 1998).

_____."A Sociobiological Defense of Aristotle's Sexual Politics" in *International Political Science Review* 15:4 (1994): 389–415.

Baldner, Steven. "An Argument for Substantial Form" in *The Saint Anselm Journal* 5:1 (Fall 2007): 1–12 (available on-line at http://www.anselm.edu/library/saj/pdf/51Baldner.pdf).

© Springer International Publishing Switzerland 2016

S. Borden Sharkey, *An Aristotelian Feminism*, Historical-Analytical Studies on Nature, Mind and Action 1, DOI 10.1007/978-3-319-29847-4

_____."St. Albert the Great and St. Thomas Aquinas on the Presence of Elements in Compounds" in *Sapientia* 54 (1999): 41–57.

Balme, David M. "Aristotle's Biology was not Essentialist" in *Philosophical Issues in Aristotle's Biology*, ed. Allan Gotthelf & James Lennox (New York: Cambridge University Press, 1987), 291–312.

Bar On, Bat-Ami (ed). *Engendering Origins: Critical Feminist Readings in Plato and Aristotle* (Albany, NY: State University of New York Press, 1994).

Barnes, Jonathan. "Aristotle and Women" [review of G.E.R. Lloyd's *Science, Folklore and Ideology*] in *London Review of Books* (16–29 February 1984): 9.

Beer, Alan E., Julia Kantecki, & Jane Reed. *Is your Body Baby-Friendly?: "Unexplained" Infertility, Miscarriage and IVF Failure explained* (Houston: AJR Pub., 2006).

Belenky, Mary F., Jill Mattuck Tarule, Nancy Rule Goldberger, Blythe McVicker Clinchy. *Women's Ways of Knowing: The Development of Self, Voice, and Mind* (New York: Basic Books, 1986).

Bell, Susan Groag. "Medieval Women Book Owners" in *Sisters and Workers in the Middle Ages*, ed. Judith M. Bennett, Elizabeth A. Clark, et. al. (Chicago: University of Chicago Press, 1976).

Benhabib, Seyla. "The Generalized and the Concrete Other: The Kohlberg-Gilligan Controversy and Feminist Theory" in *Feminism as Critique*, ed. Seyla Benhabib & Drucilla Cornell (Minneapolis: University of Minnesota Press, 1987): 77–95.

Bleier, Ruth. *Science and Gender: A Critique of Biology and Its Theories on Women* (New York: Pergamon, 1984).

Blundell, Sue. *Women in Ancient Greece* (Cambridge, MA: Harvard University Press, 1995).

Bobik, Joseph. *Aquinas on Matter and Form and the Elements: A Translation and Interpretation of the de Principiis Naturae and the De Mixtione Elementorum of St. Thomas Aquinas* (Notre Dame, IN: University of Notre Dame Press, 1998).

Boxer, Marilyn J. "For and About Women: The Theory and Practice of Women's Studies in the United States" in *Signs* 7:3 (Spring 1982): 661–695.

Broughton, John M. "Women's Rationality and Men's Virtues: A Critique of Gender Dualism in Gilligan's Theory of Moral Development" in *Social Research* 50:3 (Autumn 1983): 597–642.

Butler, Judith. *Gender Trouble: Feminism and the Subversion of Identity* (New York: Routledge 1990).

Cahill, Lisa Sowle. *Sex, Gender, and Christian Ethics* (New York: Cambridge University Press, 1996).

*Studies in the Philosophy of Science presented to William Humbert Kane, O.P.*, ed. James A. Weisheipl ([Washington]: Thomist Press, 1961): 121–149.

Cantarella, Eva. *Pandora's Daughters: The Role and Status of Women in Greek and Roman Antiquity* (Baltimore: John Hopkins University, 1987).

Carr, Anne. *Transforming Grace: Christian Tradition and Women's Experience* (San Francisco: Harper and Row, 1988).

Clark, Stephen R. "Aristotle's Woman" in *History of Political Thought* 3 (1982): 177–192.

Clarke, W. Norris. *Explorations in Metaphysics: Being—God—Person* (Notre Dame: University of Notre Dame Press, 1994).

_____.*The One and the Many: A Contemporary Thomistic Metaphysics* (Notre Dame, IN: University of Notre Dame Press, 2001).

_____.*Person and Being* (Milwaukee: Marquette University Press, 1998).

Clifford, Anne M. *Introducing Feminist Theology* (Maryknoll, NY: Orbis Books, 2002).

Cobban, A.B. *The Medieval Universities: Their Development and Organization* (Chatham, Great Britian: Methuen and Co., Ltd., 1975).

Code, Lorraine. "The Impact of Feminism on Epistemology" in *APA Newsletter on Feminism and Philosophy* 88:2 (March 1989).

Cohen, Joshua. "Okin on Justice, Gender, and Family" in *Canadian Journal of Philosophy* 22:2 (June 1992): 263–286.

Colborn, Theo; Dianne Dumanoski; & John Peterson Myers. *Our Stolen Future: Are We Threatening our Fertility, Intelligence, and Survival?—A Scientific Detective Story* (New York: Dutton Book, 1996).

Cole, Eve Browning. "Women, Slaves, and 'Love of Toil'" in *Engendering Origins: Critical Feminist Readings in Plato and Aristotle*, ed. Bat-Ami Bar On (Albany, NY: State University of New York Press, 1994), 127–144.

Cook, Kathleen C. "Sexual Inequality in Aristotle's Theories of Reproduction and Inheritance" in *Feminism and Ancient Philosophy*, ed. Julie K. Ward (New York: Routledge, 1996), 51–67.

Cooper, John. "Metaphysics in Aristotle's Embryology" in *Biologie, logique et métaphysique chez Aristotle*, ed. Daniel Devereux & Pierre Pellegrin (Paris: Éditions du CNRS, 1990).

Coulam, Carolyn B. & Nancy Hemenway. "Immunology May be Key to Pregnancy Loss (updated)," available on the InterNational Council on Infertility Information Dissemination, Inc. website at http://www.inciid.org/article.php?cat=immunology&id= 374 (accessed August 19, 2009).

Crocker, David. "Functioning and Capability: The Foundations of Sen's and Nussbaum's Development Ethic, Part I" in *Political Theory* 20:4 (1992): 584–612.

Daly, Lowrie. *The Medieval University* (New York: Sheed and Ward, 1961).

Dean-Jones, Lesley Ann. *Women's Bodies in Classical Greek Science* (Oxford: Clarendon Press, 1994).

de Marcellus, Beatriz Vollmer. *On the ontological differentiation of human gender: a critique of the philosophical literature between 1965 and 1995* [Ph.D. dissertation, philosophy, Pontificae Universitas Gregoriana] (Philadelphia: Xlibris, 2004).

Decaen, Christopher. "Elemental Virtual Presence in St. Thomas" in *The Thomist* 64 (2000): 271–300.

DeCrane, Susanne M. *Aquinas, Feminism, and the Common Good* (Washington, DC: Georgetown University Press, 2004).

Deslauriers, Marguerite. "Sex and Essence in Aristotle's *Metaphysics* and Biology" in *Feminist Interpretations of Aristotle*, ed. Cynthia A. Freeland (University Park, PA: The Pennsylvania State University Press, 1998), 138–167.

Elshtain, Jean Bethke. "Against Androgyny" in *Real Politics: At the Center of Everyday Life* (Baltimore, MD: John Hopkins University Press, 1997), 229–248.

Fausto-Sterling, Anne. "The Five Sexes: Why male and female are not enough" in *The Sciences* (May/April 1993): 20–24.

_____."The Five Sexes, revisited" in *The Sciences* 40:4 (2000): 18–23.

_____.*Myths of Gender: Biological Theories about Women and Men* (New York: Basic Books, 1992).

_____.*Sexing the Body: Gender Politics and the Construction of Sexuality* (New York: Basic Books, 2000).

Femenías, María Luisa. "Women and Natural Hierarchy in Aristotle" in *Hypatia* 9:1 (Winter 1994): 164–172.

Firestone, Shulamith. *The Dialectic of Sex: The Case for Feminist Revolution* (New York: Farrar, Straus and Giroux, 1970).

FitzGerald, John J. "'Matter' in Nature and the Knowledge of Nature: Aristotle and the Aristotelian Tradition" in *The Concept of Matter*, ed. Ernan McMullin (Notre Dame, IN: University of Notre Dame Press, 1963), 79–98.

Flanagan, Owen & Kathryn Jackson. "Justice, Care and Gender: The Kohlberg-Gilligan Debate Revisited" in *Ethics* 97:3 (1987): 622–637.

Fortenbaugh, W.W. "Aristotle on Slaves and Women" in *Articles on Aristotle, vol. 2: Ethics and Politics*, ed. Jonathan Barnes, Malcolm Schofield, & Richard Sorabji (London: Gerald Duckworth & Co., 1977), 135–139.

Freeland, Cynthia A. "Aristotle on the Sense of Touch" in *Essays on Aristotle's De Anima*, ed. Martha C. Nussbaum & Amélie Oksenberg Rorty (Oxford: Oxford University Press, 1992), 227–248.

_____.(ed). *Feminist Interpretations of Aristotle* (University Park, PA: The Pennsylvania State University Press, 1998).

_____."Nourishing Speculation: A Feminist Reading of Aristotelian Science," in *Engendering Origins: Critical Feminist Readings in Plato and Aristotle*, ed. Bat-Ami Bar On (Albany, NY: State University of New York Press, 1994), 145–187.

_____."On Irigaray on Aristotle" in *Feminist Interpretations of Aristotle* ed. Cynthia A. Freeland (University Park, PA: The Pennsylvania State University Press, 1998), 59–92.

Garnsey, Peter. *Food and Society in Classical Antiquity* (New York: Cambridge University Press, 1999).

Gilbert, Neil. *A Mother's Work: How Feminism, the Market, and Policy Shape Family Life* (New Haven, CT: Yale University Press, 2008).

Gilligan, Carol. *In a Different Voice: Psychological Theory and Women's Development* (Boston: Harvard University Press, 1982).

Gilson, E. *From Aristotle to Darwin and Back Again*, trans. J. Lyon (Notre Dame: University of Notre Dame Press, 1984).

Gladwell, Malcolm. "John Rock's Error: What the co-inventor of the Pill didn't know about menstruation can endanger women's health" in *New Yorker* (March 10, 2000), at http://www.gladwell.com/2000/2000_03_10_a_rock.htm (accessed March 11, 2009).

Gorecki, Meg. "Legal Pioneers: Four of Illinois' First Women Lawyers" in *Illinois Bar Journal* (October 1990): 510–515, found at http://womenslegalhistory.stanford.edu/articles/legalpioneers.pdf (accessed May 2, 2009).

Gotthelf, Allan & James Lennox (eds). *Philosophical Issues in Aristotle's Biology* (New York: Cambridge University Press, 1987).

Green, Judith. "Aristotle on Necessary Verticality, Body-Heat, and Gendered Proper Places in the Polis: A Feminist Critique" in *Hypatia* 7 (1992): 70–96.

Groenhout, Ruth. "The Virtue of Care: Aristotelian Ethics and Contemporary Ethics of Care" in *Feminist Interpretations of Aristotle*, ed. Cynthia A. Freeland (University Park, PA: The Pennsylvania State University Press, 1998), 171–200.

Harding, Sandra & Hintikka, Merrill B. (eds). *Discovering Reality: Feminist Perspectives on Epistemology, Metaphysics, Methodology, and Philosophy of Science*, 2nd ed. (Dordrecht: Kluwer, 2003).

Haslanger, Sally. "Feminism in Metaphysics: Negotiating the Natural" in *The Cambridge Cambridge University Press, 2000), 107–126.

_____."Feminist Metaphysics" in *Stanford Encyclopedia of Philosophy* (published February 27, 2007), at http://plato.stanford.edu/entries/feminism-metaphysics/, accessed May 27, 2009.

_____."Ontology and Social Construction" in *Philosophical Topics* 23:2 (Fall 1995): 95–125.

_____."Social Construction: Who? What? Where? How?" in *Theorizing Feminisms*, ed. E. Hackett & S. Haslanger (Oxford: Oxford University Press, 2006), 16–23.

Hass, Marjorie. "Feminist Readings of Aristotelian Logic" in *Feminist Interpretations of Aristotle* ed. Cynthia A. Freeland (University Park, PA: The Pennsylvania State University Press, 1998), 19–40.

Hewlett, Sylvia Ann. *Creating a Life: What every Woman needs to know about having a Baby and a Career* (New York: Miramax Books, 2003).

Horowitz, Daniel. *Betty Friedan and the Making of the Feminine Mystique: The American Left, The Cold War, and Modern Feminism* (Amherst, MA: University of Massachusetts Press, 1998).

Horowitz, Maryanne Cline. "Aristotle and Woman" in *Journal of the History of Biology* 9:2 (Fall 1976): 183–213.

Husserl, Edmund. *Ideas Pertaining to a Pure Phenomenology and to a Phenomenological Philosophy: First Book [General Introduction to a Pure Phenomenology]*, trans. F. Kersten (The Hague: Martinus Nijhoff, 1983).

_____.*Ideas Pertaining to a Pure Phenomenology and to a Phenomenological Philosophy: Second Book [Studies in the Phenomenology of Constitution]*, trans. Richard Rojcewicz & André Schuwer (Boston: Kluwer, 1989).

_____.*Logical Investigations*, Volumes I & II, trans. J.N. Findlay (New York: Humanities Press, 1970).

Irigaray, Luce. "Place, Interval: A Reading of Aristotle, *Physics IV*" in *Feminist Interpretations of Aristotle*, ed. Cynthia A. Freeland (University Park, PA: The Pennsylvania State University Press, 1998), 41–58.

Jaggar, Alison M. *Feminist Politics and Human Nature* (Totowa, NJ: Rowman & Allanheld, 1983).

_____."Human Biology in Feminist Theory: Sexual Equality Reconsidered" in *Beyond Domination: New Perspective on Women and Philosophy*, ed. Carol C. Gould (Totowa, NJ: Rowman & Allanheld, 1983), 21–42.

Jaggar, Alison M. & William L. McBride. "'Reproduction' as Male Ideology," in *Hypatia Reborn: Essays in Feminist Philosophy*, ed. Azizah Y. Al-Hibri & Margaret A. Simons (Bloomington, IN: Indiana UP, 1990), 249–269.

Keuls, Eva. *The Reign of the Phallus: Sexual Politics in Ancient Athens* (Berkeley: University of California Press, 1993).

Kidder, Paulette. "Cross-Cultural Judgments of the Human Good: the Debate Over Capabilities Ethics," paper presented at the Lonergan Workshop, Boston College (June 2003).

_____."Healing and Creating in the Work of Martha Nussbaum" in *Method: Journal of Lonergan Studies* 17 (1999): 47–59.

_____."Woman of Reason: Lonergan and Feminist Epistemology" in *Lonergan and Feminism*, ed. Cynthia S.W. Crysdale (Toronto: University of Toronto Press, 1994), 33–48.

King, Jacqueline E., *Gender Equity in Higher Education 2006* (Washington, DC: American Council on Education, 2006), available at http://www.acenet.edu/bookstore/pdf/Gender_ Equity_6_23.pdf (accessed August 18, 2009).

Klein, Nancy A. "Prevention of Infertility Source Document: The Impact of Age on Female Fertility" (American Society of Reproductive Medicine document, available at http://www. protectyourfertility.org/docs/age_femalefertility.doc, accessed March 12, 2009).

Lange, Lynda. "Woman is not a Rational Animal" in *Discovering Reality: Feminist Perspectives on Epistemology, Metaphysics, Methodology, and Philosophy of Science*, 2nd ed., ed. Sandra Harding & Merrill B. Hintikka (Dordrecht: Kluwer, 2003), 1–15.

Lebech, Mette. *On the Problem of Human Dignity: A Hermeneutical and Phenomenological Investigation* (Würzburg: Königshausen & Neumann, 2009).

Lefkowitz, Mary R. & Fant, Maureen B. *Women's Life in Greece and Rome. A Source Book in Translations* (Baltimore: John Hopkins University, 1982).

Lennox, James G. "Aristotle on the Biological Roots of Virtue: The Natural History of Natural Virtue" in *Biology and the Foundation of Ethics*, ed. Jane Maienschein & Michael Ruse (New York: Cambridge University Press, 1999), 10–31.

Levy, Harold L. "Does Aristotle Exclude Women from Politics?" in *Review of Politics* 52:3 (Summer 1990): 397–416.

Ling, L.H.M. "Hegemonic Liberalism: Martha Nussbaum, Jörg Haider, and the Struggle for Late Modernity," conference proceedings, International Studies Association, 41st Annual Convention (March 14–18, 2000), available at http://www.ciaonet.org.isa/li101/, accessed April 1, 2009.

MacIntyre, Alasdair. *Dependent Rational Animals: Why Human Beings Need the Virtues* (Chicago: Open Court, 1999).

Mason, Mary Ann & Eve Mason Ekman. *Mothers on the Fast Track: How a New Generation can balance Family and Careers* (New York: Oxford University Press, 2007).

Matthews, Gareth B. "Gender and Essence in Aristotle" in *Australasian Journal of Philosophy*, supplement to volume 64 (June 1986): 16–25.

Mayhew, Robert. *The Female in Aristotle's Biology: Reason or Rationalization* (Chicago: University of Chicago Press, 2004).

McReynolds, Phillip. "Nussbaum's Capabilities Approach: A Pragmatist Critique" in *The Journal of Speculative Philosophy* 16:2 (2002): 142–150.

Michael, Emily. "Descartes and Gassendi on Matter and Mind: From Aristotelian Pluralism to Early Modern Dualism" in *Meeting of the Minds: The Relations between Medieval and Classical Modern European Philosophy*, ed. Stephen F. Brown (Brepols, 1998), 141–161.

Modrak, Deborah. "Aristotle: Women, Deliberation and Nature," in *Engendering Origins: Critical Feminist Readings in Plato and Aristotle*, ed. Bat-Ami Bar On (Albany, NY: State University of New York Press, 1994), 207–222.

_____."Aristotle's Theory of Knowledge and Feminist Epistemology" in *Feminist Interpretations of Aristotle*, ed. Cynthia A. Freeland (University Park, PA: The Pennsylvania State University Press, 1998), 93–117.

Moschella, Melissa. "Personal Identity and Gender: A Revised Aristotelian Approach" in *Gender Identities in a Globalized World*, ed. Ana Marta González & Victor J. Seidler (Amherst, NY: Humanity Books, 2008), 75–108.

Murphy, James Bernard. "Aristotle, Feminism, and Biology: A Response to Larry Arnhart" in *International Political Science Review* 15:4 (1994): 417–426.

Nichols, Terence. "Aquinas's Substantial Form and Modern Science" in *International Philosophical Quarterly* 36 (1996): 305–318.

Nussbaum, Martha. "Aristotle, Feminism, and Needs for Functioning" in *Feminist Interpretations of Aristotle*, ed. Cynthia A. Freeland (University Park, PA: The Pennsylvania University Press, 1998), 248–259.

_____."Aristotle on Human Nature and the Foundations of Ethics" in *World, Mind and Ethics: Essays on the Ethical Philosophy of Bernard Williams*, ed. J.E.J. Altham & Ross Harrison (Cambridge: Cambridge University Press, 1995), 86–131.

_____."Aristotle, Politics, and Human Capabilities: A Response to Antony, Arneson, Charlesworth, and Mulgan" in *Ethics* 111 (October 2000): 104–140.

_____."Emotions and Women's Capabilities" in *Women, Culture, and Development*, ed. Martha C. Nussbaum & Jonathan Glover (Oxford: Clarendon Press, 1995), 360–395.

_____.*Frontiers of Justice: Disability, Nationality, Species Membership* (Cambridge, MA: Belknap Press, 2006).

_____."Human Capabilities, Female Human Beings" in *Women, Culture, and Development*, ed. Martha C. Nussbaum & Jonathan Glover (Oxford: Clarendon Press, 1995), 61–104.

_____. *Political Theory* 20:2 (May 1992): 202–246.

_____."Nature, Function, and Capability: Aristotle on Political Distribution" in *Oxford Studies in Ancient Philosophy*, Supplementary Volume I (1988): 145–84.

_____."Public Philosophy and International Feminism" in *Ethics* 108 (July 1998): 770–804.

_____.*Sex and Social Justice* (New York: Oxford University Press, 1999).

_____.*Women and Human Development: The Capabilities Approach* (New York: Cambridge University Press, 2002).

O'Callaghan, John. "The Plurality of Forms: Now and Then" in *The Review of Metaphysics* 62:1 (September 2008): 3–41.

Offen, Karen "Defining Feminism: A Comparative Historical Approach" in *Signs: A Journal of Women in Culture and Society* 14:1 (1988): 119–157.

Okin, Susan Moller. *Justice, Gender, and the Family* (New York: Basic Books, 1989).

_____.*Women in Western Political Thought* (Princeton, NJ: Princeton University Press, 1979).

Parson, Barbara A. "Aristotle on Women" in *Women's Studies Encyclopedia. Vol. III: History, Philosophy, and Religion*, ed. Helen Tierney (New York: Greenwood Press, 1991), 32–35.

Phillips, Anne. Review of Nussbaum's *Women and Human Development* in *Ethics* 112:2 (January 2002): 398–403.

Rashdall, Hastings. *The Universities of Europe in the Middle Ages*. 3 vol., ed. F.M. Powicke & A.B. Emden (London: Oxford University Press, 1936).

Robeyns, Ingrid. "The Capability Approach: A Theoretical Survey" in *Journal of Human Development* 6:1 (March 2005): 93–114.

Rubenstein, Richard E. *Aristotle's Children: How Christians, Muslims, and Jews Rediscovered Ancient Wisdom and Illuminated the Middle Ages* (New York: Harcourt, Inc., 2003).

Ruddick, Sara. *Maternal Thinking: Toward a Politics of Peace* (Boston: Beacon Press, 1989).

Rüegg, Walter (ed). *A History of the University in Europe*. Vol. 1 (Cambridge: Cambridge University Press, 1992).

Saiving, Valerie. "The Human Situation: A Feminist View" in *Womanspirit Rising: A Feminist Reader in Religion*, ed. Carol P. Christ & Judith Plaskow (San Francisco: Harper & Row, 1979), 25–42.

Schumacher, Michele M. (ed). *Women in Christ: Toward a New Feminism* (Grand Rapids, MI: Eerdmans, 2004).

Schwarzenbach, Sibyl. *On Civic Friendship* (New York: Columbia University Press, 2009).

_____."A Political Reading of the Reproductive Soul in Aristotle" in *History of Philosophy Quarterly* 9 (July 1992): 243–264.

Scott, Joan. *Gender and the Politics of History* (New York: Columbia University Press, 1988).

Seager, Joni. *The Penguin Atlas of Women in the World*, 4th ed. (New York: Penguin Books, 2009).

Senack, Christine M. "Aristotle on the Woman's Soul" in *Engendering Origins: Critical Feminist Readings in Plato and Aristotle*, ed. Bat-Ami Bar On (Albany, NY: State University of New York Press, 1994), 223–236.

Shallat, Lezak & Ursula Paredes (eds). *Gender Concepts in Development Planning: Basic Approach* (Santo Domingo: United Nations International Research and Training Institute for the Advancement of Women, 1996).

Shank, Michael H. "A Female University Student in the Late Medieval Kraków" in *Sisters and Workers in the Middle Ages*, ed. Judith M. Bennett, Elizabeth A. Clark, et. al. (Chicago: University of Chicago Press, 1976).

Smith, Nicholas D. "Plato and Aristotle on the Nature of Women" in *Journal of the History of Philosophy* 21 (1983): 467–478.

Sparshott, F. "Aristotle on Women" in *Philosophical Inquiry* 7:3–4 (1985): 177–200.

Spelman, Elizabeth. "Aristotle and the Politicization of the Soul" in *Discovering Reality: Feminist Perspectives on Epistemology, Metaphysics, Methodology, and Philosophy of Science*, 2nd ed., ed. Sandra Harding & Merrill B. Hintikka (Dordrecht: Kluwer, 2003), 17–30.

_____."Who's Who in the Polis?" in *Engendering Origins: Critical Feminist Readings in Plato and Aristotle*, ed. Bat-Ami Bar On (Albany, NY: State University of New York Press, 1994), 97–125.

Stein, Edith. *Philosophy of Psychology and the Humanities*, ed. Marianne Sawicki, trans. Mary Catharine Baseheart & Marianne Sawicki (Washington, DC: Institute of Carmelite Studies Publications, 2000).

_____.*The Problem of Empathy*, trans. Waltraut Stein, 3rd revised edition (Washington, DC: Institute of Carmelite Studies Publications, 1989).

Tierney, Brian (ed). *The Middle Ages Vol. I: Sources of Medieval History* (New York: Alfred A. Knopf, 1970).

Thom, Paul. "Stiff Cheese for Women" in *The Philosophical Forum* 8:1 (Fall 1976): 94–107.

Thomas Aquinas. *De mixtione elementorum*, in Joseph Bobik's *Aquinas on Matter and Form and the Elements: A Translation and Interpretation of the de Principiis Naturae and the De Mixtione Elementorum of St. Thomas Aquinas* (Notre Dame, IN: University of Notre Dame Press, 1998).

Thompson, James W. & Edgar N. Johnson. *An Introduction to Medieval Europe* (New York: W.W. Norton & Company, 1937).

Tress, Daryl McGowan. "Aristotle Against the Hippocratics on Sexual Generation" in *Philosophy and Medicine. Proceedings of the Ninth International Conference on Greek Philosophy*, vol. I (Athens, Greece, 1998): 237–253.

_____."Aristotle Against the Hippocratics on Sexual Generation: A Reply to Coles" in *Phronesis* 44:3 (1999): 228–241.

_____."Aristotle's Child: Development Through Genesis, Oikos and Polis" in *Ancient Philosophy* 17 (1997): 63–84. This essay also appears as "Aristotle's Children" in *The Philosopher's Child: Critical Essays in the Western Tradition*, ed. Susan M. Turner & Gareth B. Matthews (Rochester, NY: University of Rochester Press, 1998), 19–44.

_____."Comment on Jane Flax's 'Postmodernism and Gender Relations in Feminist Theory'" in *Signs* 14:1 (Autumn 1988): 196–200.

_____."Feminist Theory and Its Discontents" in *Interpretation* 18:2 (Winter 1990–91): 293–311.

_____."The Metaphysical Science of Aristotle's Generation of Animals and Its Feminist Critics" in *The Review of Metaphysics* 46:2 (December, 1992): 307–341. See also *Feminism and Ancient Philosophy*, ed. Julie K. Ward (New York: Routledge, 1996), 31–50.

Tuana, Nancy. "Aristotle and the Politics of Reproduction" in *Engendering Origins: Critical Feminist Readings in Plato and Aristotle*, ed. Bat-Ami Bar On (Albany, NY: State University of New York Press, 1994), 189–206.

Uyan-Semerci, Pinar. "A Relational Account of Nussbaum's List of Capabilities" in *Journal of Human Development* 8:2 (July 2007): 203–221.

Vertin, Michael. "Gender, Science, and Cognitional Conversion" in *Lonergan and Feminism*, ed. Cynthia S.W. Crysdale (Toronto: University of Toronto Press, 1994), 49–71.

Walker, Susan. "Women and Housing in Classical Greece: The Archaeological Evidence" in *Images of Women in Antiquity*, ed. Averil Cameron & Amélie Kuhrt (Detroit: Wayne State University Press, 1983), 81–91.

Wallace, William A. "A Place for Form in Science: The Modeling of Nature" in *The Recovery of Form – American Catholic Philosophical Quarterly* (1996): 35–46.

Wilder, Alfred. "On the Essential Equality of Men and Women in Aristotle" in *Angelicum* 59 (1982): 200–223.

Williams, Wendy W. "The Equality Crisis: Some Reflections on Culture, Courts, and Feminism" in *Women's Rights Law Reporter* 7:3 (Spring 1982): 175–200.

_____."Equality's Riddle: Pregnancy and the Equal Treatment/Special Treatment Debate" in *Feminist Legal Theory*, ed. D. Kelly Weisberg (Philadelphia: Temple University Press, 1993), 128–155.

Wilson, Edward O. *On Human Nature* (Cambridge, MA: Harvard University Press, 1978).

*Objectivity*, ed. Louise M. Antony & Charlotte Witt (Boulder, CO: Westview Press, 1993), 273–288.

_____."Form, Normativity and Gender in Aristotle: A Feminist Perspective" in *Feminist Interpretations of Aristotle*, ed. Cynthia A. Freeland (University Park, PA: The Pennsylvania State University Press, 1998), 118–137. Also published in *Feminist Reflections on the History of Philosophy*, ed. Lilli Alanen & Charlotte Witt (Boston: Kluwer, 2004), 117–136.

Wolf, Susan. "Comments on Nussbaum" in *Women, Culture, and Development: A Study in Human Capabilities*, ed. Martha C. Nussbaum & Jonathan Glover (Oxford: Clarendon Press, 1995), 105–115.

Zinserling, Verena. *Women in Greece and Rome* (New York: Abner Schram, 1973).

# Index

© Springer International Publishing Switzerland 2016
S. Borden Sharkey, *An Aristotelian Feminism*, Historical-Analytical Studies on
Nature, Mind and Action 1, DOI 10.1007/978-3-319-29847-4

166                                                                    Index


**D**
Darwin, C., 116
Democritus, 87, 100
Desert Fathers, 6
Dualism, 30, 37, 50, 99, 102, 105, 128
Dynamisms, 4

**E**
Empedocles, 87, 100, 116

**F**
Fausto-Sterling, A., 21–25, 51, 63
Femininity, 32, 49, 52, 54
Feminism
    Aristotelian feminism, 1–28, 30, 56, 59,
        60, 74, 79, 129, 135, 137, 153, 155
    global feminism, 15
    radical feminists, 29, 33
    traditionalism, 57
    Western feminism, 15
Firestone, S.
    *The Dialectic of Sex*, 29
Form
    common human form, 53, 102, 104
    species-form, 47, 69, 87, 93, 115,
        116, 122–125
    substantial form, 37, 39–42, 44, 101,
        102, 124
Freedom, 5, 10, 14, 36, 44, 53, 55, 56, 60, 69,
    94, 108, 135

    119, 134
Friedan, B.
    *The Feminine Mystique*, 15, 60

**G**
Garnsey, P.
    *Food and Society in Classical Antiquity*,
        126
Gender
    biological determinism, 16, 18, 32, 55, 135
    gender development, 19, 31, 54, 55, 63, 65,
        66, 69, 71–73
    social constructivism, 16, 19, 32
Gilligan, C.
    *In a Different Voice*, 70

**H**
History of the universities, 138
Hobbes, T., 13

Holistic development, 8, 78, 79, 138,
    139, 154
Hume, D., 76, 100
Hylomorphism
    flexibility in physical expression, 127
    qualified hylomorphists, 36, 37, 64, 65, 73
    strict hylomorphists, 64, 65, 73

**J**
Judge Bradley, 33

**K**
Kohlberg, L., 47, 48

**L**
Liberalism, 10, 12, 14, 16
Locke, J., 37, 76, 100

**M**
MacIntyre, A., 14, 44, 111, 133
Male and female patterns for fertility, 142, 144
Marx, K., 3
Masculinity, 32, 49, 52, 54
Materialism, 37, 50, 99
Matter
    biological matter, 27, 41, 43–45, 50–56,
        60–74, 77, 127, 129
    environmental and cultural matter, 41–44,

        143, 144
    formed/secondary matter, 39–44, 69, 124
    prime matter, 39, 40
    Sexually-differentiated biological matter,
        61, 65–67, 69–72, 77
    sexually-relevant biological matter, 70, 71
*Monism*, 37, 50

**N**
Naïve realist, 124
Nussbaum, M.
    *Sex and Social Justice*, 4, 5, 8, 9, 12, 13,
        17, 18, 20
    *Women and Human Development*, 3, 16, 77

**P**
Passivity, 55, 85, 114, 133, 134
Plato, 11, 12, 30, 76, 87, 97, 102, 105, 106,
    109, 110, 119, 122, 128, 132, 140

Printed in the United States
By Bookmasters